Contents

Course overview

American English File
THIRD Edition

Welcome to **American English File Third Edition**. This is how to use the Student Book, Online Practice, and the Workbook in and out of class.

Student Book

All the language and skills you need to improve your English, with Grammar, Vocabulary, Pronunciation, and skills work in every File.

Use your Student Book in class with your teacher.

Workbook

Grammar, Vocabulary, and Pronunciation practice for every lesson.

Use your Workbook for homework or for self-study to practice language and to check your progress.

Go to
americanenglishfileonline.com
and use your Access Code
to log into the
Online Practice.

ACTIVITIES   AUDIO   VIDEO   RESOURCES

ONLINE

LOOK AGAIN

- Review the language from every lesson.
- Watch the video and listen to all the class audio as many times as you like.

PRACTICE

- Improve your skills with extra Reading, Writing, Listening, and Speaking practice.
- Use the interactive video to practice Colloquial English.

CHECK YOUR PROGRESS

- Test yourself on the language from the File and get instant feedback.
- Try a Challenge activity.

SOUND BANK

- Use the Sound Bank video to practice and improve your pronunciation of English sounds.

Online Practice

Look again at Student Book language you want to review or that you missed in class, do extra *Practice* activities, and *Check your progress* on what you learned so far.

Use the Online Practice to learn outside the classroom and get instant feedback on your progress.

americanenglishfileonline.com

G question formation   **V** figuring out meaning from context   **P** intonation: showing interest

1 READING & SPEAKING

a Look at the photos of Simone Biles and Dan Stevens and read their biographical info. Have you watched any of her competitions, or seen any of his TV shows or movies? What did you think of them?

b Now read the interviews and complete the questions.

c Read the interviews again and focus on their answers. Write **S** (Simone) or **D** (Dan). Which question(s) helped you answer **S** or **D**?

Who do you think…?
1 ☐ doesn't eat any animal products
2 ☐ doesn't have a partner right now
3 ☐ is currently living in California
4 ☐ doesn't like insects
5 ☐ is romantic
6 ☐ is very family-oriented
7 ☐ becomes emotional when they're tired
8 ☐ likes to make the last point in a discussion

d Which of the questions in the interviews do you think are…?

- the most interesting
- the least interesting
- too personal to ask a person if you don't know them well

e Choose six questions from *Q&A* to ask your partner.

> 🔍 **Politely refusing to answer a question**
>
> If you are asked a question you think is inappropriate, or simply don't want to answer, you can say, *I'd prefer not to answer that* or *I'd rather not answer that if you don't mind.*

Glossary
decorated (adj.) given a medal as a sign of respect
podium (noun) a small platform that a person stands on to give a speech or receive a medal

Q&A

Every week the newspaper *The Guardian* chooses people who have been in the news recently, and publishes a short interview with them called **Q&A**.

Simone Biles is a gymnast who was born in the state of Ohio in 1997. Biles has competed at the World Championships since 2013, and is now the most decorated gymnast in World Championship history. She has also won gold in the Olympic Games, and written an autobiography called *Courage to Soar*.

1 _____'s your most treasured possession?
My Olympic medals.

2 **What** _____ **you want to be when you were growing up?**
A nurse.

3 **What** _____ **you like about yourself?**
I like to have the last word.

4 **What** _____ **your most embarrassing moment?**
I was on the podium at the 2014 World Championships in China when a bee appeared out of nowhere and took a liking to my flowers.

5 **What or** _____ **is the greatest love of your life?**
Food.

6 **What** _____ **your superpower be?**
To be a witch. A good witch, of course. It would be cool to control things with my mind and do spells.

7 _____ **did you last cry, and why?**
Just a few days ago. I was overtired.

8 _____ **would you like to be remembered?**
As a confident, inspirational, and very bubbly person.

9 _____ **word or phrase do you most overuse?**
"Oh my gosh."

Adapted from The Guardian

Dan Stevens, the actor, was born in England in 1982. He played Matthew Crawley on the TV show *Downton Abbey*, until his character died suddenly in a special Christmas episode. He has since starred in many successful TV shows and movies, including *Beauty and the Beast*, *Legion*, and *The Call of the Wild*.

1 _____ were you happiest?
My wedding day, eight years ago.

2 What _____ you owe your parents?
A lot – and probably quite a lot of money.

3 _____'s your wallpaper?
A photo of my kids, Willow, Aubrey, and Eden, who are eight, five, and one.

4 _____ keeps you awake at night?
My three kids.

5 _____ would you most like to say sorry to?
To *Downton Abbey* fans, for ruining their Christmas one year.

6 What single thing _____ improve the quality of your life?
One of those robot vacuum cleaners.

7 _____ do you relax?
I go for walks in Griffith Park, in LA.

8 What _____ love feel like?
As if somebody's painted the world a different color.

9 _____ you have a "guilty pleasure"?
Yes, vegan cheesecake.

2 GRAMMAR question formation

a 🔊 1.2 Listen to some journalists interviewing a famous actress who has just arrived in Toronto. Write down the four questions they ask.

b Answer the questions below with a partner.
Which question is an example of…?
- a question that ends with a preposition
- a subject question, where there is no auxiliary verb
- a question that uses a negative auxiliary verb
- an indirect question

c Ⓖ p.132 **Grammar Bank 1A**

d Ⓒ **Communication** Indirect questions **A** p.106 **B** p.110 Ask and answer indirect questions.

3 PRONUNCIATION intonation: showing interest

a 🔊 1.5 Listen to some people asking questions 1–5. Who sounds more interested each time, **a** or **b**?
1 Do you have a big family?
2 What don't you like about the place where you live?
3 What sports or games are you good at?
4 Do you think you have a healthy diet?
5 What makes you feel happy?

b 🔊 1.6 Listen and repeat the questions with interested intonation.

> 🔍 **Reacting to what someone says**
> When you ask someone a question and they answer, it is normal to show interest or sympathy. You can use:
> - expressions such as *Oh, really? I'm sorry. What a shame!*
> - exclamations such as *Wow! Me too! How interesting!*
> - follow-up questions such as *Why (not)? Why is that? Why do you say that?*

c 🔊 1.7 Now listen to five conversations using the questions in **a**. Complete the expressions or questions that the people use to react to the answers.
1 *Wow*! That's a huge family.
2 _____? What's wrong with them?
3 _____! We could play a game one day.
4 _____! How long have you been a vegan?
5 _____? I can't think of anything worse!

d 🔊 1.8 Listen and repeat the responses. Copy the intonation.

e Ask and answer the questions in **a** with a partner. Use interested intonation, and react to your partner's answers.

4 READING & VOCABULARY figuring out meaning from context

a   Look at the cartoon. How do you think the candidate is feeling? How would you react if it happened to you?

b   Read the title of the article and the first paragraph. Then look at interview questions A–G. With a partner, say how you would answer them. Which question would you least like to be asked?

A   What do you usually do after a bad day at work?
B   What's your biggest weakness?
C   How would your enemy describe you?
D   You have 50 red and 50 blue balls. How could you divide these between two containers to give the maximum probability of picking one of the colors?
E   What's the most selfish thing you've ever done?
F   Are you a nice person?
G   What on your résumé is the closest thing to a lie?

Would YOU get the job?

Interviews are a source of anxiety for most job-seekers. Job website Glassdoor has created a list of some of the toughest interview questions from the elite companies where they were asked, and offers an expert opinion on the best possible answers.

1 _____ (The Phoenix Partnership)

How to answer: If you answer "nothing," then you may look too defensive, as if you are hiding something, even if you are innocent. The best tactic would be to reply that everyone presents the best side of themselves on a résumé – that is the point of the document – but that you think lying, and even exaggeration, is wrong.

2 _____ (Condé Nast)

How to answer: You could just tell the interviewer that you are not the sort of person to make enemies, but that sometimes you've enjoyed a good-natured rivalry with someone, for example, in a sport. This will show your competitive side and your drive to succeed.

3 _____ (Page Group)

How to answer: This is an occasion when you could give a light-hearted response. Something like, "I don't consider myself to be selfish, but I always make sure I have some time during the week for myself, so I can practice art / tennis / soccer / singing."

4 _____ (Palantir Technologies)

How to answer: Everyone should be prepared to answer this question, whatever job you're interviewing for. There's no foolproof answer – it's a good idea to have thought about a list of areas that are not your biggest strengths, but that wouldn't affect the role that you are interviewing for.

Applying for a job at IKEA

Make a chair and take a seat

CANARY PETE

5 _____ (Clearwater Analytics)

How to answer: If you are a serious math geek, then you might have a decent chance of answering this one. One answer would be to put a single red ball in one container and all of the other balls in the other container.

6 _____ (Switch Consulting)

How to answer: Don't be afraid to talk about what you do to relax, and show how you have a healthy work–life balance. It's also a chance to say something about your personal life, which could be very helpful for making a good impression. For example, you could mention how you go to the gym to relax.

7 _____ (Badoo)

How to answer: Don't just answer "yes" or "no." Think about your personality type and the culture of the company where you are interviewing. What is your gut feeling about the type of people that do well at the company? This should help you to give an appropriate answer.

Adapted from Mail Online

c Read the article once and complete it with questions A–G. Would you now feel more confident about answering the questions?

d Read the article again. With a partner, try to figure out what the highlighted words and phrases mean, and how you think they are pronounced. What helped you to figure them out?

e Now match the highlighted words and phrases to 1–8.

1 _____ (noun) a reaction based on feelings and emotions rather than thought and reason
2 _____ (adj.) designed so that it cannot fail
3 _____ (phrase) an answer that is intended to be amusing rather than serious
4 _____ (noun, informal) a person who is very interested in and who knows a lot about a particular subject
5 _____ (phrase) the number of hours per week you spend working compared with the number of hours you spend with your family, relaxing, etc.
6 _____ (phrase) the main reason for something
7 _____ (phrase) friendly competition
8 _____ (noun) people who are looking for a job

f Look at some more genuine interview questions. What do you think they would tell you about the candidate? Why? Do you think these kinds of questions really help interviewers to choose the best person for the job?
- What would you do if you were the one survivor of a plane crash? (Airbnb)
- Who do you think would win in a fight between Spider-Man and Batman? (Stanford University)
- What did you have for breakfast? (Banana Republic)
- Describe the color yellow to somebody who's blind. (Spirit Airlines)
- How many people flew out of Chicago last year? (Redbox software)
- What am I thinking right now? (TES Global)
- Who is your hero, and why? (General Electrics)
- Tell me something about your childhood. (Next)

g Choose two questions in **f** to ask a partner.

5 LISTENING

a Have you ever had an interview for a job or acceptance into a school? What kinds of questions did they ask you? Did you get the job or the acceptance?

b 🔊 1.9 Listen to four people talking about a strange question they were asked in an interview. Complete questions 1–4.

What strange question were they asked?	How did they answer?	What happened in the end?
1 If you could _____ _____ with _____ _____ from the past, who would you choose and why?		
2 Do you _____ a _____? Are you planning to _____ _____?		
3 Do you still _____ _____?		
4 _____ _____ would you like to be reincarnated as?		

c Listen again and make notes in the rest of the chart.

d Which of the questions do you think were acceptable to ask at an interview?

6 SPEAKING

a 🄲 **Communication** Tough questions **A** p.106 **B** p.110 Ask your partner some difficult interview questions.

b Invent a tough interview question of your own, which you think might tell you something interesting about another person.

c Ask your question to as many other students as possible and answer theirs.

d Which questions did you think were the most interesting? Why?

> When you have eliminated the impossible, whatever remains, however improbable, must be the truth.
> *Sherlock Holmes in* The Sign of Four *by Arthur Conan Doyle*

G auxiliary verbs, *the...*, *the... +* comparatives **V** compound adjectives, modifiers **P** intonation and sentence rhythm

1 READING & LISTENING

a Look at the names below. Do you know what they have in common? Do you know anything about them?

the *MARY CELESTE*   the *USS CYCLOPS*   Amelia Earhart

b 🔊1.10 Listen and find out. Do you think we will ever know what happened?

c 🔊1.11 Read and listen to *The mystery of the lighthouse keepers*. Then cover the text and answer the questions with a partner.

The facts

1 What was the mystery and who discovered it?
2 What was strange about...?
  • the lighthouse door
  • a chair
  • the rain jackets
  • the clocks
  • the logbook

The theories

3 What theories did people come up with?
4 Which of the theories do you think could be true? Why?
5 Which do you think are impossible? Why?

d Find words in the article that mean...

Paragraph 1

1 _____ (*noun*) something that is difficult to understand or explain (SYN *mystery*)
2 _____ (*verb*) to confuse somebody completely

Paragraph 2

3 _____ (*adj.*) far away from places where other people live

Paragraph 3

4 _____ (*adj.*) unexpected, surprising, or strange
5 _____ (*noun*) a mark, object, or sign that shows that somebody or something existed or was present (*He disappeared without a ~.*)

Paragraph 4

6 _____ (*verb*) to find the correct answer or explanation for something

THE MYSTERY OF THE LIGHTHOUSE KEEPERS

The mystery of the Flannan Islands lighthouse keepers is one of the greatest puzzles in history, a case that has baffled real and amateur detectives for more than a century.

The Flannan Islands are seven uninhabited rocks that rise out of the sea. They form part of the Outer Hebrides, a chain of remote islands off the west coast of Scotland. For centuries, they were a danger for ships, so in 1899, a 75-foot lighthouse was built on the largest of the islands, and three lighthouse keepers were employed.

On December 26th, 1900, a steamship sailed to the island carrying three new lighthouse keepers to relieve the men who had spent three months alone in the Atlantic. But when they arrived at the lighthouse, they made an extraordinary discovery – there was nobody there! The lighthouse door was unlocked, and inside everything was neat, but one of the chairs was knocked over. One rain jacket was hanging on its hook, but the other two had disappeared.

The clocks had stopped. The last entry in the logbook was 9 a.m. on December 15th. But of the three keepers, Ducat, Marshall, and MacArthur, there was not a trace.

When the news of the keepers' disappearance reached the mainland, there was a huge amount of media speculation. Some suggested that the men had argued about a woman, and that one had murdered the other two before throwing himself into the sea. Others wondered whether perhaps they had been kidnapped by German agents who were planning an invasion of Britain, using submarines. Some thought they might have been carried away by a sea serpent, or a giant seabird, or even by a boat full of ghosts. An Edinburgh police officer, Robert Muirhead, was sent to the island to solve the mystery.

STRANGE AFFAIR AT A LIGHTHOUSE.

Three Keepers Disappear.

[P.A. TELEGRAM]

Intimation has been received at the Northern Lighthouse Board, Edinburgh, of the loss of the lighthouse staff at the Flannan Islands lighthouse.

The station was established in December last year, and was staffed by four men, three taking duty and the other having relief.

When the Board's steamer yesterday went to the islands to land the relieving keeper, it was found that the three men last on duty had disappeared, leaving no trace behind. They are the principal keeper (James Ducat) and Thomas Marshall and Don[...] an occasional keep[...] member of the re[...]

It is surmised [...] during the storm [...] attempting to sav[...] render assistance t[...]

The relieving ke[...] been temporarily [...] incident [...]

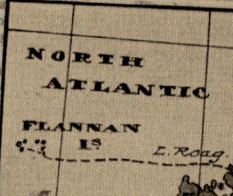

NORTH ATLANTIC

FLANNAN IS

L. Roag

Lewis

Adapted from The Times

e 🔊 1.12 Listen to the rest of the story. What was Muirhead's theory? What did people think of it at the time? What is the modern explanation?

> **Glossary**
> **Queen Elizabeth II** (known as the QE2) a famous transatlantic cruise ship
> **White Cliffs of Dover** very tall cliffs on the English coastline across from France

f Listen again. Why are the following mentioned?

1 a huge rock
2 *Queen Elizabeth II*
3 a paper in a scientific journal
4 1901
5 one man's rain jacket and the bodies of the men

2 GRAMMAR auxiliary verbs

a Talk in small groups.

Have you (or has anybody you know)…?
- seen or heard something that can't be explained, e.g., a ghost or a UFO
- had a strange coincidence, e.g., meeting someone in an unexpected place
- visited a fortune-teller, psychic, or faith healer

> 🔍 **Reacting to a story about something strange**
> When somebody talks about something strange or difficult to explain, we often react with these phrases.
>
> | *How / That's* | *strange / bizarre / odd / weird / spooky.* |
> | *What a / an* | *weird story / amazing coincidence.* |

b Look at the conversations and try to fill in the blanks with an auxiliary verb (*do*, *did*, *is*, *was*, etc.).

1 A I heard a weird noise in the middle of the night.
  B You ¹_____? What kind of noise?
2 A You don't believe in ghosts, ²_____ you?
  B No, I don't.
3 A I've never been to a fortune-teller.
  B Neither ³_____ I.
  C I ⁴_____. It was really interesting.
4 A I don't believe you really saw a UFO.
  B I ⁵_____ see one! It couldn't have been anything else.

c 🔊 1.13 Listen and check. Then in pairs, decide which highlighted phrase (1–5) is used…

A ☐ to add emphasis
B ☐ to say that you are different
C ☐ to check information
D ☐ to show surprise
E ☐ to say that you are the same

d Ⓖ p.133 **Grammar Bank 1B**

3 PRONUNCIATION & SPEAKING
intonation and sentence rhythm

a 🔊 1.15 Listen to the conversations. Underline the highlighted auxiliary verbs (*did*, *don't*, *do*) that are stressed.

1 A I dreamed that I saw a ghost last night.
  B You did? So did I. How spooky!
2 A I don't believe in fortune-telling.
  B You don't? I do.
3 A You don't like horror movies, do you?
  B I do like them. It's just that sometimes they're too scary!

b Practice the conversations with a partner. Copy the rhythm and intonation.

c Complete sentences 1–8 so that they are true for you.

1 I'm not very good at _____.
  (activity)
2 I'm going to _____ tonight.
  (verb phrase)
3 I love _____.
  (a kind of music)
4 I don't like _____.
  (a kind of food)
5 I've never read _____.
  (a famous book)
6 I'd love to live in _____.
  (a town or country)
7 I was very _____ as a child.
  (adj. of personality)
8 I didn't _____ yesterday evening. (verb phrase)

d Work in pairs, **A** and **B**. **A** read your sentences to **B**. **B** respond with a reply question and then say whether you are the same or different. Then switch roles.

I'm not very good at cooking.
    You aren't? Neither am I.

I'm going to watch Netflix tonight.
    You are? I'm not. I'm going to study.

e Ⓒ **Communication** You're psychic, aren't you? **A p.106 B p.110** Make guesses about your partner.

a Look at the photo of a forest. How do you think you would feel if you were walking in it?

b 🔊 1.16 Now look at the photo and listen. Follow the instructions. Write your answers below.

A walk in the forest

1
2
3
4
5
6

c Listen again and check what you have written. Make sure you have answered all parts of the questions.

d 🔊 1.17 Now listen to an explanation of what you have written. Make notes in the chart.

A walk in the forest
1 the person =
2 the animal = how you interact with it =
3 the house = no fence = a fence =
4 the table =
5 the cup =
6 the water = how wet you get =

e Now use the notes to interpret what you wrote in **b**. Then compare with a partner and say what you agree with and what you disagree with.

I put that the animal was a…, and it says that means…, but I don't think that's true.

f Do you believe in this kind of personality test? Do you believe that you can learn anything about someone's personality by…?

- analyzing their handwriting (graphology)
- looking at their hands (palmistry)
- analyzing the position of the sun, moon, and planets at the exact time of their birth (astrology)
- online personality quizzes, e.g., Buzzfeed

g Grammar in context *the…, the…* + comparatives

> *The bigger* the animal,
> *the more problems* you have.
>
> *The harder and more resistant* the cup is,
> *the stronger* your relationship is.

Use *the* + comparative adjective or adverb, or *the more / less* (+ noun) to show that one thing depends on another, e.g.,

- *The earlier we start, the sooner we'll finish.* = If we start early, we'll finish early.
- *The more money you spend now, the less you'll have for your vacation.* = If you spend a lot of money now, you'll have less for your vacation.

Rewrite the sentences using *the…, the…* + comparative.

1 If you study a lot, you learn a lot.

The _____,

the _____.

2 If I drink a lot of coffee, I sleep badly.

The _____,

the _____.

3 If you have a lot of time, you do things slowly.

The _____,

the _____.

4 If you are in shape, you feel good.

The _____,

the _____.

🔊 **1.18** Now listen and check. Notice the stress and intonation pattern in the sentences.

h Complete the sentences in your own words. Then read your sentences to a partner.

1 The more money I have,…
2 The earlier I get up,…
3 The faster American people speak,…
4 The less I eat,…
5 The harder I work,…
6 The more I exercise,…

---

5 VOCABULARY compound adjectives

a Look at some extracts from the listening in **4**. Can you remember what words go in the blanks?

1 If there was no fence around the house, it means you are very open-_____, and welcome new ideas.

2 If you hardly got wet at all, it means that you depend less on your friends and are more self-_____.

b 🔊 **1.19** Listen and check. Do the compound adjectives in **a** have a positive or negative meaning?

> 🔍 **Compound adjectives**
>
> Compound adjectives have two parts. The second part often ends in *-ed* or *-ing*, e.g., *good-natured*, *slow-moving*. The words are usually linked by hyphens.

c 🔊 **1.20** Listen to some more compound adjectives. Which word has the main stress?

absentminded   bad-tempered   big-headed   easygoing
good-tempered   laid-back   narrow-minded   open-minded
self-centered   strong-willed   tight-fisted   two-faced
well-balanced   well-behaved

d With a partner, use the two parts of the words to try to figure out their meaning. Which do you think are positive and negative characteristics? Are there any that you think can be either?

(I think a bad-tempered *person is somebody who gets angry easily…*

> 🔍 **Modifiers**
>
> We often use modifiers with adjectives of personality to make them stronger or less strong.
>
> **With positive characteristics**
>
> | My mom is | really / incredibly / extremely very pretty | good-tempered. |
> |---|---|---|
>
> **With negative characteristics**
>
> | My sister is | really / incredibly / extremely very rather / pretty a little / kind of | bad-tempered. |
> |---|---|---|

e Tell your partner about people with the characteristics below. Give examples of their behavior.

Do you know somebody who is…?

- very open-minded
- extremely absentminded
- a little tight-fisted
- pretty laid-back
- kind of two-faced
- very good-tempered
- incredibly strong-willed
- really self-centered

(My cousin is pretty laid-back. She didn't even get angry when her boyfriend crashed her car!

🔄 **Go online** to review the lesson

1 ▶ THE INTERVIEW Part 1

a Read the biographical information about Jeff Neil. How do you think his previous experience helps him in his present job?

Jeff Neil is a career coach and the founder of a company called New Career Breakthrough in New York City. His job involves helping people to discover the right career options for them, and then to help them actually get a job, by advising them on their résumés and on interview techniques. His specialty is helping people who are making career transitions, e.g., from one industry to another. Before setting up his company, he worked for seven years as an HR (Human Resources) director.

b Watch Part 1 of an interview with him, where he talks about helping candidates when they are applying for a job. Check (✓) the three things he talks about.

1 ☐ Checking what there is about you on the Internet.
2 ☐ Choosing the right jobs to apply for.
3 ☐ Choosing what photos to send with your résumé.
4 ☐ Thinking about the skills and abilities a job needs.
5 ☐ Writing a good cover letter.
6 ☐ Writing a good résumé.

c Now listen again. Take notes about the advice he gives in the three areas you checked.

Glossary
résumé (BrE **curriculum vitae** or **CV**) a written record of your education and the jobs you have done that you send when you are applying for a job
cover(ing) letter a letter containing extra information that candidates send with their résumé

▶ Part 2

a Read five tips for the day of the interview. Now watch Part 2, where Jeff talks about the day of the interview. Are they **T** (true) or **F** (false)? Correct the F ones.

1 It's better to dress too formally than too casually.
2 You should try to find out beforehand what the company's dress style is.
3 You should arrive at the place where the interview is going to take place at least half an hour before the interview.
4 Don't take any electronic devices with you to the interview.
5 Be careful how you talk to other company employees before an interview.

b Watch again for more detail. Do you agree with all the tips?

Glossary
LinkedIn a social networking service for professional people

▶ Part 3

a Now watch Part 3 where Jeff talks about the interview itself. Complete the advice he gives.

1 If you want to ask about _____ and _____, either do this late in the interview, or wait for the employer to mention them.
2 _____ language and the _____ of your voice are just as important as what you actually say.
3 Be aware that the way you answer an "extreme" interview question can reveal things about your _____ .

b Listen again and answer the questions.

1 What's the biggest mistake job candidates make during an interview?
2 What's the most important thing for them to communicate in the interview?
3 Why does he mention people who were "slouched"?
4 What do you need to communicate with your tone of voice?
5 What "extreme" question did Jeff once ask?
6 What possible answers does he suggest? Why?

2 ▶ LOOKING AT LANGUAGE

> 🔍 **Make or do?**
> Jeff uses several expressions with *make* and *do*. These verbs are very common in expressions related to work, and are sometimes confused by learners of English because they just have one verb in their first language.

a Complete the extracts from the interview with the right form of *make* or *do*. Watch and check.

1 "...so some of the biggest mistakes that, that I've seen that people _____ on their résumé is they include everything."
2 "...as an employer, I don't care what you _____ 20 years ago or 30 years ago."
3 "You also want to _____ a Google search on your own name."
4 "...and to take an eight and a half sheet of paper and _____ three columns..."
5 "You want to _____ sure your cell phone is turned off."
6 "They're _____ a lot of eye contact directly with me."

b Now complete some more sentences related to the world of work.

1 They are going to _____ a decision about who gets the job by the end of the week.
2 Can I _____ a suggestion about how to re-organize the HR department?
3 We must _____ much more market research before we develop the new product.
4 All the new employees are going to _____ a training course next month.
5 Everyone in the company has _____ a big effort this year.
6 George is _____ a great job and I think he deserves to earn a higher salary.
7 I need to _____ a few phone calls before the meeting starts.

3 ▶ THE CONVERSATION

a Watch the conversation. How do they respond to the question? Write **D**, **S**, and **A** on the line in the appropriate place.

Yes, definitely	It depends	Absolutely not

b Watch it again. Match the sentence halves.

1 **Alice** Admitting you can't do something is OK if ☐
2 **Alice** If you say you can speak French on your CV and you can't, ☐
3 **Sarah** It's OK to exaggerate a bit about something if ☐
4 **Sarah** If speaking a language was essential for a job, ☐
5 **Debbie** If you lie and say you can do something, ☐
6 **Debbie** If you don't have many hobbies, ☐

A it's not very important for the job.
B you will have wasted the interviewer's time and given a bad impression of yourself.
C it's a good idea to exaggerate a bit.
D you say you are prepared to learn.
E it might be expensive for the company when they discover the truth.
F I wouldn't say I could do it.

c Do <u>you</u> think it's OK to slightly exaggerate on your résumé? Who do you agree with most, and why?

d Watch three extracts where the speakers are emphasizing something and complete the gaps.

1 I think it's a _____ _____ idea to even slightly exaggerate...
2 ...you might find yourself in a situation where you've wasted their time and you've just made yourself look _____ _____ silly.
3 I've _____ exaggerated on a CV.

e Now watch two more extracts. What does the speaker do with the missing word to make it more emphatic?

1 ...but I wouldn't do that if I knew the job was going to require me _____ that language...
2 ...you shouldn't outright lie because you _____ get caught out and a lot of the times it could cost a company a lot of money...

f Now have a conversation in groups of three.

1 Do you think that to get a job today, who you know is still more important than what you know?
2 Do you think résumés and interviews are a reliable way of selecting people for a job?

🔄 **Go online** to watch the video, review the lesson, and check your progress

> Never go to a doctor whose office plants have died.
> *Erma Bombeck, American journalist*

| G present perfect simple and continuous | V illnesses and injuries | P /ʃ/, /dʒ/, /tʃ/, and /k/ |

1 VOCABULARY illnesses and injuries

a Take the first-aid quiz with a partner. As you read the options, try to figure out the meaning of the highlighted words and phrases.

b **C Communication** Medical myths or first-aid facts? **A** p.106 **B** p.110 Check your answers to the quiz and explain the reasons to your partner.

c **V** p.152 **Vocabulary Bank** Illnesses and injuries

d What illnesses or injuries might you get if you are…?

| eating out | hiking in the mountains |
| playing sports | visiting a tropical country |

MEDICAL MYTHS OR FIRST-AID FACTS?

First aid can help treat a minor injury, or even save a life in a medical emergency. However, it's important to know what **NOT** to do. Sometimes, incorrect first aid can actually be more harmful than helpful. So how useful is the advice you've heard? Take our quiz to find out.

For each question, decide which answers are myths (**M**) and which are facts (**F**).

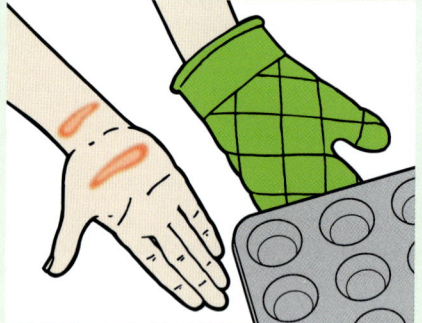

1 What's the first thing you should put on a burn?
a butter
b cool running water
c an ice pack

2 How should you treat a sprained ankle?
a put a hot, damp cloth on the ankle
b put an ice pack on the ankle
c put the leg up, e.g., on a chair

3 What's the best thing to do for someone with hypothermia?
a rub their arms and legs to warm them up
b give them hot coffee
c cover them in something warm, e.g., a coat or a blanket

4 What's the first thing to do if someone is choking?
a stand behind them and press their stomach inwards
b make them continue to cough hard
c hit them hard on the back

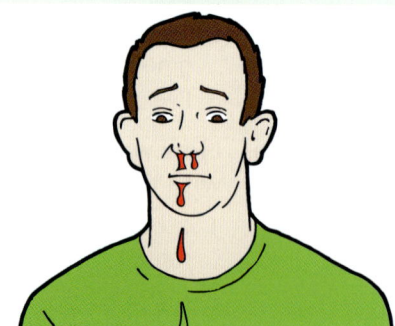

5 What's the best way to stop a nosebleed?
a tip your head forwards
b pinch the soft part of your nose
c tip your head backwards

6 After you have cleaned a bad cut, what should you do…?
a put on a bandage
b put on antibiotic ointment
c leave it open to the air

2 PRONUNCIATION /ʃ/, /dʒ/, /tʃ/, and /k/

1 ʃ	2 dʒ	3 tʃ	4 k

a How do you pronounce sounds 1–4 in the chart? Write the words from the box in the correct column.

ache   allergic   bandage   choking
emergency   infection   injury   pressure   rash
sick   stomach   temperature   unconscious

b ◗ 2.5 Listen and check. Practice saying the words.

c Use the words in **a** to answer questions 1–3 about the sound-spelling rules.

1 What ways can you spell the /ʃ/ sound? Which do you think is the most common?
2 How do you often pronounce g before i and e?
3 Which two ways can ch be pronounced? Which do you think is the more common?

d ℗ p.166–7 **Sound Bank** Look at the typical spellings for /ʃ/, /dʒ/, /tʃ/, and /k/, and more examples. Practice saying the words.

e ◗ 2.6 Look at some more medical words. Are they the same in your language? Which sounds in **a** do they contain? Listen and check.

cholesterol   indigestion   injection
operation   scratch   surgeon   syringe

3 LISTENING & SPEAKING

a Talk in pairs. What would you do and why?

If you were on the street and saw someone who had a medical problem, what would your immediate reaction be?
a I wouldn't do anything myself, but I would wait to see if someone else was able to help.
b I'd call an ambulance and stay with the person until it came.
c I'd go up to the person and see if I could do any first aid.

b ◗ 2.7 You are going to listen to Bettina, Umesh, and Alison talking about a time when someone needed first aid. First, listen to some extracts and complete the expressions.

Bettina
1 ...he didn't have a _____, so I thought he was probably _____ _____ _____ _____.
2 ...he took her to one side to _____ _____ _____...
3 I kept going until the _____ _____ _____...
4 ...because obviously she was _____ _____.

Umesh
5 ...an old lady stepped off the sidewalk in front of me and she _____ _____ _____ onto the street.
6 She'd fallen pretty hard, but she _____ _____ _____...
7 It was obviously an effort for her to sit up, it was _____ _____...

Alison
8 Then all of a sudden, he stopped walking and _____ _____...
9 Some teenagers in line _____ _____ _____...
10 ...then they put him on a stretcher and _____ _____ _____.

c ◗ 2.8 Now listen to their stories. When the incident happened, did they help? Why (not)?

d Listen again and answer the questions for each story.

1 What was he / she doing when it happened?
2 Who needed first aid? Why?
3 What did he / she do?
4 What happened in the end?
5 How did he / she feel a) during the event, b) after the event?

e Talk in small groups.

Have you ever been in a situation where you had to give first aid? Who to? Where were you? What happened? How did you feel?

Has anyone ever had to give you first aid? Why? Where were you? What happened?

Have you ever received any first-aid training? If no, would you like to? In which jobs should people be given mandatory first-aid training?

What could you do if someone...?
• had a severe allergic reaction
• had a high temperature
• got very bad sunburn
• felt faint and dizzy
• got a big blister on their foot
• got food poisoning
• had an epileptic seizure

4 GRAMMAR present perfect simple and continuous

a 🔊 2.9 Listen to a conversation between a doctor and a patient and answer the questions.

1 What symptoms does the patient have?
2 What does he think might be wrong with him?
3 What does he think he needs?
4 What does the doctor suggest?

b 🔊 2.10 Listen to what the doctor and receptionist say after Mr. Payne has left. What do they think of him? Do you know the name for someone like this?

c 🔊 2.11 Now listen to some extracts from the conversation in **a** and circle the correct form, present perfect simple or continuous. Are there any where you think both options would also be possible?

1 *I haven't been feeling / I haven't felt* well for a few days.
2 *I've been coughing / I've coughed* a lot and I keep getting headaches.
3 What *have you been taking / have you taken* for the headaches?
4 How many tablets *have you been taking / have you taken* today?
5 And *have you taken / have you been taking* your temperature this morning?
6 Yes. *I've been taking it / I've taken it* five or six times already.
7 I think I need a blood test. I *haven't had / haven't been having* one for two months.

d 🇬 p.134 Grammar Bank 2A

e In pairs, use the prompts to ask and answer the questions. The first question should be simple present and the second should be present perfect simple or continuous.

1 / often *get* colds?   How many colds / *have* in the last three months?
2 / *take* any vitamins or supplements?   How long / *take* them?
3 / *drink* much water?   How many glasses / *drink* today?
4 / *exercise*? What?   How long / *do* it?
5 / *eat* a lot of fruit and vegetables?   How many servings / *have* today?
6 / *walk* to school (or work or college)?   How far / *walk* today?
7 How many hours / *sleep* a night?   / *sleep* well recently?
8 / *be* allergic to anything?   / ever *have* a serious allergic reaction?

5 READING & SPEAKING

a Look at the title of the article on p.19 and read the first paragraph. With a partner, try to complete the definition of a *cyberchondriac*. Do you think the tone of the article is humorous or serious?

cyberchondriac /ˌsaɪbərˈkɒndriæk/ (*noun*) a person who compulsively searches the internet for information about _____

b Now read the whole article. Complete the summary of each paragraph with phrases a–e.

1 When the writer found out that she had a fast heart rate, she ▨
2 At the hospital, she discovered that she ▨
3 Since she returned from the hospital, she ▨
4 It's difficult to know from online information whether a condition ▨
5 A lot of online medical information ▨

a has been obsessively checking her symptoms online.
b googled the possible causes.
c isn't very reliable or up to date.
d was suffering from a chest infection and cyberchondria.
e is rare or very common.

c The highlighted phrases in the article are related to medicine. Match them to definitions 1–7.

1 _____ the medical treatment of a heart problem that involves an operation
2 _____ successful treatments for an illness that was thought to be impossible to cure
3 _____ IDM not feeling very well
4 _____ exaggerated reports in the news that make people worry
5 _____ the most terrible situations that could happen
6 _____ the speed at which your heart beats
7 _____ an illness that could kill you

Confessions of a *cyberchondriac*

I'm sure that's what I've got...

1 **A few weeks ago,** I was feeling under the weather. After days of intensive internet diagnosis, I finally went to see my doctor. After examining me, she told me that my heart rate was a little fast and sent me off to the hospital for some tests. Did I go straight there? Of course not. First I took out my phone, logged on to Google, and found out that the technical term for a fast heart rate is *supraventricular tachycardia*. Then I typed these two words into Google. Sadly, the problem with Dr. Google is that he isn't exactly a comfort in times of crisis. One website immediately scared me with a list of 407 possible causes.

2 I raced to the hospital, convinced that I probably needed open-heart surgery. Four hours later, I got a diagnosis. I had a chest infection...and a bad case of *cyberchondria*. The only consolation for the latter condition is that I'm in good company. A Microsoft survey of one million internet users last year found that 2% of all searches – a not-insignificant number – were health-related.

3 Unfortunately, once you have it, cyberchondria can be hard to cure. Since my trip to the hospital, I have been obsessively checking my pulse, swapping symptoms in chat rooms, and reading all about worst-case scenarios. What if the doctors got it wrong? What if the EKG machine was faulty? It's exhausting trying to convince yourself that you might have a life-threatening illness.

4 The Microsoft study also revealed another serious problem – that online information often doesn't discriminate between common and very rare conditions. One in four of all articles thrown up by an internet search for *headache* suggested a brain tumor as a possible cause. Although it is true that this may be the cause, in fact, brain tumors develop in fewer than one in 50,000 people. People also assume that the first answers that come up in searches refer to the most common causes, so if you type in *mouth ulcer* and see that *mouth cancer* has several mentions near the top, you think that it must be very common. However, this is not the case at all.

5 Another problem for cyberchondriacs is that online medical information may be from an unreliable source, or out of date. A recent American study showed that 75% of the people who use the internet to look up information about their health do not check where that information came from, or the date it was created. "Once something has been put up on the internet, even if it's wrong, it's difficult to remove," says Sarah Jarvis, a doctor. "This is a problem, especially with scare stories, and also with some alternative remedies that claim to be miracle cures, but which may actually do you harm." Check the information? Sorry, I don't have time – I'm off to buy a heart-rate monitor!

Adapted from The Sunday Times

Please **Do Not** Confuse Your **Google Search** With My Medical Degree

d Now read each paragraph again carefully and choose a, b, or c.

1 The problem with Dr. Google is that the information is _____.
   a insufficient   b worrying   c false
2 Microsoft's survey discovered that _____ searches are about health.
   a very few
   b a lot of
   c the majority of
3 The information the writer has found since coming back from the hospital has _____.
   a made her cyberchondria worse
   b made no difference to her cyberchondria
   c cured her cyberchondria
4 One of the problems with internet searches is that they _____.
   a don't rank answers in order of probability
   b only focus on common illnesses
   c don't always give an answer
5 Most people are unlikely to check _____ health information was posted.
   a why and by who
   b how and when
   c when and by who

e In small groups, answer the questions. Ask for and give as much information as possible.

1 Do you know anyone who you think is a hypochondriac or a cyberchondriac? What kinds of things do they do?
2 Do you think people in your country worry a lot about their...?

| blood pressure | cholesterol level |
| digestive system | liver |

Give examples if you can. Are there other things related to health that they worry about?

6 WRITING

W p.115 **Writing** An informal email
Write an email to a friend explaining that you haven't been well, and saying what you've been doing recently.

> **Glossary**
> **EKG machine** electrocardiogram machine, used to test people's heart rate

Go online to review the lesson

G using adjectives as nouns, adjective order   **V** clothes and fashion   **P** vowel sounds

1 READING & SPEAKING

a Think of an older person you know who seems much younger than they actually are. (Circle) any of the adjectives below that you would use to describe them.

active brave energetic funny glamorous impulsive
independent lively open-minded sociable

b Describe the person to a partner, and say what they do that makes them seem younger than their age.

c Look at the photo of Dilys and Sian. Approximately how old do you think they are?

The joy of the age-gap friendship

Modern life makes it hard for the old and the young to meet, and even harder to become best friends. What's the secret?

Dilys on Sian

I met Sian at an event where we were both speakers, and we just clicked. I could see she was just a great person, and smarter than most. She was a glamorous, lively woman, who talked about being an entrepreneur and her love for her father.

She started inviting me to different places. I went to the races with her – not the sort of thing I usually do. She brought fun back into my life when I was working hard to run a charity. The new experiences we share help to keep me alive. When I was sick last Christmas, she really rescued me. She came in like a hurricane, with decorations, firewood… I was feeling sad and afraid, and she told me that wasn't allowed.

▲ Dilys and Sian

"She brought fun back into my life."

Sian's full of energy and warmth. I feel I understand her because she represents my younger self. Mine wasn't a typical path; I always wanted to be a little different. I was a dancer and taught the art of movement. I got married within six weeks, but divorced when my only son was seven. I've got the life I wanted, but it isn't always easy. I try to offer that perspective to Sian.

Sian on Dilys

I met Dilys in Cardiff, where we both live, at an event called Superwoman. We were both invited to speak and were at the same table. Dilys did a lot of charity work with disabled people, as well as being the world's oldest female solo skydiver. I was there to talk about my media marketing company. We hit it off; I thought she was amazing and the way I want to be as I grow older.

We love to sit with take-out food and listen to Mozart. We like movies and the theater. She has a huge amount of energy and can dance for longer than me. She even persuaded me to do a skydive, despite my fear of heights. When we're in a cab, taxi drivers ask how we met, but we never think of our age gap. She advises me on my love life, work, and how to be a better person.

"She's the way I want to be as I grow older."

I often walk into Dilys's house when I'm stressed and within seconds I'm more relaxed. She calms me down when I'm angry, and teaches me to see things from other people's point of view. Now, she's the first person I call when anything good or bad happens. My family says how much good she does me.

> **Glossary**
> **the races** a series of horse races that happen at one place on a particular day

Adapted from The Guardian

d Now read the article, where each woman talks about how they met and about their relationship. Who are the following sentences true for? Write **S** (Sian), **D** (Dilys), or **B** (both of them).

1 ___ She admires the other person.
2 ___ She cheered the other person up on one specific occasion.
3 ___ She got along immediately with the other person.
4 ___ She has done an extreme sport.
5 ___ She has helped the other person to be more open-minded.
6 ___ She has introduced the other to things she hadn't tried before.
7 ___ She likes cultural activities.
8 ___ She manages an organization that helps people.
9 ___ She runs a company.
10 ___ She's good at giving advice.
11 ___ She's very energetic.
12 ___ She doesn't like being in high places.

e Look at your answers to **d**. What do you think is the secret of Dilys and Sian's friendship?

f Now look at the photo of Dave and John. What do you think the age difference is between them?

▲ Dave and John

g **©** **Communication** The joy of the age-gap friendship
A p.107 B p.111 Read about Dave and John and compare what they say about each other.

h Complete some phrases from the four texts. Compare with a partner and explain what they mean in your own words.

1 **Dilys** We just cl_____.
2 **Sian** We h_____ it off.
3 **Sian** We never think of our age g_____.
4 **Sian** She…teaches me to see things from other people's p_____ of v_____.
5 **Dave** I've learned never to t_____ sides.
6 **John** (He loves cars;) I couldn't c_____ less.
7 **John** I l_____ up to him.

i Talk to a partner.
- Are you good friends with anyone who is a lot older or younger than you?
- If yes, how did you meet? Why do you get along well? What kind of things do you do together?
- If no, what advantages do you think there are to having a friend of a different generation?
- Is there a family member from a different generation who you are close to? What do you like about them?

2 GRAMMAR using adjectives as nouns, adjective order

a Look at the sentences in 1 and 2 below and decide if you think they are right (✓) or wrong (✗). Compare with a partner and say why you think the ✗ ones are wrong.

1 a ___ In general, it's difficult for the old and the young to be good friends.
  b ___ In general, it's difficult for the old people and the young people to be good friends.
  c ___ In general, it's difficult for old people and young people to be good friends.
2 a ___ Sian is a lively, dark-haired, Welsh woman.
  b ___ Sian is a Welsh, lively, dark-haired woman.
  c ___ Sian is a dark-haired, Welsh, lively woman.

b **©** **p.135 Grammar Bank 2B**

c Discuss the statements below in small groups. Do you agree? Why (not)?
- Young people don't respect the old as much as they used to.
- Politicians should be at least 40 years old – the young don't have enough experience for such a responsible job.
- Rich people are often less generous than poor people.
- The unemployed should take any job they can. Any job is better than no job.
- The homeless should be allowed to live rent-free in empty second homes.

3 VOCABULARY clothes and fashion

a Look at the title of an article about fashion. What's your answer to the question?

b Look at the photo of the Hoppen family and read the article. Complete the highlighted phrases with the clothes in the box.

---
dress   jacket   jeans   sandals
sweater   top   sneakers

Can the same clothes work for all ages?

It's odd to imagine wearing the same clothes as your 55-year-old mother or even your 80-year-old grandmother, but fashion, it seems, has finally crossed the age divide. "It's not about what you 'should' wear when you're young or old," says designer Emilia Wikstead. "It's about finding the things that really suit you, regardless of your age."

The Hoppen family:
Plum Hoppen (21),
her mother Jenny (60),
her sister Daisy (31)
[= from left to right]

When three women of the same clothing and shoe size live under the same roof, clothes are bound to go missing. "I remember seeing this girl in the park and thinking, 'That's a nice dress; it looks like one of mine,'" says Jenny Hoppen. "And I realized it was Daisy, going to a wedding, wearing my dress and shoes." But even if they borrow from each other, the same piece looks different on them all.

In the photo, they are all wearing the same ¹cropped _____. Plum wears hers with ²a leather _____ and ³patterned _____, but they look just as good on Jenny with ⁴a silk V-neck _____ and ⁵red velvet _____, or on Daisy with ⁶a see-through black _____ worn over ⁷a black turtle-neck _____. "The principle we learned from our mother," says Daisy, "is to have our own sense of style and be adventurous."

c Whose "look" do you prefer? Do you ever borrow clothes or accessories from people in your family, or friends?

d **V** p.153 **Vocabulary Bank** Clothes and fashion

4 PRONUNCIATION vowel sounds

a 2.21 Look at the pairs of sound pictures below. Put two words from the box in each column. Listen and check.

---
awful cotton dotted hooded jeans
leather linen long loose patterned
sandals sleeveless slippers suit vest wool

boot	bull	tree	fish

egg	cat	clock	saw

b **P** Sound Bank p.166 Look at the typical spellings for these sounds.

c 2.22 Listen to some phrases describing clothes. Is anyone in the class wearing them, or something similar?

d Talk in pairs. What would or wouldn't you wear…?

---
to a formal interview   on the beach
to work or school / college
to a wedding   sightseeing in a city
---

5 LISTENING & SPEAKING

a Look at the clothes in the photos. What age group do you associate them with?

1 a cardigan and fur slippers
2 a leather miniskirt
3 very short shorts
4 tight jeans and a T-shirt with a slogan
5 a blazer and chinos

I'M NEVER RONG.

b 🔊 **2.23** Listen to a radio discussion about dressing your age. Match the clothes 1–5 in **a** to what the journalists say about them, A–F. There is one comment you don't need.

A ___ "They never suit an older person."
B ___ "They make younger men look older than they are."
C ___ "A woman in her 70s looked great in one."
D ___ "Middle-aged men tend to wear them a lot."
E ___ "Older people should never wear clothes made of this material."
F ___ "Your grandma probably won't like them as a present."

c Listen again and mark the opinions **T** (true) or **F** (false). Correct the **F** ones.

Liza thinks that…
1 90% of women dress younger than their age.
2 teenage girls would never dress older than their age.
3 it's fine for older women to wear trendy clothes.

Adrian thinks that…
4 very few men admit to dressing younger than their age.
5 Mick Jagger looks awful in many of the clothes he wears.
6 men usually wear a suit and tie to work.

d In pairs, think about what the journalists said, and try to complete their fashion rules.

Liza	Wear whatever you think _____ and makes you _____.
Adrian	Dress for the age _____, not for the age _____.

e 🔊 **2.24** Listen to the end of the discussion and check. Who do you agree with more, Liza or Adrian?

f Work in groups of three, and discuss three of the topics below. Take turns being the host. The host chooses the topic and manages the discussion. Try to use the language from the box.

- People should stop buying new clothes and buy more second-hand and vintage clothes.
- Men are just as interested in shopping for clothes as women.
- These days, nobody is prepared to suffer in order to look good. The most important thing is comfort.
- You can tell a lot about someone's personality from the clothes they wear.
- Cheap fashion means exploiting people in less developed countries.

> 🔍 **Managing discussions**
> Let's start with you, (Liza).   So, to sum up…
> (Adrian,) what about…?   Can you let (Liza) finish?
> Let's go back to…   Sorry. Go ahead.
>
> **Politely disagreeing**
> Sorry, but I don't agree.   I'm not sure about that.
> True, but…   I agree up to a point, but…

6 WRITING

a Imagine you have decided to sell two items of clothing on eBay. Write detailed descriptions, using the example below as a model. Set a starting price.

Blue and white striped cotton shirt – Size M
Condition: New without tags

"Never worn! Would look great with jeans. Perfect for the summer."

$12.99

b Now read some other students' ads. What would you like to bid for?

7 ▶ VIDEO LISTENING

a Watch an interview about the Hiut jeans company. What do you think is the unique selling point (USP) of their jeans?

b Watch the interview again. Then make notes under the following categories.

Description of jeans
1 Material: *denim*
2 Style:
3 Celebrity wearer:
History of company
4 When David and Clare started it and why:
5 Who they employ:
6 How many pairs of jeans they produce per week:
7 How they try to make their jeans environmentally friendly:

c Would you like to have a pair of Hiut jeans? Would you be prepared to join the no-wash club? Why (not)?

🔄 **Go online** to watch the video and review the lesson

GRAMMAR

a Complete the sentences with one word.

1 What were you and Sarah talking _____?
2 You didn't like her latest novel, _____ you?
3 My father loves opera and so _____ my mother.
4 **A** I've been to India twice.
   B You _____? I'd love to go.
5 What have you _____ doing since last week?

b Circle a, b, or c.

1 Could you tell me what time ____?
   a the bus leaves   b leaves the bus
   c does the bus leave
2 How many people ____ this computer?
   a do use   b use   c does use
3 You're not eating much. ____ like the food?
   a You don't   b Don't you   c Aren't you
4 **A** Why didn't you call me?
   B I ____, but your phone was off.
   a do call   b did called   c did call
5 The slower you work, ____ you'll finish.
   a later   b the later   c the later than
6 ____ three cups of coffee already this morning.
   a I've been having   b I've had   c I have
7 That was probably the worst movie ____!
   a I've ever seen   b I've never seen
   c I've ever been seeing
8 I met ____ in my language class today.
   a a Japanese
   b the Japanese
   c a Japanese woman
9 Some people think that ____ don't pay enough tax.
   a the rich   b the rich people   c rich
10 I got a ____ bag for my birthday.
   a beautiful leather Italian
   b Italian leather beautiful
   c beautiful Italian leather

VOCABULARY

a Complete the compound adjectives.

1 My boss is very bad-_____. When things go wrong, he starts shouting at everyone.
2 I'm very _____minded. I tend to forget things.
3 I think Paul is very tight-_____. He never spends money unless he absolutely has to.
4 Sylvia won't have any problems at the interview – she's very self-_____.
5 That sweater is very old-_____. It looks like the kind of thing my grandpa would wear.

b Write words for the definitions.

1 bl_____ (*verb*) to lose blood from an injury
2 sw_____ (*adj.*) bigger than normal, especially because of an injury or infection
3 b_____ (*noun*) a piece of cloth used to tie around a part of the body that has been hurt
4 t_____ (*noun*) a pain in one of your teeth
5 r_____ (*noun*) an area of red spots caused by an illness or allergy

c Circle the correct verb or verb phrase.

1 I *have / feel* a little dizzy. I need to sit down.
2 She *burned / sprained* her ankle when she was jogging.
3 It was so hot in the room that I nearly *fainted / choked*.
4 This skirt doesn't *fit / suit* me. It's too big.
5 Can I go in jeans? I don't feel like getting *dressed / changed*.

d Circle the word that is different.

1 striped   dotted   plain   patterned
2 silk   cotton   fur   plaid
3 collar   sleeveless   hooded   long-sleeved
4 Lycra   scarf   vest   cardigan
5 fashionable   scruffy   stylish   trendy

e Complete with one word.

1 My mother had a very bad case of the flu last week, but she's beginning to get _____ it now.
2 Please lie _____ on the couch over there.
3 I'm feeling sick. I think I'm going to _____ up.
4 Do we really need to dress _____ for the party tonight?
5 Please _____ up your clothes in the closet.

PRONUNCIATION

a Circle the word with a different sound.

1		ache choke change matches
2		unconscious rash fashion suede
3		injury striped silk blister
4		jeans leather velvet denim
5		cough flu suit loose

b Underline the main stressed syllable.

1 in|cre|di|bly   3 an|ti|bi|o|tics   5 fa|shio|na|ble
2 big-|hea|ded   4 swim|suit

CAN YOU understand this text?

a Read the article once. Do the scientists who have studied Scott Kelly agree about the effect of space travel on the human body?

b Read the article again and choose a, b, or c.

1 Scientists expected that, after spending a year in space, Scott Kelly would be…
   a more intelligent.
   b taller and lighter.
   c younger.

2 Telomeres prevent…
   a aging.
   b radiation.
   c damage to our chromosomes.

3 Scientists are afraid that astronauts…
   a will not want to do long space flights.
   b will have a lot of long-term health problems.
   c won't be able to travel further than Mars.

4 In space, astronauts…
   a must use the gym twice a week.
   b exercise more than when they are in training.
   c are not allowed to eat whatever they like.

▶ CAN YOU understand these people?

🔊 2.25 Watch or listen and choose a, b, or c.

1 Sean   2 Harry   3 Maria   4 Mark

1 One of the questions Sean was asked at a job interview was ____.
   a whether he liked working in restaurants
   b what his favorite basketball team was
   c who his favorite superhero was

2 In the house where Harry grew up, there is a ghost that ____.
   a all of her family has seen
   b all of her family has heard
   c all of her family is afraid of

3 Maria gave her little brother first aid when ____.
   a her mother was not at home
   b his older brother had hit him on the head
   c he fell off the sofa and cut himself

4 Mark meets younger friends ____.
   a through classes he teaches
   b at the theater
   c when he exercises

Astronaut returns from space younger than his twin

American astronaut Scott Kelly, and his identical twin **Mark**, also a retired astronaut, may be the most studied siblings in the history of science. Each time one of them went into space while the other remained on Earth, both men would carry out dozens of experiments, including cognitive exercises, genetic sequencing, and testing for bacteria on their bodies. When Scott landed in Kazakhstan last year, after 340 days in space, he came back two inches taller, fifteen pounds lighter, and with a strong desire to jump into a swimming pool. Changes like these were predictable and temporary. Now, however, scientists have found the first signs of a change that no one expected – during his year on board the International Space Station, Scott's body had become younger.

One of the genetic indicators of human aging is the length of our telomeres. Telomeres are the caps at the end of each strand of DNA that protect our chromosomes, like the plastic tips at the end of shoelaces. Usually, telomeres get shorter as we age; they are about 11,000 molecules long when we are born and only about 4,000 long in old age, and this means that our DNA is increasingly vulnerable to damage as we get older. However, an analysis of Scott Kelly's cells, led by Susan Bailey, professor of radiation cancer biology at Colorado State University, showed that the 52-year-old astronaut's telomeres got longer while he was in space, before shrinking back again after returning to Earth.

In theory, expanding telomeres indicate the reversal of part of the aging process. However, they are also strongly linked to cancer. NASA is aiming to send humans to Mars and beyond, but many scientists worry that long-haul trips into space could cause astronauts to suffer from chronic and severe health problems. So this is definitely not good news, and it could have serious implications for the future of space travel.

Christopher Mason, assistant professor of physiology and biophysics at Cornell Weill Medicine in New York, takes a different view. Professor Mason's team also found changes in Scott Kelly's genes while he was in space. But he thinks this may be less a result of simply being in space, and more due to the intense NASA fitness regime. "On Earth, you might go to the gym on Tuesday and then decide you can't be bothered on Thursday and go out for a big dinner, but on the space station, the astronauts exercise extremely regularly, and all food and exercise is very controlled."

Adapted from The Times

> Airplane travel is nature's way of making you look like your passport photo.
> *Al Gore, US politician and environmentalist*

G narrative tenses, past perfect continuous, *so / such...that* **V** air travel **P** irregular past forms, sentence rhythm

1 LISTENING & VOCABULARY air travel

a 🔊 **3.1** Listen to some announcements. Would you hear them when traveling by train or by plane? Write **T** or **P**.
A ☐ B ☐ C ☐ D ☐ E ☐ F ☐ G ☐ H ☐ I ☐ J ☐

b 🔊 **3.2** Listen again to the ones you would hear when traveling by train (or subway). What do you need to know if you want to travel on...?

1 the 9:04 train to Waterbury
2 the Hudson Line service to Grand Central Terminal
3 the 10:25 to Chicago, in the dining car
4 the J, M, and Z trains

c 🔊 **3.3** Listen again to the ones you would hear when traveling by plane. Answer the questions for each one.

- Would you hear it in the airport terminal or on the plane?
- What is it asking people to do?

d 🔊 **3.4** Listen to some extracts from the announcements 1–6 in **c**. What do these formal words and phrases mean?

1 approximately   4 place, personal electronic devices
2 locate   5 requiring
3 proceed to   6 disembark, rear

e **V** p.154 **Vocabulary Bank** Air travel

2 READING

a When you travel by plane, bus, or train, do you usually prefer to sit in the front, in the middle, or in the back? Do you prefer a window seat or an aisle seat? Why?

b Look at the seating diagram of a plane and the seats marked with an X. Then read the article about where to sit on a plane and match the seat numbers to the correct paragraphs.

How to get the best seat

Every time you fly and have to choose a seat, you ask yourself, "Which is the best seat to choose?" The answer is that it depends entirely on your priorities as a passenger. *Telegraph Travel* has sifted through the research to reveal the top spots.

If you want a speedy exit ☐
You're on a three-day weekend trip to Chicago, and you're traveling light with just a small carry-on bag in the [1]_____. You want to maximize the amount of time you spend at your destination and minimize the time spent on the plane. Verdict? You need to grab an aisle seat towards the front of the plane on the left, which is where the main exit is located and where passengers leave the aircraft from.

If you want to sleep ☐
Sleep is hard to come by at an [2]_____ of 35,000 feet. There are so many things conspiring against you that it's hard to nod off: the hum of the engines, the passenger next to you needing to get out, the lack of neck support in your seat. Some places, however, are better than others, for example, some areas of the [3]_____ are less noisy. Window seats give you control of the window blind and a place to rest your head; they also mean you don't need to be woken up every time the passenger next to you needs to go to the bathroom. The verdict? A window seat at the front of the plane, where it is also quieter.

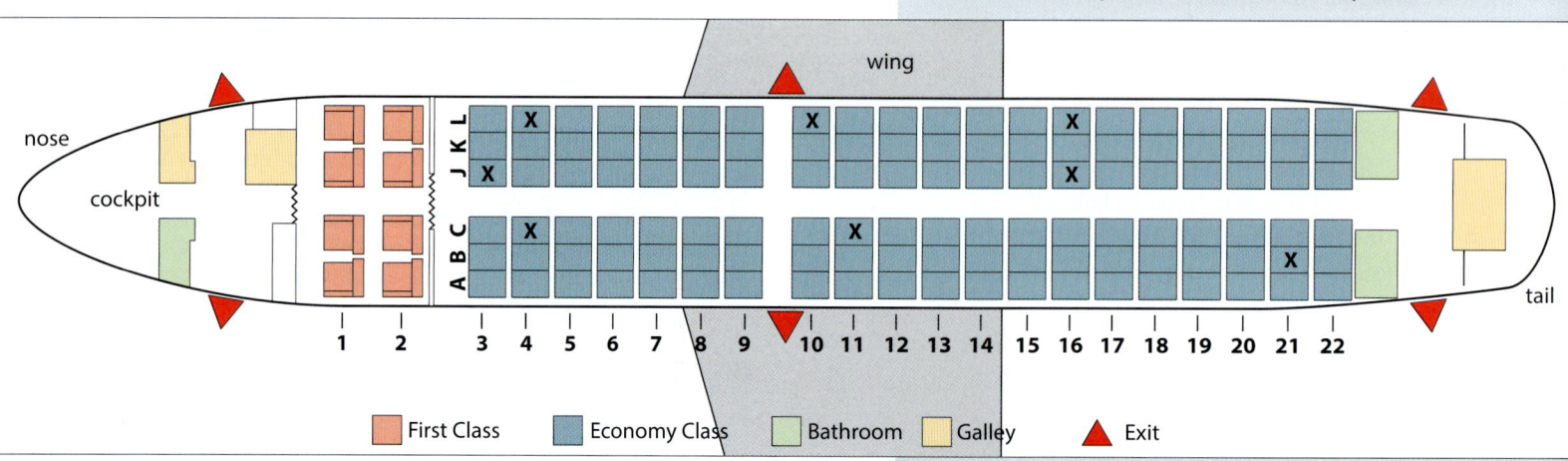

nose · cockpit · wing · tail

1 2 3 4 5 6 7 8 9 10 11 12 13 14 15 16 17 18 19 20 21 22

☐ First Class ☐ Economy Class ☐ Bathroom ☐ Galley ▲ Exit

Adapted from The Telegraph

If you don't like turbulence ☐
Turbulence does, of course, shake the entire aircraft, but experts claim there are some seats on a plane where bumps will feel less intense. The verdict? Sit in the middle of the plane, above the wings, which help keep the plane steady when the going gets tough.

If you need more legroom ☐
Seats in exit rows have more legroom than most. These seats are, however, in such high demand that some airlines, especially 4 _____ ones, charge more for them. They also come with restrictions: passengers in exit rows, for instance, must be willing to assist in the 5 _____ of the aircraft during an emergency, so they are not available for children or people needing 6 _____. The verdict? If you're traveling without children, if you're in shape, and you can afford it, choose a seat in an exit row.

If you want a better dining experience ☐
According to Professor Charles Spence – author of *Gastrophysics: The New Science of Eating* – plane food tastes better at the front of the aircraft, where it is quieter and the air is more humid. "Dry cabin air and the loud 7 _____ noise all contribute to our inability to taste and smell food and drink," he told *Telegraph Travel*. Verdict? Sit as close to the cockpit as possible if you want to make plane food taste better. More often than not, you'll also get served first.

If you're safety-conscious ☐
Airlines and plane manufacturers will tell you that all seats are equal when it comes to matters of safety. However, some seats are more equal than others. A 2007 study by the magazine *Popular Mechanics* found that passengers sitting near the 8 _____ of a plane were 40 percent more likely to survive a crash than those sitting in the first few rows. Verdict? Sit as far back as possible.

If you want to have an empty seat next to you ☐ ☐
If you are flying with a companion, try booking both the aisle and the window seat. You will often find that the middle seat – because it is the least favored by passengers traveling solo – has been left empty. Relax and enjoy it.

c Now read the article again and complete it with a word or phrase from the box.

> altitude   cabin   engine   evacuation
> low-cost   overhead compartment
> special assistance   tail

d According to the information in the article, which do you now think would be the best seat for you?

---

e **Grammar in context** *so / such…that…*

> There are **so many** things conspiring against you **that** it's hard to nod off…
>
> These seats are, however, in **such high demand that** some airlines, especially low-cost ones, charge more for them.

We often use *so / such…that* to express a consequence.

- Use *so* + adjective or adverb, e.g., *The taxi driver drove so quickly (that) we got to the airport on time.*
- Use *so much* + uncountable noun and *so many* + plural countable noun, e.g., *There was so much traffic / There were so many buses on the road (that) we nearly missed our flight.*
- Use *such a* + adjective + single countable noun, e.g., *It was such a great hotel (that) we want to go back there.*
- Use *such* + adjective + uncountable or plural noun, e.g., *We had such terrible weather / such small rooms (that) we didn't enjoy the vacation.*

Complete with *so, so much / many, such,* or *such a.*

1 The flight was _____ long that I got really bored.
2 I had _____ noisy child behind me that I couldn't sleep.
3 I slept _____ badly on the flight from New York that the jet lag was worse than usual.
4 There were _____ people at check-in that we had to stand in line for nearly 45 minutes.
5 We had _____ luggage that we had to get two carts.
6 We met _____ nice people in the hotel that we were never bored.

3 SPEAKING

In pairs, ask and answer the questions.

If you have flown several times
1 How often do you fly? What kinds of airlines do you usually use?
2 When was the last flight you took? Where did you go? What for? Where did you sit?
3 Have you ever flown long-haul? Where did you go? How long was the flight? Did you get jet lag?
4 How do you feel about flying? Have you ever had a very bad experience on a flight?

If you have never / hardly ever flown
1 When was the last time you went on a trip? Where did you go? What for?
2 How do you usually travel a) short distances, b) longer distances? Why do you choose to travel this way?
3 What's the farthest you've ever traveled? Why did you go there?
4 What's your favorite way of traveling? Why?

Have you ever…
- been very delayed when traveling? How long for?
- missed a flight, train, or bus? Why? What did you do?
- had to sit near a screaming baby (or a child that kept kicking your seat) on a plane, train, or bus? What did you do?
- had to catch a connecting flight, train, or bus with very little time to spare? Did you catch it?

4 LISTENING

a You are going to listen to an airline pilot talking on a radio program. Before you listen, discuss questions 1–6 with a partner and imagine what the answers will be.

1 What weather conditions are the most dangerous when you are flying a plane?
2 Is turbulence really dangerous?
3 Which is more dangerous, take-off or landing?
4 Why do passengers have to turn off electronic devices and put their tray tables up during take-off and landing?
5 Is it really worth listening to safety demonstrations?
6 Do you ever get scared?

b 🔴 **3.9** Listen to the program. How many of the pilot's answers did you predict correctly?

c Listen again and take notes. How does he explain his answers?

d What did the pilot say that might make you feel more relaxed the next time you fly?

5 GRAMMAR narrative tenses, past perfect continuous

a Read a newspaper story about a Spirit Airlines flight. What had made its way onto the plane? What happened during the flight?

b Read the story again and circle the correct form of the verbs 1–8.

c Now look at a sentence from the story. What was the flight like before the bat appeared? What tense do you think the highlighted verb is?

> The plane had been flying for nearly 30 minutes before the creature made its appearance in the passenger cabin. Up until that point, the flight had been routine.

d 🔵 p.136 Grammar Bank 3A

e In pairs or groups, try to complete the two sentences in four different ways, using the four narrative tenses.

1 The police stopped the driver because he…
2 I couldn't sleep last night because…

Routine flight goes "batty"

Passengers on a Spirit Airlines flight from Charlotte, North Carolina to Newark, New Jersey on July 31, 2018, were surprised when a bat was spotted flying on board. The plane had been flying for nearly 30 minutes before the creature made its appearance in the passenger cabin. Up until that point, the flight had been routine. Most passengers [1] *had sat / were sitting* quietly in their seats, enjoying a drink and a snack. Once passengers [2] *realized / had realized* that a bat was on the plane, they began taking videos as it frantically swooped through the cabin. One video posted to social media shows a passenger running down the aisle as others [3] *had screamed / were screaming.*

Peter Scattini, one of the passengers on board, [4] *tweeted / was tweeting* a video of the bat with the following text, "Me, twice a year: 'I'll never fly Spirit again.' Me, this morning, after deciding I'd rather save 12 dollars." Another passenger, who [5] *had filmed / was filming* the bat, posted a video that showed people laughing as they watched the bat fly through the cabin.

A spokesperson for Spirit Airlines said, "The bat was eventually corralled into a lavatory and [6] *removed / had removed* once on the ground by animal control officers. The aircraft was disinfected and searched as a precaution." The spokesperson continued, "It is believed the bat started its journey in Charlotte, flying into an overhead bin while our crews [7] *had done / were doing* overnight maintenance. No one was hurt in this incident, including the bat."

Videos of the bat [8] *went / were going* viral on social media, prompting hundreds of people to make jokes about the airline, including Stephen Colbert, host of The Late Show, who tweeted, "I can't believe there was a bat on a Spirit Airlines flight. I've only ever seen raccoons."

Adapted from The Independent

6 PRONUNCIATION irregular past forms, sentence rhythm

a Write the simple past of the following verbs in the chart, according to the pronunciation of the vowel sound.

become catch cut drive fall fight fly hear
hide hold hurt keep leave lie read
ride say sleep tell think throw write

1 🥾	2 🐟	3 🪚	4 🐦
		caught	
5 ☎	6 ↑	7 🍷	8 🚂
			became

b Look at the verbs in **a** again. Which ones have a past participle that is different from the simple past form? Write these past participles in the chart.

c ◐ 3.12 Listen and check. Then listen and repeat.

d Read a short anecdote about a flight. With a partner, guess what the missing verbs might be.

This ¹_____ when my **wife** and I were on a **flight** to **New York**, and we'd been ²_____ for a **few hours**. I was ³_____, and my **wife** was ⁴_____ a **movie**, when **suddenly**, we ⁵_____ an **announcement** – "Is **there** a **doctor** on **board**?" It ⁶_____ **out** that a **woman** was ⁷_____ a **baby**! Luckily, two **doctors** ⁸_____ **forward**, and the **baby** was ⁹_____ **safely**.

e ◐ 3.13 Listen and fill in the blanks. Practice reading the anecdote aloud with the correct rhythm, with light stress on the main verbs and other **bold** words.

7 SPEAKING

a ◉ **Communication** Flight stories **A** p.107 **B** p.112
Read a newspaper story. Then tell your partner the story.

b You are going to tell an anecdote. The story can either be true or invented. If it's invented, you must try to tell it in such a convincing way that your partner thinks it's true. Choose <u>one</u> of the topics below and plan what you're going to say. Use the language in the **Telling an anecdote** box to help you, and ask your teacher for any other words you need.

Talk about a time when you…

were robbed or lost something important when you were traveling or on vacation.

got completely lost while traveling in another city or country.

arrived home from a trip and had a surprise.

> 🔍 **Telling an anecdote**
> **Setting the scene**
> *This happened (to me) when I was…*
> *I was…-ing when…*
> *I…, because I had / hadn't…*
>
> **The main events**
> *I decided to…, because…*
> *So then I…*
> *Suddenly / At that moment,…*
>
> **What happened in the end**
> *In the end / Eventually,…*
> *It turned out that…*
> *I felt…*

c In pairs, **A** tell **B** your story. **B** show interest and ask for more details. Decide whether you think the story is true or not. Then switch roles.

This happened to me a few years ago, when I was on vacation in Florida. I was swimming in the ocean one day when I saw a shark.

Really? How big was it?

◉ **Go online** to review the lesson

A good story should make you laugh, and a moment later break your heart.
Chuck Palahniuk, US author

| **G** the position of adverbs and adverbial phrases | **V** adverbs and adverbial phrases | **P** word stress and intonation |

1 GRAMMAR the position of adverbs and adverbial phrases

a Read four 50-word stories. With a partner, predict how you think each story ends.

fiftywordstories.com

fiftywordstories.com is a website to which people from all over the world contribute 50-word stories in English.

1 Sweet talking

"What are you reading there? It looks serious – you must be **incredibly** smart." He uses his usual pick-up lines on the train. Ask them a simple question. Then pay them a compliment. It **always** works. **Sadly** not this time.

2 Departed

"Is Mommy gone?"
"**Unfortunately** she is, sweetie."
"I miss Mommy."
"So do I, sweetie. Don't cry."
"Let's go and get Mommy, **right now**!"
"We can't do that, sweetie."
"Where is she?"
"She's in a **much** better place."
"WHERE?"

3 Can't live without it

Absolutely alone. Silence imprisons her. Suffocating silence.
She gets up and crosses the room. She presses the button.
Waits.
Three. Two. One.
At once, there is noise! Footsteps running down the stairs.
Shouts and wonderful chaos **at last**! She smiles. Three voices shout in unison,

4 Revenge is sweet

"You're sitting in my seat!" the woman said. She showed me her ticket and shouted **rudely**, "See? It's mine. Move."
I looked at the ticket **carefully**. Then I stood up **silently**.
As the train left the station, I whispered to her,

b Read the four final sentences and match them to the stories. Which one do you think has the best ending?

A "She's gone to have a facial in a nice, *quiet* beauty salon."

B "Mom! The internet's not working!"

C "You have the right seat, but the wrong train."

D "My divorce papers," she replied <mark>angrily</mark>, and turned away.

c Look at the <mark>highlighted</mark> adverbs or adverbial phrases in the stories. Think about what they mean and write them in the correct place in the chart.

Types of adverbs
Time (when things happen, e.g., *immediately*)   <u>right now</u> _____ _____
Manner (how you do something, e.g., *slowly*)   <u>rudely</u> _____ _____ _____
Degree (describing / modifying an adjective, e.g., *very*) <u>incredibly</u> _____   _____
Comment (giving an opinion, e.g., *luckily*)   <u>sadly</u> _____
Frequency (how often things happen, e.g., *rarely*) _____

d With a partner, decide where the **bold** adverbs should go in these sentences.

1 He speaks French and Spanish. **fluently**

2 I use public transportation. **hardly ever**

3 I thought I'd lost my phone, but it was in my bag. **fortunately**

4 It's important that you arrive on time. **extremely**

5 When I find out, I'll tell you. **immediately**

e 🅖 **p.137 Grammar Bank 3B**

f 🔊3.15 Listen to some sound effects and short conversations. Then use the **bold** adverb to complete the sentence.

1 When she got to the bus stop, the bus… **just**

2 They were having a party when… **suddenly**

3 He thought he had lost his boarding pass, but… **luckily**

4 The woman thought Andrea and Tom were friends, but in fact… **hardly**

5 The driver couldn't see where he was going because… **hard**

6 Salvatore couldn't understand the man because… **incredibly**

2 VOCABULARY adverbs and adverbial phrases

a Read another 50-word story. What do you think the missing word is?

Hard rock

I <mark>nearly</mark> forget his birthday! I rush to the store. <mark>Lately</mark>, he enjoys listening to music, so I choose a Bluetooth speaker. I regret it now. His bedroom is <mark>near</mark> mine. The music is really loud! I open the door, and shout, "_____, it's <mark>late</mark>. Please turn the volume down!"

b Look at the <mark>highlighted</mark> adverbs. What's the difference between…?

a *near* and *nearly*   b *late* and *lately*

c 🅥 **p.155 Vocabulary Bank** Adverbs and adverbial phrases

3 PRONUNCIATION word stress and intonation

a 🔊3.18 <u>Underline</u> the stressed syllables in these adverbs. Listen and check.

ab|so|lute|ly   ac|tu|a|lly   a|ppar|ent|ly   ba|si|ca|lly   de|fi|nite|ly
e|spe|cia|lly   e|ven|tual|ly   fortu|nate|ly   gra|dua|lly   i|de|a|lly
in|cre|di|bly   lu|cki|ly   ob|vi|ous|ly   un|fortu|nate|ly

b 🔊3.19 Listen and repeat the sentences, copying the stress and intonation of the adverbs.

1 There was a lot of traffic, and unfortunately, we arrived extremely late.

2 We definitely want to go abroad this summer, ideally somewhere hot.

3 It's incredibly easy – even a child could do it!

4 I thought Roberto was Portuguese, but actually he's Brazilian.

5 Apparently, Jack has been offered a promotion at work, but it will mean moving to New York.

6 I absolutely love Italian food, especially pasta.

4 WRITING

a You are going to write a 50-word story. It must be 50 words exactly (not including the title) and you must include at least two adverbs. Contracted forms (e.g., *I'd*) count as one word. First, in pairs, choose one of the titles below.

A summer romance   A day to remember
The lie   Never again

b Brainstorm ideas for the plot. Then together, write a first draft. Don't worry about the number of words.

c Now edit the story to make it exactly 50 words.

d Read two other pairs' stories. Which do you like best?

5 SPEAKING

a Look at the questions about reading habits and answer them with a partner.

Reading habits

- **Which of the following do you read? How often?**

  PRINT
  comics or magazines
  fiction, e.g., classic or modern novels, short stories, graphic novels
  nonfiction, e.g., self-help books, history books, travel writing, guidebooks
  textbooks, manuals, or instructions

  ONLINE
  blogs   chat rooms / forums
  news reports and articles
  recipes   shopping websites
  social media   song lyrics
  study- or work-related articles

- **Why do you choose to read some things in print and some on-screen?**

- **What do you read, if anything, specifically to improve your English?**

b **○ Communication** Reading habits p.108 Compare your reading habits.

6 READING & LISTENING

🔍 **Reading for pleasure**

When you read this story, you will understand it better and enjoy it more if you ask yourself questions from time to time. Think about…

- the setting of the story: Where and when does it take place?

- the characters: Who are they? What do they look like? What kinds of people are they? How do you feel about them?

- the events of the story: What is happening at each stage? What might happen next?

- the ending: What might have happened after the end of the story? What is the writer trying to say?

Glossary

franc /fræŋk/ (*noun*) French currency, until the euro was introduced in 2002

The Necklace
BY GUY DE MAUPASSANT

Part 1

Mathilde Loisel was a pretty and charming girl, but born into a poor family. She was ambitious, and thought she deserved to be part of the highest level of French society. As she grew up, she was increasingly ashamed of her circumstances, but there was little she could do about it. Eventually, she married a clerk at the Ministry of Education.

They led a simple life, and Mathilde suffered. She felt that she deserved a life of luxury, and their poor house and ugly furniture, and just one young servant, made her miserable. She had no dresses, no jewelry, nothing. She never visited her one rich schoolfriend, Madame Forestier, because she could not bear to see the life that she herself would never have.

One evening, her husband came home, proudly holding in his hand a large envelope.

"Here," he said, "here's something for you."

She quickly opened it. It was an invitation from the Minister of Education to a party at the palace of the Ministry. But instead of being delighted, as her husband had hoped, she threw the invitation on the table.

"What do you want me to do with this?"

"My dear, I thought you would be pleased. You never go out, and this is a great occasion. I went to a lot of trouble to get the invitation. Everybody wants one and not many are given to the clerks. You will meet all kinds of important people there."

She looked at him impatiently and said, "What do you want me to wear to the party?"

He had not thought of that; he hesitated.

"The dress you wear to the theater—"

He stopped, as he saw that his wife was crying.

"What's the matter? What's the matter?"

Mathilde wiped her eyes and replied calmly, "Nothing. Only I have no dress, so I cannot go to this party. Give your invitation to some colleague whose wife has better clothes than I."

Her husband was heartbroken.

"Look here, Mathilde, how much would this cost, a proper dress?"

She thought for a few seconds, and answered, "I don't know exactly, but I think I could do it with four hundred francs."

He grew a little pale. He had saved exactly this amount for a short trip the following summer with his friends. But he said, "All right. I will give you four hundred francs. But make sure you get a pretty dress."

But as the day of the party drew near, Mathilde was still not happy. Although she now had her dress, she had no jewelry to go with it. When she told her husband, he suggested that she ask her friend Jeanne Forestier to lend her something.

Pleased with the idea, she went to her friend's house, and told her about her distress. Madame Forestier agreed to lend her something. She tried on several pieces, but nothing was right, until she suddenly saw a magnificent diamond necklace. To her joy, her friend let her borrow it.

a 🔊 **3.20** Read and listen to Part 1 of a short story. With a partner, continue sentences 1–8 **in your own words**.

1 Mathilde was unhappy because…
2 She never visited Madame Forestier because…
3 Her husband was proud when he came home one night because…
4 Mathilde threw the invitation on the table because…
5 Her husband was really upset because…
6 He was able to give her the money for a dress because…
7 Mathilde was still unhappy because….
8 She was delighted when she visited Madame Forestier because …

When do you think the story takes place? What kinds of people are Mathilde and her husband? Who do you sympathize with more?
Do you think Mathilde will enjoy the party?

b 🔊 **3.21** Now listen to Part 2. Answer the questions with a partner.

1 Did Mathilde enjoy the party? Give examples.
2 How did they get home?
3 What did she discover when they got home?
4 What did her husband do?
5 What did they decide to do in the end?
6 How did they raise the money?
7 How did Madame Forestier react?

How do you think their lives will change now?

> **Glossary**
> **clasp** /klæsp/ (*noun*) a device that fastens something, such as a handbag, or the ends of a piece of jewelry
> **Palais Royal** /ˈpæleɪ rɔrˈjæl/ an expensive area of Paris

c 🔊 **3.22** Read and listen to Part 3. Answer the questions with a partner.

1 How did life change for Mathilde?
2 How did it change for her husband?
3 What had they achieved at the end of the ten years?
4 How had Mathilde changed over the ten years?

Who do you think suffered the most, Mathilde or her husband? Why?
What do you think would have happened if Mathilde hadn't lost the necklace? How do you think the story ends?

d 🔊 **3.23** Listen to the end of the story. Did it end the way you expected?

Do your feelings for Mathilde change during the story?
What do you think might have happened after the final conversation?
What do you think the message of the story is?

> **Glossary**
> **Champs-Elysées** /ʃɑmz eiˈlizei/ the most famous and beautiful avenue in Paris, which goes from the Place de la Concorde to the Arc de Triomphe

7 WRITING

Ⓦ **p.116 Writing** A short story   Write a short story of 140–190 words.

Part 3

Mathilde now learned the terrible life of the really poor. Heroically, she made the best of it. The debt must be paid. She would pay it. They dismissed their servant; they left their house and rented a small attic under the roof.

She learned how to do housework, and how to cook. She washed the dishes, wearing out her pink nails on the greasy pots and the bottoms of the pans. She washed their dirty sheets and clothes. She took their rubbish down to the street every morning, and she carried up the water, pausing for breath on every floor. Wearing old, worn-out clothes, she went out to the greengrocer, the grocer, the butcher, with a basket on her arm, bargaining, insulted, fighting to save a sou here or there.

Every month, they had to pay back part of the money they had borrowed. Her husband worked in the evening, doing the accounts for a shopkeeper, and at night, often, he did copying at five sous the page.

This life lasted ten years. At the end of ten years, they had paid everything back, everything, with all the accumulation of interest.

With her badly combed hair, and her red hands, Mathilde now looked like an old woman. But sometimes, when her husband was at the office, she sat down by the window, and she thought of that evening long ago, of that party, where she had been so beautiful and so admired.

What would have happened if she had not lost that necklace? Who knows? Who knows?

> **Glossary**
> **sou** /su/ (*noun*) an old French coin worth very little (100 sous = 1 franc)

🔘 **Go online** to review the lesson

1 ▶ THE INTERVIEW Part 1

a Read the biographical information about Marion Pomeranc. In what way are the two parts of her career connected?

> **Marion Pomeranc** is the manager of literary programs at a non-profit organization in New York City called Learning Leaders. The programs involve encouraging children to read by providing books for children who don't have much access to them, and getting adults to come in and read to them, and discuss the books. She is also the author of three children's books, *The Hand-Me-Down Horse*, *The American Wei*, and *The Can Do Thanksgiving*. She believes in dealing with serious topics in her books such as hunger and immigration, but in a way that children can relate to.

b Watch Part 1 of an interview with her. Why does she mention these four books?

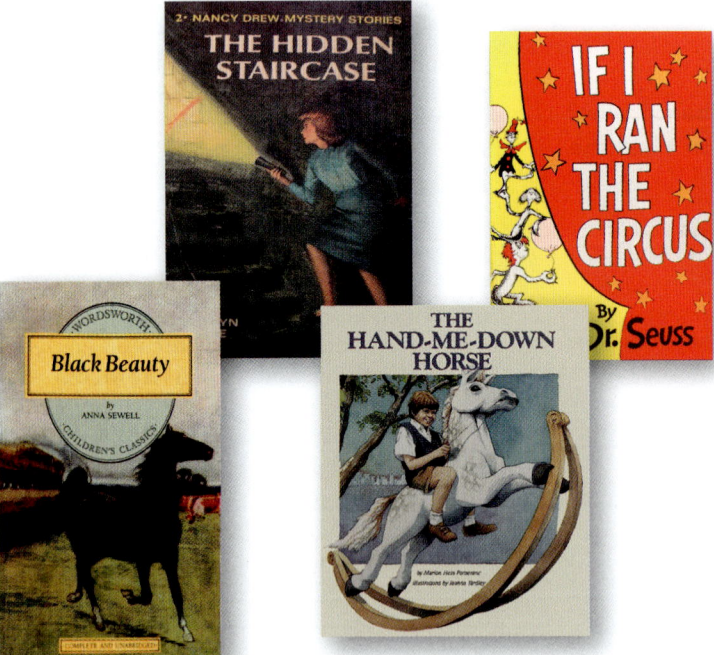

c Now watch again and mark the sentences **T** (true) or **F** (false). Say why the **F** sentences are false.

1 What Marion loved about *If I Ran the Circus* was the pictures.
2 She helped her parents to become readers.
3 She read to her son a few times a week.
4 Her son reads mainly fiction these days.
5 Marion doesn't like the fact that children's authors today write about real life.

> **Glossary**
> ***Corduroy*** a children's book by Don Freeman about a teddy bear
> **fiction** a type of literature that describes imaginary people and events

▶ Part 2

a Now watch Part 2. What does Marion say is important for getting a) teenagers to read more b) younger children to read.

b Watch again. Check (✓) the things that she says are good for encouraging teenagers and children to read.

Teenagers
1 ☐ Not insisting on them finishing a book.
2 ☐ Getting them to buy e-books.
3 ☐ Suggesting that they read in bed at night.
4 ☐ Accepting that they don't just have to read books to become good readers.
5 ☐ Series of books where the same characters reoccur.

Children
1 ☐ Having a lot of books in the house.
2 ☐ Going to visit libraries or publishers.
3 ☐ Always buying them books as birthday presents.
4 ☐ Hearing authors talk about their books.
5 ☐ Books where children have a more active role than the adults.
6 ☐ Books with beautiful illustrations.

> **Glossary**
> **ads** abbreviation for advertisements
> **goofy** silly or foolish

▶ Part 3

a Now watch Part 3. Is Marion positive or negative about new technology and the future of books?

b Watch again and answer the questions.

1 Why does she prefer to read on an e-reader these days?

2 Why does she think all children should have an e-reader ?

3 In what way does she think social media can be positive for kids?

4 How often does she read for pleasure? Where, when, and why?

2 ▶ LOOKING AT LANGUAGE

> 🔍 **Ways of giving yourself time to think**
> Marion often gives herself time to think when she is answering questions by repeating the question or stopping and starting again. She also uses filler sounds such as "um" and "uh," and certain words or phrases, e.g., *you know*, etc. that don't add meaning but that are used for this purpose.

🔊 **3.27** Watch some extracts from the interview and complete the missing words or phrases.

1 I What was it that you liked about Dr. Seuss?
   M _____ _____ _____ about Dr. Seuss is his use of language…

2 " _____ _____, the made-up words, the way the words flow together and sound."

3 "…or you can read the side of a cereal box. _____ _____, that's all reading."

4 "And I think if you'd look carefully at books that kids really like, it's the one where, where youth dominates. And _____ _____ rules the world a little bit."

5 I Do you think social media has decreased or increased people's literacy?
   M _____ _____ I think social media has had a positive effect on children.

3 ▶ THE CONVERSATION

a Watch the conversation. Who (E, D, or I)…?

☐ recommends one book

☐ recommends more than one book

☐ doesn't recommend a specific book

b Watch again. Answer the questions with **A** (Harry Potter), **B** (*The Diving Bell and the Butterfly*), or **C** (*Everything I Know About Love*).

Which book…?

1 ☐ did Emma tell lots of friends to read

2 ☐ has Ida never heard of

3 ☐ isn't very long

4 ☐ has David never read

5 ☐ does Ida think has influenced people from all over the world

6 ☐ is about the author's life and upbringing

7 ☐ was David both moved and uplifted by

8 ☐ does Emma think sounds good because you learn from other people's experiences

9 ☐ is set in the present day

c Have you read any of the books they mention? If no, did what they say make you want to read them? Is there a book you think everyone should read?

d Watch an extract and ⊙circle the vague language you hear. Are the other options also possible?

Emma I think, from, like, all of my friends that are my age, we all kind of read it when we were young and it just becomes, [1] *I mean / like*, everyone knows what you mean when you talk about your Hogwarts house, for example.

Ida Yeah.

Emma And you just [2] *kind of / sort of* lose yourself in this fantasy. The book that you read as a child, I still kind of re-read it every few years and a lot of people have said that it's helped them deal with, like, grief and…

David Wow!

Emma …[3] *stuff like that / things like that*. So, I think it's actually quite powerful.

Ida I think also because, like you were saying, you, you, [4] *kind of / sort of* grew up with it.

e Now have a conversation in groups of three.

1 Do you think people who read are normally more intelligent than people who don't?

2 Do you think that young people have problems reading long or difficult texts because of the kind of reading they do on social media? Is this a problem?

🔄 **Go online** to watch the video, review the lesson, and check your progress

G future perfect and future continuous   **V** the environment, weather   **P** vowel sounds

> You cannot go through a single day without having an impact on the world around you.
> *Jane Goodall, UK anthropologist*

1 SPEAKING

a What do you understand by the expression *environmentally friendly*? Can you think of any synonyms? On a scale of 1–10, how environmentally friendly do you think a) your friends and family are, b) people in your town are?

b Complete the questionnaire and figure out your score. Then compare with a partner. Give examples to explain your answers.

c **Ⓒ Communication** Your score p.108   Read about what your score means.

Are you <u>really</u> as environmentally friendly as you think you are?

A Your "values"

Circle the statement (1–5) that best describes your habits. Write the number in the box.

1 I don't really do anything environmentally friendly.

2 I do one or two things that are environmentally friendly.

3 I do quite a few things that are environmentally friendly.

4 Most things I do are environmentally friendly.

5 Everything I do is environmentally friendly.

Your value score = ☐

B Your "actions"

How often do you do each of the following? Score each action from 1 (never) to 5 (always).

a ☐ turn off lights when you leave a room

b ☐ put on a sweater rather than turning up the heat

c ☐ avoid buying something with a lot of packaging

d ☐ take your own shopping bag

e ☐ use public transportation instead of driving

f ☐ walk or ride your bike

g ☐ buy recycled toilet paper

h ☐ avoid taking airline flights

i ☐ avoid leaving your TV on when you're not watching it

j ☐ turn the faucet off when brushing your teeth

Your action score = ☐

Your overall score

First, figure out your "actions" score. Take the average of section **B** (add up and divide by 10) and write the number in the box.

Subtract your "value" score **A** from your "action" score **B**.

2 GRAMMAR future perfect and future continuous

a Look at the title of the infographic. What predictions do you think it will make about the things in the box?

energy   waste   transportation   food and water   the weather

b Now read the infographic. How many of your predictions were there? With a partner, say which ones…

1 you think are likely to happen in the next 20 years.
2 you think will definitely happen in the next 20 years.
3 you think probably won't ever happen.
4 you would most and least like to come true.

How will we be living in 20 YEARS?

ENERGY

Fossil fuels, like coal and gas, will be very expensive. Most people ¹ will have installed solar panels or wind turbines on their houses or apartment buildings to generate their electricity.

WASTE

People ² will be recycling nearly 100% of their waste (and those who don't will have to pay a fine). All stores and cafés ³ will have stopped using plastic bags and single-use containers, like to-go coffee cups.

TRANSPORTATION

Governments ⁴ will have invested a lot of money in public transportation. Everyone ⁵ will be riding their bikes, walking, or using the bus and train more. Low-cost airlines ⁶ will have disappeared and flights will be much more expensive.

FOOD AND WATER

Farmers ⁷ will have stopped producing meat commercially and many kinds of fish ⁸ will have died out. Fresh water ⁹ will be running out in many parts of the world, and we ¹⁰ will be getting much of our water from the ocean (through desalination plants).

THE WEATHER

We ¹¹ will be having more extreme weather, and heatwaves, hurricanes, floods, etc., will be frequent occurrences. Many ski resorts ¹² will have closed because of a lack of winter snow, and some low-lying beaches and vacation resorts ¹³ will have disappeared completely.

c Look at the highlighted verbs in the predictions. Which ones refer to…?

a an action or situation that will be finished in the future
b an action or situation that will be in progress in the future

d 🄶 p.138 Grammar Bank 4A

e Talk to a partner and say if you think the following predictions will happen. Explain why (not).

In 20 years…

- everyone will be using their own reusable shopping bags, cups, and bottles.
- most people will have stopped eating any animal products and will be eating a vegan diet.
- all private swimming pools and golf courses will have been banned.
- people will be taking more vacations in their own country and fewer abroad.
- car companies will only be selling electric cars.
- most people in office jobs will be working from home.

> 🔎 *definitely, probably,* and *likely / unlikely*
> We often use verb + *definitely* or *probably,* and be *likely / unlikely* + infinitive when talking about the future, especially when we are making predictions.
>
> **I think…**
> it'll definitely happen.
> it's (very) likely to happen.
> it'll probably happen.
> it probably won't happen.
> it's (very) unlikely to happen.
> it definitely won't happen.

f Now make your own predictions about things in the box.

fashion   health and medicine   housing
politics   shopping   social media

3 VOCABULARY weather

a Look at the photos. What kinds of weather events can you see? When did you last see them where you live?

b Ⓥ p.156 Vocabulary Bank Weather

4 PRONUNCIATION vowel sounds

a Look at the groups of words. What is the common sound in each group? Write the sound words for 1–10.

1 _owl_   shower drought
2 _____   below snow
3 _____   cool humid monsoon typhoon
4 _____   flood thunder
5 _____   heavy weather
6 _____   heat wave breeze freezing
7 _____   pouring storm scorching warm
8 _____   drizzling chilly
9 _____   bright icy lightning mild
10_____   clear zero

b 🔊 4.6 Listen and check. Practice saying the groups of words.

5 READING

a Read the introduction to the website of the Climate Stories Project. What is the project about?

b Now look at the photos and read what six people from different continents have to say about climate change. Then with a partner, try to label the photos with the countries where they are from.

c Read the stories again. Then look at the things in the list. For each one, say who mentions them and why they are significant.

1 one month's rainfall
2 September 21st
3 Los Angeles and Manhattan
4 the river
5 _przedwiośnie_
6 beautiful properties and parks

d Which person mentions things that are also happening where you live?

Climate Stories Project

Today, more and more of us are feeling the effects of climate change on a personal and community level. The Climate Stories Project allows people from around the world to share their stories about climate change and explain the impact that it is having on our lives.

Diana Maciaga
from _____

We don't have major hurricanes or wildfires, but you can see that the weather patterns have been changing. For example, the winters are much milder than they used to be 20 years ago, and in the summers, we often have a huge heat wave. We used to have a special name for a period that is between winter and spring: we call it _przedwiośnie_, and now it doesn't really happen. So for me, this is one of the most significant examples of the changes in climate.

Umberto Crespo Palmarito
from _____

Here, the rainy season used to start in March and the rain stopped in November. Now, the heavy rain only starts in June. Years ago, it would be pouring rain every day. And now there can be a week, 15 days, without any rain. My grandfather and my father lived their life according to the weather because it was like a clock: it was never wrong. We used to say that September 21st was the day the weather changed. And now people don't say it. It's completely different from before.

6 LISTENING

a You're going to listen to Matt Wallace, a meteorologist, talking about his job. First, in pairs, read the questions and guess what he's going to answer.

1 What's the difference between a meteorologist and a TV weatherman?
2 How far ahead can you accurately predict the weather?
3 Are long-term forecasts ever accurate?
4 What's your favorite kind of weather?
5 In what ways have you noticed that the weather has changed in the last ten years?
6 Are you optimistic or pessimistic about climate change?

b 🔊 4.7 Listen to the interview once. Did you guess correctly in **a**?

c Listen again. What examples does he give for the following?

1 an occasion when it's difficult to predict the weather
2 how weather in one part of the world affects another part
3 why thunderstorms are exciting to watch at night
4 some unusual weather this year in the US
5 the effects of climate change on the US weather

d Do you think Matt enjoys his job? Why?

7 SPEAKING

Talk to a partner.

Let's talk about the weather
- What's your favorite kind of weather? And your least favorite?
- How does the weather affect your mood?
- Do people in your country complain much about the weather? What kind of weather in particular?
- In what ways has climate change affected the weather in your country?
- Are you optimistic or pessimistic about climate change?

Have you, or has anyone you know, ever been somewhere when...?
- it poured rain for days and days
- there was a flood
- there was a hurricane or it was incredibly windy
- it was absolutely freezing
- it was very foggy, or there was bad smog
- there was a terrible heat wave
- you were caught outside in a thunderstorm

🔍 **Modifiers with strong adjectives**
When you are talking about extreme situations, e.g., very bad weather, you can use:

1 normal adjectives with a modifier (*very, really, extremely, incredibly, unbelievably*), e.g., *It was incredibly cold / extremely hot / unbelievably windy*, etc.
2 strong adjectives, e.g., *It's boiling here – 100 degrees. It's freezing today*, etc.
3 Strong adjectives with *absolutely*, e.g., *It was absolutely freezing. The midday heat was absolutely scorching.*

Nadine Lefort
from _____

For many years, we had less snow in the winter, and then this past year we had an extreme winter – freezing, with terrible blizzards – so weather patterns are changing and it's less predictable. Another thing I notice is that the coasts seem to be eroding much more quickly than they were in the past. It's sad, because so many beautiful properties and parks are right on the coast and it will be a shame to see them gone. People are saying that they'd never buy or build in those places because they'll be gone in the future.

Harou Abass Hadiza
from _____

When I was in elementary school, my friends and I used to go to the river. It was green, and the air was cool and fresh. Some of us were afraid to go far from the riverbank when we were swimming, because the river was deep and had a strong current. However, in the last few years, we've been experiencing increasingly hot weather – extreme heat. Now the river isn't so deep, and it's dusty and dirty. Air quality in my city has also declined. There is more dust, due to desertification.

Efleda Bautista
from _____

I come from Tacloban City, the city that was hit by Typhoon Haiyan, and this is really a prime example of what climate change can do to destroy a community. We had a long drought, and then rainfall equivalent to one month's rainfall falling in one or two days in the city, and everywhere was flooded. That never happened before, and it's closely connected with climate change.

Jordan Hamada
from _____

There hasn't been a big snowstorm here for over ten years. This area is known for its rain, and there hasn't been much for the past few months, and I'm pretty surprised, because it's been so dry this winter. It's definitely not something I think about all the time, but I've seen some articles recently talking about how Los Angeles and Manhattan will eventually be under water, possibly in our lifetime, or the next generation's lifetime, and that makes it seem very real – that's definitely a scary thought.

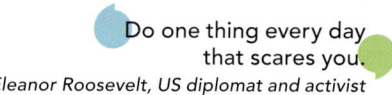

| **G** zero and first conditionals, future time clauses | **V** expressions with *take* | **P** linked phrases |

1 LISTENING

a Look at the things on the list. How risky do you personally think they are? Why? Score them 1–5 (1 = not risky at all, 5 = very risky). Then compare in small groups. How similar are you in your attitude to risk?

- ☐ having cosmetic surgery
- ☐ riding a bike in your city
- ☐ smoking
- ☐ eating street food when you're traveling
- ☐ buying a used car
- ☐ hiking in the mountains
- ☐ online dating
- ☐ telling a lie on your résumé

b 🔊 **4.8** Listen to four people answering the question *Are you a risk-taker?* Write ✓, ✗, or ✓/✗ in the box. Which of the topics in the box does the risk they talk about relate to?

a job	a sport	a relationship	money

1 Holly ☐ _____
2 Natalie ☐ _____
3 Tom ☐ _____
4 Jeanie ☐ _____

c Listen again and write **H** (Holly), **N** (Natalie), **T** (Tom), or **J** (Jeanie).

Who…?

1 ☐ thinks his / her attitude about risk hasn't changed at all throughout his / her life
2 ☐ thinks that the risk varies depending on the price
3 ☐ had to make a life-changing decision
4 ☐ is surprised about how positive he / she felt after doing a risky activity
5 ☐ thinks most people take this kind of risk these days
6 ☐ decided not to go right into working in an office
7 ☐ wonders whether things might have been different if he / she hadn't taken the risk
8 ☐ thinks the risk was worth taking because he / she learned some useful things for the future

d Which speaker do you think took the biggest risk? Why?

2 SPEAKING

a Work with a partner. **A** interview **B** with the questions in the green circles. After each question, write *R* if you think that **B** is prepared to take risks in that area. Then **B** interview **A** in the same way with the blue circles.

b Now compare your answers in each area. Decide which of you is the bigger risk-taker.

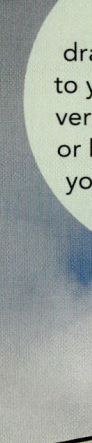

Appearance

Have you ever done something dramatically different to your hair, e.g., had a very different hairstyle or hair color? How did you feel immediately afterwards?

Would you ever get a tattoo or a piercing?

On the road

Do you drive a car or ride a motorcycle? Do you ever go really fast and break the speed limit?

Do you walk by yourself late at night, or take late-night taxis?

Where do you usually cross the street – at a traffic light or crosswalk, or just anywhere?

Shopping and money

Do you have different PINs and passwords, or do you always use the same one?

Do you use internet or mobile banking? Do you think it's safe? Have you ever lost any money from computer fraud?

Have you ever bought something expensive on eBay or a similar site? Would you?

3 GRAMMAR zero and first conditionals, future time clauses

a Match the sentence halves.

1 If my dad finds out I've been hitchhiking, ☐
2 When you're crossing the street in the US, ☐
3 As soon as I've passed my driver's test, ☐
4 If it's still snowing tomorrow, ☐
5 When we've booked the flights, ☐
6 Unless you lend her that money, ☐
7 If his temperature hasn't gone down, ☐
8 If it doesn't rain by the end of the week, ☐

A all the plants in the garden will have died.
B he'll be furious.
C I'm going to buy a car.
D make sure you look left and right.
E she won't be able to buy a train ticket.
F we need to start looking for hotels.
G we won't be driving anywhere.
H he isn't going to school tomorrow.

b Look at the highlighted verbs. In first conditional sentences and future time clauses, what forms or tenses can you use...?

1 after *if*, *when*, etc. (1–8)
2 in the main clause (A–H)

c Now look at two more conditional sentences. Do the **bold** clauses refer to a) something that is a possible consequence of the *if*-clause, or b) something that is always a consequence of the *if*-clause?

1 If you don't take out travel insurance, **you run the risk of paying expensive medical fees**.
2 If you use online banking, **it's essential to never share your password**.

d **G** p.139 **Grammar Bank 4B**

e In pairs, complete each sentence in your own words.

1 Don't buy a used car unless...
2 You shouldn't think about getting a tattoo if...
3 Keep a first-aid kit in your house in case...
4 Children shouldn't use social media until...
5 Always take out travel insurance in case...
6 As soon as you've received your new credit card,...
7 Don't go hiking in the mountains on your own unless...
8 If you are taking a new job abroad,...

Food

If you were offered very unusual food that you'd never had before, would you try it? Why (not)?

If food is past its sell-by date, would you still eat it? Have you ever had food poisoning from eating something that wasn't fresh?

Travel

Have you ever gone on vacation with someone you didn't know very well?

Have you ever taken selfies on vacation in a dangerous place, e.g., on the edge of a cliff?

Do you usually take out insurance when you travel?

If you're traveling somewhere, do you usually get to the station or airport with plenty of time, or do you always arrive at the last minute?

Work and study

Would you accept a job abroad in a country where you didn't speak the language?

Have you ever put off studying for an exam to the last minute? Did you pass?

4 PRONUNCIATION linked phrases

a 🔊 4.12 Listen and complete the sentence below with three words. Can you explain why a) the first and second words are linked together, b) the second and third words are linked together?

I'll call you _____ _____ _____ the mail's been delivered.

b 🔊 4.13 Listen and complete the sentences with more linked phrases.

1 Don't call me _____ emergency.
2 As _____ concerned, you have to be crazy to want to do an extreme sport.
3 Be careful with your wallet, _____, don't use your phone on the street.
4 It was _____ experience that I've never forgotten it.
5 I dyed my hair blue a _____, and I hated it!
6 I was scared at first, but it was _____ the end.
7 _____, let's try to find a cheap hotel.
8 _____ world, everyone would earn a salary.

c In pairs, practice saying the highlighted phrases quickly, trying to link the words together. Then make personal sentences with as many of the phrases as you can.

I never go to the doctor unless it's an emergency.

5 READING

a Look at the photos and label them with a sport from the box. What other extreme sports do you know?

bungee jumping   paragliding   skydiving   wingsuit flying

b Now look at the title of an article about extreme sports, and read the article. Check (✓) the three reasons it gives.

1   More and more celebrities are taking them up.
2   Once some people have tried it, they can't stop.
3   People find traditional sports, like soccer, not challenging enough.
4   People want to have new experiences.
5   They are better known because you can watch other people doing them live online.
6   It's cheaper to do extreme sports than ever before.

c Look at 1–7 below and think about what information is missing: a name or a number. Then read the article again and fill in the blanks.

1 _____: the typical speed of a wingsuit flyer
2 _____: the age that Zanon was when he died
3 _____ and _____: the two men killed wingsuit flying in the US a few years ago
4 _____: the number of people who parachuted for the first time last year
5 _____: the percentage of female climbers now
6 _____: the woman who paraglided off a mountain in Turkey
7 _____: one of world's best female wingsuit flyers

d Read the last paragraph again. What do you think the writer means when he says *Maybe the future of extreme sports is about learning to be less extreme*? Do you agree?

e Talk to a partner.

Have you ever done an extreme sport?
Did you enjoy it? Why (not)?
Which extreme sport that you have never done would you most / least like to try?

Glossary

Taft Point a very high granite rock in Yosemite /yuˈsɛmɪti/ National Park, California
GoPro a compact action camera capable of taking photos and videos in extreme conditions

WHY ARE DEADLY EXTREME SPORTS MORE POPULAR THAN EVER?

Two men leap from the top of the mountain and spread their wings to fly down one of the most dangerous routes in one of the world's most dangerous sports. Dario Zanon and Graham Dickinson are experts at wingsuit flying. Using pieces of cloth that join their arms and legs, they fly past cliff edges and between trees at over 110 mph. Then they release their parachutes and drift down to land. This video has been watched over ten million times on social media.

A few months later, Zanon returned to Chamonix and climbed the Aiguille du Midi on the other side of the valley, for a solo flight. On that Sunday, his body was found on the glaciers 5,000 feet below. He was 33. Most likely no one will ever know exactly which small thing went wrong. Small things become big quickly at 110 mph. It does happen to the best. Mark Sutton, the man who parachuted into the London Olympics stadium dressed as James Bond, was killed wingsuit flying in the Swiss Alps, while filming for EpicTV. Dean Potter, a famous US wingsuit flyer, died with his friend Graham Hunt. They had jumped from Taft Point in California.

Today extreme sports are booming. Skydiving is a good example – in 2006, the British Parachute Association recorded 39,100 first jumps, but last year there were 59,679. The number of people climbing Everest has rocketed since the 1990s, and the proportion of women climbers is increasing, up from about 16% in 2002 to 36% now.

"You just get into it and then progressively build up," says Jess Cox, 27, an instructor at her father's paragliding business. "Better flights involve going higher, further, doing acrobatic stuff." She shows me a video on her phone, of when she and a friend jumped off a mountain in Turkey. "Woo-hoo!" she squeals, watching. "I'd say that was one of the best days of my life. It's completely addictive. Some people become completely obsessed, quit their jobs, and just travel around the world, leaping off things." Science teacher Becky, on the other hand, didn't get addicted. "I did a skydive once and I've also done bungee jumping. The skydive was good, yes. I've no particular need to do it again. But," she says, "life would be a bit boring if people didn't try new things."

Extreme sports constantly push people to test the ultimate limits of their own safety. They are jumping blindfolded, or with their dog, or skydiving without a parachute into a giant net – and you'll find all these online, thanks to action cameras. One hundred hours of GoPro video are uploaded onto YouTube every minute, and sales of these cameras are growing at 50% a year. Watching other people do these things is attracting many more new participants.

A good soccer player or tennis player always wants to be tested against better opponents, but their opponents are human. In extreme sports, the opponent is danger. So how can you get better without killing yourself? Steph Davis, one of the world's best-known climbers and wingsuit flyers, wrote, "Perhaps getting better means becoming more elegant." Maybe the future of extreme sports is about learning to be less extreme.

Adapted from The Guardian

6 VOCABULARY expressions with *take*

a ◀)) 4.14 Listen to Sophie Rees, who works in the ski industry, answering six questions about extreme sports. Match her answers 1–6 to questions A–F.

A ☐ Are you ever afraid that you might get injured or killed?

B ☐ Do you think extreme sports are more popular with men than with women?

C ☐ What other extreme sports have you done?

D ☐ What's the first extreme sport you did? When was it?

E ☐ Why do you enjoy extreme sports?

F ☐ Why do you think extreme sports are becoming more popular?

b Listen again. How does she answer each question?

c Look at three extracts from the interview with Sophie. Can you remember what the missing words are?

1 I take _____ my dad – we're both sports-crazy.

2 I think it's because I love taking _____; I love the adrenaline rush.

3 I think more and more people are taking _____ in extreme sports…

d Look at some more expressions and phrasal verbs with *take*. With a partner, try to figure out their meaning from the context.

Expressions with *take*

1 My neighbor takes care of my son while I'm at work.

2 You should take advantage of that job offer. It's a great opportunity.

3 The concert will take place on March 6th.

4 You don't need to hurry. Take your time.

5 Regarding evaluation, coursework is taken into account, as well as exam results.

6 Lina took part in a charity walk and raised $500 for a local animal shelter.

7 The dog looked so hungry that I took pity on it, and gave it some of my food.

Phrasal verbs with *take*

8 Take your jacket off – it's hot in here.
The flight will take off in about 20 minutes.

9 I'd love to take up snowboarding – it sounds really exciting.

10 My boyfriend's little sister has really taken to me – she always wants to play with me.

11 Our company is growing quickly. We're planning to take on three new employees in the marketing department.

12 Elias is taking me out for dinner tonight to a great new restaurant.
Please take the trash out. It's beginning to smell.

e 🄲 **Communication** I'll take a question **A** p.108 **B** p.111 Ask and answer questions with *take*.

7 WRITING

🅦 **p.117 Writing** For and against Write a blog post.

8 ▶ VIDEO LISTENING

a Watch a documentary about Grace Doyle. How did surfing help her through a difficult time in her life?

> **Glossary**
> **surfboard** a long narrow piece of hard material that you stand on to surf (also **body~**, a short, light board that you ride lying on your front)
> **wipe out** to fall, especially when doing a sport such as surfing or skiing

b Watch the documentary again and complete the information with one or two words.

1 Grace is from a small town in _____.

2 She originally trained to be a _____.

3 She got interested in surfing when she was young because of her _____ _____.

4 Grace has surfed abroad in places such as Central America, _____, and _____.

5 The global surfing business is worth about a _____ billion _____.

6 Grace thinks that media coverage is one reason why surfing has become _____ _____.

7 According to Grace, people are attracted to surfing because it's _____ and _____.

8 If you fall off a big wave, you need to hold your _____ and _____.

9 Grace enjoys the balance between the danger of injury and the chance she might get the _____ _____ of her life.

10 In highly competitive surfing, there's a real risk that you could get _____ or even _____.

c Do you think doing something that gives you an "adrenaline rush" is always more enjoyable? What things do you do that are "both healthy and fun?"

🅖 **Go online** to watch the video and review the lesson

GRAMMAR

a (Circle) a, b, or c.

1 When we got to Terminal 2, the flight from Seoul ____.
   a had already landed   b had already been landing
   c already landed

2 When we arrived at the airport, we ____ that our flight was delayed.
   a had discovered   b were discovering
   c discovered

3 We ____ for about an hour when suddenly the plane began to lose altitude.
   a had been flying   b were flying   c flew

4 Nico's father ____.
   a speaks English fluently   b speaks English fluent
   c speaks fluently English

5 ____. I just need another five minutes.
   a I'm finished almost   b Almost I'm finished
   c I'm almost finished

6 The driver ____ in the accident.
   a seriously was injured   b was injured seriously
   c was seriously injured

7 The car ____ 50,000 miles – we'll need to get it serviced.
   a will soon have reached   b will soon reach
   c will soon be reaching

8 You can watch TV as soon as ____ your homework.
   a you'll finish   b you're finishing   c you've finished

9 If the tickets cost more than $100, ____.
   a I don't go   b I'm not going to go
   c I won't have gone

10 She won't get accepted into a good college ____ she works really hard next year.
   a until   b unless   c in case

b Complete the sentences with the correct form of the verb in **bold**.

1 Imagine! This time tomorrow we _____ on the beach. **lie**

2 The game starts at 7:00. By the time I get home, it _____ already. **start**

3 You can't use your cell phone until the plane _____. **land**

4 Many people have problems sleeping if they _____ coffee after midday. **drink**

5 I want to spend a year traveling when I _____ from college. **graduate**

VOCABULARY

a Write words for the definitions.

1 g_____ the place where you wait to board your flight

2 b_____ c_____ the place where you pick up your luggage after you've arrived

3 a_____ the passage between the rows of seats inside a plane

4 t_____ a series of sudden and violent changes in wind direction that affects flights

5 j_____ l_____ the feeling of being tired and confused after a long-haul flight

b (Circle) the correct word.

1 **A** How was your *trip / travel*?   **B** Great, thanks.

2 Gina and I haven't seen each other much *late / lately*.

3 Our hotel has a great view! We can *even / ever* see the Eiffel Tower!

4 I've been working too *hard / hardly* lately.

5 I love all pasta, but *especially / specially* lasagna.

c Complete with the verb in the past tense.

1 The wind bl_____ so hard that two trees fell down.

2 The taxi dr_____ me off outside the terminal.

3 It p_____ rain last night and I got really wet coming home from work.

4 She g_____ on the bus, but there was nowhere to sit.

5 We t_____ advantage of the good weather and spent the day at the beach.

d (Circle) the word that is different.

1 breeze   wind   hurricane   blizzard
2 chilly   boiling   hot   scorching
3 fog   damp   mist   smog
4 cold   freezing   bright   icy
5 hail   thunder   lightning   drought

e Complete with one word.

1 We checked _____ as soon as we got to the airport.

2 The most dangerous moments during a flight are when the plane is taking _____ or landing.

3 I've decided to take _____ running. I need to lose some weight.

4 Who do you take _____ most in your family?

5 The final will take _____ in Vancouver next Saturday.

PRONUNCIATION

a Circle the word with a different sound.

1		**p**ouring	st**or**m	h**ar**dly	w**ar**m
2		w**ea**ther	h**ea**vy	chang**ea**ble	pl**ea**sant
3		l**ou**nge	sn**ow**	c**o**ld	cl**o**sed
4		l**u**ggage	fl**oo**d	th**u**nder	h**u**mid
5		r**ai**n	**ai**sle	l**a**tely	del**ay**ed

b Underline the main stressed syllable.

1 e|ven|tua|lly   3 e|specia|lly   5 hurr|i|cane
2 gra|dua|lly   4 pa|ssen|ger

CAN YOU understand this text?

a Read the article once. Which volcano is the most challenging to climb?

b Read the article again. Answer the questions with Misti (**M**), Ngauruhoe (**N**), or Teide (**T**).

1 It's famous because it was in a movie.
2 It's no longer an active volcano.
3 It can be freezing there, even in the summer.
4 It's the highest of the three volcanoes.
5 You don't have to have a guide.
6 You can see volcanic activity during the hike.

▶ CAN YOU understand these people?

🔊 4.15 Watch or listen and choose a, b, or c.

1 Claudia   2 Rafael   3 Diarmuid   4 Julia

1 When Claudia flew to Shanghai, ____.
   a the flight started in London
   b she was able to eat on the plane
   c the flight took off in the morning
2 Rafael ____.
   a often reads novels
   b doesn't read very fast
   c never reads online
3 When Diarmuid was living in Japan, and there were typhoons, ____.
   a he wasn't allowed to leave the house
   b a lot of people panicked
   c his building was destroyed
4 Julia enjoyed waterskiing ____ the dangers.
   a because she was addicted to
   b despite knowing about
   c because she was ignorant of

INCREDIBLE VOLCANOES TO CLIMB

Mount Misti is Peru's most famous volcano. It is also its most active, so climbers must be aware of any eruption threats before attempting the exhilarating two-day hike to the summit. Due to the challenging environmental conditions, few people reach the top of the volcano. Ice picks and crampons are often a necessity, making this a difficult hike for a climbing novice, but a welcome challenge for anyone wanting to test their limits. You will need a guide, who will provide you with safe overnight accommodations. Along the way, look for hot gases hissing through volcanic cracks. From the summit, at 19,101 feet, you can look down at the city of Arequipa and see neighboring volcanoes Chachani and Pikchu Pikchu.

Mount Ngauruhoe has become one of New Zealand's most popular climbing locations since its star turn as Mount Doom in Peter Jackson's *The Lord of the Rings* trilogy. After its last eruption in 1975, Mount Ngauruhoe's Volcanic Alert Level has dramatically reduced, although it is still listed as an active volcano. Ngauruhoe is 7,515 feet high, and a 90-minute walk takes you to the foot of the volcano. The hike takes about eight hours altogether. The first 45 minutes are suitable for children and the elderly, but the climb then becomes more dramatic, with a steep slope and few opportunities to rest. It's a challenging hike across loose rock surfaces, ice caps and at times sub-zero temperatures, even in summer. This is one for adrenaline seekers. You will also need a guide.

Mount Teide is Europe's highest volcano. It lies 12,198 feet above sea level on Tenerife, the largest island in the Canaries. Last erupting in 1909, it is now a dormant volcano that attracts eager climbers each year. Hikers can attempt to reach Teide's summit throughout the year, but due to the scorching summer heat, it is best to climb it during the spring (April–May) and fall (September–October) when the weather is mildest. The terrain is not too treacherous, and the low altitude trails are accessible to climbers of all abilities. The five- to seven-hour trek to the summit is a challenging expedition, but when you reach the top and gaze down at Tenerife and its neighboring islands, all your efforts will be worthwhile.

🖱 **Go online** to watch the video, review Files 3 & 4, and check your progress

5A I'm a survivor

G unreal conditionals V feelings P word stress in three- or four-syllable adjectives

> Survival can be summed up in three words – never give up.
> That's the heart of it, really. Just keep trying.
> *Bear Grylls, adventurer, writer, and TV host*

1 SPEAKING

a Read survival questions 1–6. How do you think you would you feel in each situation: calm, nervous, scared, or terrified?

1 **What would you do if you woke up in the middle of the night and thought that you could hear an intruder?**
   a I'd confront the intruder.
   b I'd keep still and quiet and hope that the intruder would go away.
   c I'd lock myself in a room and call the police.

2 **What would you do if you were driving and your brakes stopped working?**
   a I'd put the car in neutral gear.
   b I'd put the car in a lower gear.
   c I'd put the emergency brake on.

3 **What would you do if you were caught out in the countryside in a thunderstorm?**
   a I'd go down on my knees and make myself into a ball.
   b I'd lie flat on the ground.
   c I'd shelter under a tree.

4 **What would you do if you fell through ice into a lake?**
   a I'd take off my clothes and shoes and try to keep afloat.
   b I'd try to climb onto the ice from the place where I'd fallen in.
   c I'd keep as still as possible and shout for help.

5 **What would you do if you were hiking alone in the mountains and you got completely lost (and there was no cell phone signal)?**
   a I'd stay where I was and wait to be rescued.
   b I'd keep walking and try to find my way to my destination.
   c I'd try to find my way back to where I'd started from.

6 **What would you do if you were skiing out of bounds and were buried in an avalanche?**
   a I'd push my ski poles up through the snow to attract attention.
   b I'd curl into a ball and cover my head and wait to be rescued.
   c I'd use swimming movements to try to get to the surface.

b Now answer the questions, choosing a, b, or c. Compare answers in groups of three and give reasons.

c **ⓒ Communication** It's an emergency! **A** p.108 **B** p.111 **C** p.112 Work in the same groups of three. Read the answers to the situations, then explain what you should and shouldn't do.

d Did you choose the correct answers to the questions in **b**?

2 READING & LISTENING

a Read the description of a reality TV show. Do you have any similar programs in your country?

> ***The Island with Bear Grylls*** is a reality TV program narrated by Bear Grylls, a well-known adventurer. It features two groups of participants who are placed on a remote, uninhabited Pacific island for five weeks, to test their survival skills. They are left alone, with only the clothes they are wearing and some basic tools and training. In season five, the groups were divided according to whether they were high or low earners.

b Read the first part of an interview with Ali Brookes on p.47. Would you like to learn any of these survival techniques? What do you think you would miss if you were on the island?

c Read the interview again. Choose the best words to complete the gaps.

1 challenge   program   aim
2 because   since   so
3 actually   anyway   apparently
4 complicated   difficult   easy
5 across   over   through
6 hurt   injured   sick
7 if   unless   until
8 Although   As   However
9 as well   even   though
10 definitely   ideally   obviously

d 🔊 5.1 Listen and check your answers. With all things considered, do you think she was positive or negative about the whole experience?

ALI BROOKES,

A 29-YEAR-OLD DOCTOR, WAS A PARTICIPANT IN SEASON FIVE, IN THE "HIGH EARNERS" GROUP.

Why did you decide to apply?

I'd always really enjoyed watching *The Island with Bear Grylls*. And I think it's really the ultimate ¹_____, being stranded on a desert island, having to survive there with no help at all. I love being outdoors and going on adventures, ²_____ that side of it really appealed to me as well. So I sent off my application form, and the next thing I knew, I had a couple of interviews, and then I got a phone call saying they wanted me to go on *The Island*! Never in a million years, when I applied, did I think I'd ³_____ get to go. So I was absolutely stunned when they told me they wanted me to go on the program, but at the same time, I was thrilled! And two weeks later, we were off on a plane to the island.

What survival techniques did you learn?

So we learned a whole range of survival techniques. We learned how to make fire, which was actually quite complicated. You had to get the right wood from a particular type of tree on the beach, and then use pieces of that wood, and a shoelace to make fire. In our training, they made it look very ⁴_____, they had the fire lit within a few minutes. But in reality, it took us a couple of days before we made fire, but we did get it, which was amazing. Once we had fire, we could then boil water for drinking. The water we found was brown and green and had stuff floating in it, so we would filter it ⁵_____ a pair of pants or a shirt to get rid of the big clumps of dirt, and then we would boil it to kill off any bacteria or parasites. Amazingly, nobody got ⁶_____ from drinking the water during our whole five weeks on the island. They also taught us how to build shelters to protect ourselves from the bad weather. In practice, the shelters were not that waterproof and we had a lot of very wet, cold nights. They taught us how to navigate by the sun and how to build up a map of the island as we explored it. It didn't stop us from getting lost though.

Who or what did you miss most?

Before I went on the show, I said I'd miss my husband the most. But in fact, the thing I missed the most was most definitely food. It was all I could think about, and ⁷_____ I couldn't sleep, I would go through a list of different pizza toppings in my head to try and get to sleep. I really missed having a good nights' sleep. ⁸_____ we did build shelters off the ground to stop us from getting bitten by the insects and other creepy crawlies, it was really uncomfortable. Having clean clothes, I missed that ⁹_____. Putting on dirty, wet socks every morning is one of the worst feelings. Of course, I missed my friends and family too, but actually what I realized was that I didn't miss many things. I ¹⁰_____ didn't miss having a phone, or a computer, or the internet. Though as I said, I did miss clean, dry socks.

e You're going to listen to Ali talk about her best and worst experiences on the island. First, read some things she mentions. Do you think they were things she enjoyed (✓), or things she found difficult (✗)?

- [ ] most of what we ate was yucca, which is like a potato
- [ ] the water we had to wash in was the ocean
- [ ] when it rained
- [ ] we were meeting all these new people we'd never met before
- [ ] (He) threw us out of the boat and told us to swim to the island
- [ ] we had a sports day and we had a talent show
- [ ] leaving the island

f 🔊 **5.2** Now listen to the second part of the interview with Ali and check your ideas in **e**.

g Listen again. What does she say about…?

1 a few coconuts
2 a wild boar
3 tension and arguments
4 a communal shelter
5 35 days

h How many of the 16 people survived the whole five weeks? What general lesson did the participants learn as a result of their time on the island? Do you think you could survive on the island?

3 VOCABULARY & PRONUNCIATION
feelings; word stress

a 🔊 **5.3** Listen to two extracts from the interview. How did Ali feel? Fill in the blanks with adjectives.

> So, I was absolutely ¹_____ when they told me they wanted me to go on the program, but at the same time, I was ²_____.

> …seeing Bear pull up on his boat to come and collect us was just an amazing feeling. I felt both really ³_____ and super ⁴_____.

b ⓥ **p.157 Vocabulary Bank** Feelings

c 🔊 **5.7** Listen to some conversations and look at the extracts. <u>Underline</u> the stressed syllable in the **bold** adjectives.

1 Please come quickly. I'm **des|pe|rate**.
2 You weren't **o|ffen|ded** by what I said, were you?
3 To be honest, I was a little **dis|a|ppoin|ted**.
4 I'm completely **be|wil|dered** by so much information.
5 I was **a|sto|nished** – I really wasn't expecting it.
6 Yes, we'd be **de|ligh|ted** to. Thank you so much.
7 They were **de|va|sta|ted**. It was such a shock.
8 I was absolutely **horr|i|fied**. It was an awful accident.
9 I'm completely **o|ver|whelmed** – I don't know what to say.

d Practice saying the extracts, copying the intonation and stressing the correct syllable in the adjectives.

e Choose three adjectives from **c** and tell your partner about a time or a situation when you felt like that.

4 READING & LISTENING

a How much do you know about the Amazon rainforest? In small groups, complete the missing words.

1 The Amazon rainforest is in the continent of South America. It is roughly the size of **A**_____.
2 It covers a total of nine countries, including **Br**_____, Bolivia, **P**_____, Ecuador, **C**_____, Venezuela, Guyana, Suriname, and French Guiana.
3 The Amazon River, which flows through the northern part of the forest, is the **s**_____-**l**_____ river in the world.
4 The tree canopy is so thick that the forest floor is always **d**_____. Some trees grow up to 200 feet high.
5 There are about 50 indigenous **tr**_____ living in the forest that have never had any **c**_____ with the outside world.
6 Some of the most dangerous animals in the world live in the forest; these include poisonous **sn**_____, **fr**_____, and **sp**_____, as well as jaguars and piranhas.

b Read the beginning of a true survival story and then answer the questions below.

1 What was the three friends' original plan? How did this change?
2 What caused tensions between…?
   a the three men and the guide b Kevin and Marcus
3 Why did they finally separate into two pairs? How did they decide to travel?

Which pair would you have chosen to go with? Why? How would you have felt if you had been in Marcus's situation?

c You are going to listen to part of a documentary and find out what happened to the four men. After each part, answer the questions with a partner.

🔊 **5.8**

1 What happened to Kevin and Yossi on the raft?
2 What piece of luck did Yossi have?

Whose situation would you rather have been in, Kevin's or Yossi's? Why?

🔊 **5.9**

3 How were Kevin and Yossi feeling?
4 What happened to Yossi on his first night alone in the jungle?

What would you have done if you had been in Yossi's situation?

LOST IN THE JUNGLE

FOUR YOUNG MEN WENT INTO THE AMAZON JUNGLE ON THE ADVENTURE OF A LIFETIME. ONLY TWO OF THEM WOULD COME OUT ALIVE…

In 1981, three friends went backpacking in the Amazon rainforest in a remote area of Bolivia: Yossi Ghinsberg, 22, and his two friends Kevin Gale, 29, and Marcus Stamm, 29. They hired an experienced guide, an Austrian named Karl Ruprechter, who promised that he could take them deep into the rainforest to an undiscovered Indian village. Then they would raft nearly 125 miles back downriver. Karl said that the journey to the village would take them about seven days. Before they entered the jungle, the three friends made a promise that they would "go in together and come out together."

The four men set off from the town of Apolo and soon they had left civilization far behind. But after walking for more than a week, there was no sign of the village, and tensions began to appear in the group. The three friends started to suspect that Karl, the guide, didn't really know where the Indian village was. Yossi and Kevin began to get fed up with their friend Marcus because he was complaining about everything, especially his feet, which had become infected and were hurting.

Eventually, they decided to abandon the search for the village and just hike (instead of rafting) back to Apolo, the way they had come. But Kevin was furious because he thought that it was Marcus's fault that they had had to cut short their adventure. So, he decided that he would raft down the river, and he persuaded Yossi to join him, but he didn't want Marcus to come with them. Marcus and Karl decided to go back to Apolo on foot. The three friends agreed to meet in a hotel in the capital La Paz in a week.

Early the next morning, the two pairs of travelers said goodbye and set off on their different journeys…

◀) 5.10

5 Why did Yossi's spirits change from desperate to optimistic, and then to desperate again?

How would you have felt at this point? What do you think had happened to Kevin?

◀) 5.11

6 What had Kevin been doing all this time?
7 What did Kevin decide to do?
8 Why was he incredibly lucky?

If you had been Kevin, what would you have done now?

◀) 5.12

9 How did Kevin first try to get help?
10 Why was it unsuccessful?
11 What was his last attempt to find his friend?

◀) 5.13

12 How long had Yossi been on his own in the jungle? How was he?
13 What did he think the buzzing noise was? What was it?

What do you think might have happened to Marcus and Karl?

d Do you think you would have survived if you had been in Yossi's situation? Would you have done anything differently? Who do you sympathize with most?

5 GRAMMAR unreal conditionals

a Fill in the blanks with the verbs in the correct tense.

1 What would you do if you _____ (hike) alone in the mountains and you _____ (get lost)?
2 If I thought that I could hear an intruder in my house, I _____ (call) the police and I _____ (not confront) the intruder.
3 What would you have done if you _____ (be) in Yossi's situation?
4 If Kevin hadn't looked for his friend, Yossi _____ (die).

b Look at sentences 1–4 again. Which two refer to a hypothetical situation in the past? Which two refer to a hypothetical situation in the present or future?

c **G** p.140 **Grammar Bank 5A**

d With a partner, write two conditional story chains, one with second conditionals, and one with third conditionals.

1 If I had one year off work, I'd _____.
_____.
If _____.
If _____.
If _____.
If _____.
If I had one year off work, I'd go to South Africa.
If I went to South Africa, I'd probably go on a safari…

2 If I hadn't been feeling so terrible, _____.
_____.
If _____.
If _____.
If _____.
If _____.

e Read your stories to another pair. Whose did you like best?

6 WRITING

W p.118 **Writing** A blog post Write a post about how to keep safe in different situations.

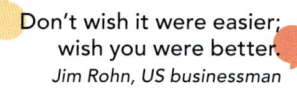

> Don't wish it were easier;
> wish you were better.
> *Jim Rohn, US businessman*

G *wish* for present / future, *wish* for past regrets | **V** expressing feelings with verbs or *-ed* / *-ing* adjectives | **P** sentence rhythm and intonation

1 GRAMMAR *wish* for the present / future

a Look at some posts on a Pinterest board. Do you ever wish for any of these things? Which ones?

I wish you knew how much I really love you.

#1574 I wish my friends' houses were connected to mine by secret tunnels.

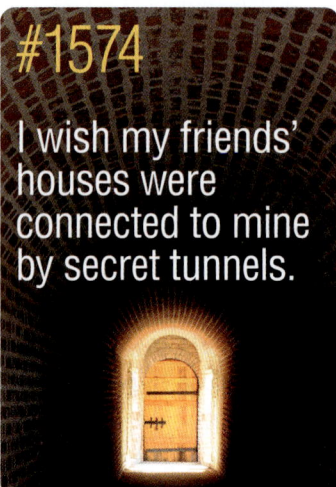

I wish I didn't have to go to work today.

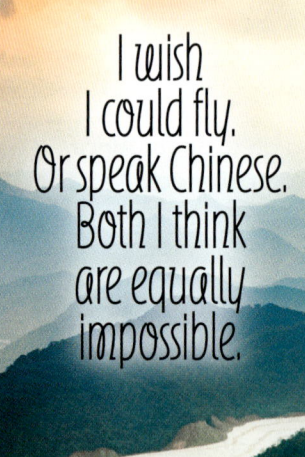

I wish I could fly. Or speak Chinese. Both I think are equally impossible.

I wish I could eat as much as I wanted **WITHOUT** gaining weight.

I wish I could text my dog when I wasn't at home with her. Tell her I miss her. See what she's doing. Ask her to take a selfie for me.

I wish my family didn't live so far away.

b Now look at a WhatsApp group where friends have shared things that annoy them. Check (✓) the things that annoy you, too.

So annoying!
You, Tony, Mia, Georgia, Ronnie,...

I just got back from the movie theater – couldn't enjoy the movie. I wish they would ban people from eating in movie theaters. Some people just can't last for two hours without eating or drinking something. Grrr. 8:58 PM ✔✔

Tony
I wish soccer commentators would stop shouting "Goooal" in that ridiculous way. If we're watching, we can see that it's a goal, and if we're not watching, it's because we don't care. 8:58 PM

Mia
I wish people wouldn't put their bags on seats to try and stop people from sitting next to them. 9:17 PM

Georgia
I wish my boyfriend wouldn't fall asleep every time I want to talk to him. 10:03 PM

Ronnie
I wish my son would occasionally remember to fill up my car with gas after he borrows it. 10:11 PM

Josie
I wish people in call centers wouldn't use my first name like we were old friends. 10:47 PM

Donna
I wish my family would take their tissues out of their pockets before they put their clothes in the washing machine. 11:02 PM

Ella
I wish people wouldn't ask me "What are you doing?" when it's completely obvious what I'm doing. 11:35 PM

Omar
I wish people wouldn't leave supermarket shopping carts in the parking lot just because they're too lazy to take them back. 12:06 AM

c Compare the things you've checked with a partner. Which are your top three, and why?

🔍 **Expressing annoyance**

It really annoys me when…	people eat potato chips at the movies.
It's so annoying when…	
It drives me crazy when…	

d Compare the Pinterest posts in **a** and the messages in **b**. Then complete the rules with *would / wouldn't* + base form or simple past.

1 We use *wish* + person + _____ to talk about things you would like to be different in the present / future (but that are impossible or unlikely).

2 We use *wish* + person + _____ to talk about things we want to happen or stop happening because they annoy us.

e 🅖 p.141 **Grammar Bank 5B** *wish* for present / future

f Write two more things that annoy you and that you would like people to change, and two things that you would like to be different about yourself or your life. Use *I wish* + *would / wouldn't* and *I wish* + simple past.

g In pairs or small groups, compare what you've written. Did anyone come up with the same things?

2 VOCABULARY & SPEAKING expressing feelings with verbs or -ed / -ing adjectives

> 🔎 **Ways of talking about how we feel**
>
> We can talk about how we feel in three different ways:
>
> 1 by using a **verb** (e.g., *annoy*)
> *People who eat in movie theaters really annoy me.*
>
> 2 by using an ***-ing*** **adjective** (e.g., *annoying*)
> *People who eat in movie theaters are really annoying.*
>
> 3 by using an ***-ed*** **adjective** (e.g., *annoyed*)
> *I get really annoyed when people eat in movie theaters.*

a Complete the sentences with the correct form of the word in **bold**.

1 It really _____ me when people drive close behind me. **infuriate**
2 I get very _____ when something goes wrong with my internet connection and I don't know how to fix it. **frustrate**
3 It's so _____ when I can't remember someone's name, but they can remember mine. **embarrass**
4 I used to love shopping at the mall, but now I find it _____. After an hour, I just want to go home. **exhaust**
5 I'm often _____ with my birthday presents. My expectations are obviously too high! **disappoint**
6 It _____ me that some people still don't do their banking online. **amaze**
7 I find speaking in public absolutely _____. I hate doing it. **terrify**
8 I've often been _____ by reading about how some successful people have overcome difficulties. **inspire**
9 I never find instructions for electronic devices helpful – in fact, usually they just _____ me. **confuse**
10 When I travel, I'm always _____ if I manage to communicate something in a foreign language. **thrill**

b 🔊 **5.19** Listen and check. Then with a partner, say if the sentences are true for you or not. Give examples or reasons.

> 🔎 **Feelings adjectives that have an *-ed* form but not an *-ing* form**
>
> A few *-ed* adjectives describing feelings don't have an *-ing* form, e.g., *impressed – impressive*
> **NOT** *impressing*

c Complete the sentences below with a form of the adjective in **bold**.

1 We are extremely **impressed** by your résumé. Your résumé is extremely *impressive*.
2 I get very **stressed** at work. My job is very _____.
3 I was really **scared** during the movie. The ending was especially _____.
4 I was **delighted** to meet Jane. She really is a _____ person.
5 I was really **offended** by what you said. What you said was really _____.

d In pairs, choose three squares and think about what you are going to say. Then talk to a partner.

an embarrassing mistake you once made	something that makes you feel depressed
a movie or a book that you found really disappointing	something that really annoys you when you're shopping
something that you find frustrating about learning English	something that really stresses you in your daily life
someone who inspires you	some physical activity that you did that left you absolutely exhausted

I'm going to tell you about an embarrassing mistake I once made. I was emailing a colleague...

a You are going to read an article about regrets. Which three areas of life do you think people tend to have the most regrets about? Choose from the box below.

career   education   family   health   love   money   travel

b Read the article once and check. How did the writer change someone's life?

Regrets

Recently, I helped my son move into his freshman year dorm room at his college in Chicago and we discussed his hopes and plans for the next four years. That evening, I found myself thinking about how to help him make decisions he would never regret. I went to Twitter and typed, "What is your biggest regret?" The response was huge and devastatingly honest. I had asked a question that, surprisingly, a lot of people really wanted to answer.

I loved the light-hearted responses...

> "Not flying on Concorde to New York with Lionel Richie. He wanted to take me for dinner. I was working. #idiot"

But very few of them were like that. What emerged is that real regrets are not about bad things happening to you. They are about bad choices – a deep sorrow, or anger at yourself for something you did, or something you failed to do.

Most of the replies divided into different categories. Education was high up the list – there were many more regrets to do with school and college than I had expected.

> "Never going to university. Left me disadvantaged all my life. Never lived up to my potential."

> 1

> 2

Career-choice regrets made me realize a pattern was developing: regret seems most often to be about fear. Fear of doing the wrong thing, which then leads to an unfulfilled life.

> "Not following my dream to work in radio."

> 3

> 4

And then, perhaps less surprising, there was love: a few tweets from people regretting that they had declared their love and ended up having their heart broken, but many, many more regretting not being brave – regretting having been afraid. There's definitely a lesson in there: while there's always the possibility of rejection, it's better than the regret of not having tried.

> "Not telling someone I loved them. 20 years too late now."

> 5

It was encouraging that right alongside the people who regretted a life lived in fear were others who had made a change who were now regretting the time it had taken to find their solution.

> "Worrying too much about what other people thought of me."

> 6

Intriguingly, of all the replies, only two people mentioned money – one regretting an apartment they hadn't bought, one regretting a sale.

◆ Regret seems most often to be about fear. ◆

My favorite of all the replies was from @dorey1414. She tweeted me this:

> "I'm 54, no friends, or family, only 18 Twitter followers, but I have everything I need. Biggest regret – not listening in school."

At last, here was one tiny area where I could be useful! I retweeted her words and asked Twitter if they could help. Ten minutes later, her follower count had gone up to 24. By the morning, it was 360. She now has more than 900 and is massively excited about it, starting enthusiastic conversations with dozens of her new followers. Having left school before graduating and worked for 38 years in a job she doesn't enjoy, she now has a chance to change her life.

Before I flew home from Chicago, I texted my son with this advice: "Take risks – they may go wrong but it's better than regretting not having tried. And call your mother."

Adapted from an article by Emma Freud in The Guardian

c Read the article again. Complete 1–6 with tweets A–F. What kinds of words are left out in some of the tweets?

A	"Being scared all the time. Moved to France – still scary but food and life is good!"
B	"Listening to my dad when he said my voice was too weak to be a singer."
C	"Marrying the first person who asked, because I thought no one would ever ask me."
D	"My regret: listening to teachers who said I was stupid because I can't spell. After two degrees was told I'm dyslexic. Am currently on fourth degree."
E	"Not getting a better education and working full-time from the age of 16."
F	"Not taking the job in Tokyo."

d Look at the <mark>highlighted</mark> words in the article. Which are nouns and which are adjectives? If it's a noun, write the adjective, and vice versa.

e If you had read Emma Freud's tweet *What is your biggest regret?*, what would you have written?

> *I would have written "Not starting to learn English when I was younger."*

4 GRAMMAR *wish* for past regrets

a 🔊 5.20 Listen to three people talking about regrets. What thing does each person regret?

b Listen again and complete the sentences with *wish*. What tense do we use after *wish* to talk about a regret?

 **Speaker 1**
I wish I _____.

 **Speaker 2**
I wish I _____.
I wish she _____.

 **Speaker 3**
I wish I _____.

c 🇬 **p.141 Grammar Bank 5B** *wish* for past regrets

d Write a regret with *I wish* for each of the categories below.

family	health	money	travel

5 PRONUNCIATION & SPEAKING
sentence rhythm and intonation

a 🔊 5.22 Listen and write down six more regrets with *wish*.

b Match regrets 1–6 from **a** with the sentences below.

- [ ] A Do you want me to call and make an excuse?
- [ ] B Yes, watching it on TV is never as exciting.
- [ ] C Well, it isn't too late. You're only 22.
- [ ] D Yes, you should have had more self-control!
- [ ] E Why don't you go back to the store and see if they still have them?
- [ ] F Yes, that wasn't a good move on your part. I hope she's not too upset.

c 🔊 5.23 Listen and check. In pairs, practice the conversations. <u>C</u>opy the <u>r</u>hythm and intonation.

d Work in small groups. Tell the other students about…

- a famous person from the past that you wish you'd met.
- a live event you wish you'd been to.
- something you wish you'd learned as a child.
- something you wish you hadn't bought.
- something you wish you'd spent more time on.
- a vacation or trip you wish you hadn't gone on.

6 LISTENING & WRITING

a 🔊 5.24 Listen to a poem about regret from a poetry website. What's the first line of each verse?

b Listen again, and for each verse, write down as many words as you can.

c Work with a partner. Compare the words you've written, and together, try to reconstruct the poem.

d Listen one more time and check your version.

e Together, write your own poem of at least three verses. Start each verse with *I wish I had / hadn't…*

f Read your poems aloud. Take a class vote for the best one.

🔍 **Go online** to review the lesson

1 ▶ THE INTERVIEW Part 1

a Read the biographical information about Candida Brady. Have you heard of any of the documentary films or people mentioned?

Candida Brady is a British journalist and filmmaker. She founded her film company, Blenheim Films, in 1996 and has produced and directed several films and documentaries on a variety of topics, including youth culture, music, and ballet.

In 2012, Candida completed her first full-length documentary feature film, *Trashed*, which follows the actor Jeremy Irons around the world as he discovers the growing environmental and health problems caused by waste – the billions of tons of garbage that we generate every day – and the way we deal with it. The soundtrack for the film was composed by the Greek composer Vangelis, who wrote the award-winning soundtrack to *Chariots of Fire*, and the film won several awards at film festivals. Her latest film, *Urban and the Shed Crew*, based on the memoir of writer Bernard Hare, is about a young boy's struggle to survive on the streets of Leeds in the 1990s.

b Watch Part 1 of an interview with her. Mark the sentences **T** (true) or **F** (false).

1 Candida made the film *Trashed* because she wanted people to know more about the problem of waste.
2 Jeremy Irons is a person who loves buying new things.
3 Candida was surprised that Jeremy Irons immediately loved the film proposal.
4 Vangelis is a good friend of Candida's.
5 Vangelis had previous experience working on projects related to the environment.
6 She didn't need to do much research before making the film because she was already an expert on the subject.

> **Glossary**
> **rough cut** /rʌf kʌt/ the first version of a film after the different scenes have been put together
> **Jacques Cousteau** a well-known French conservationist and filmmaker who studied the ocean and all forms of life in water

c Now watch again and say why the **F** sentences are false.

d Have you seen any documentaries about the environment? What did you learn from them?

▶ Part 2

a Now watch Part 2. Answer the questions.

1 Which was the bigger problem for Candida: making the film visually attractive, or trying not to make it too depressing?
2 What kind of pollution does she think is the most worrying: air, land, or water?

b Watch again. Complete the sentences with one word.

1 Candida had a _____ DOP (Director of Photography).
2 She wanted to film in beautiful places that had been _____ by man-made garbage.
3 She would have preferred to make a more _____ documentary.
4 They were very much aware that they wanted to offer _____ at the end of the film.
5 She says you have to dig down over a foot deep on a beach to find sand that doesn't have any _____ in it.
6 She says the pieces of plastic in the water become so fragmented that they're the same size as the zooplankton, which is in the _____ chain.

> **Glossary**
> **Saida (or Sidon)** a port in Lebanon, its third largest city
> **zooplankton** microscopic organisms that live in water

c Which kind of pollution, air, land, or water, is the biggest problem where you live?

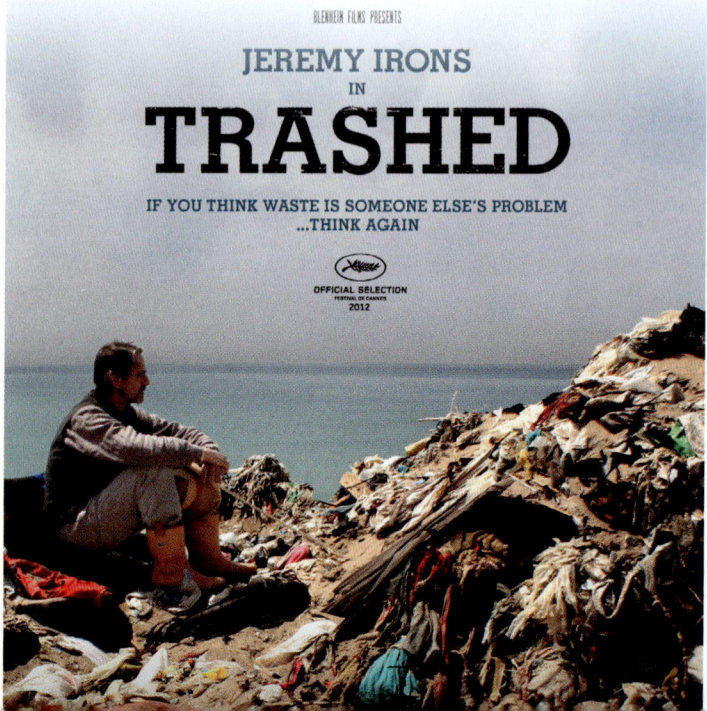

BLENHEIM FILMS PRESENTS
JEREMY IRONS
IN
TRASHED
IF YOU THINK WASTE IS SOMEONE ELSE'S PROBLEM
...THINK AGAIN
OFFICIAL SELECTION
2012

▶ Part 3

a Now watch Part 3. Answer the questions.

1 Who does she blame for the problem of waste?
2 Why does San Francisco offer a positive note at the end of the film?
3 Has the film changed her own habits?

b Watch again. What does she say about…?

1 hotels in San Francisco
2 her grandparents
3 her bicycle

> **Glossary**
> **zero waste** the recycling and re-using of all products
> **bins** containers where people throw their garbage

c How much recycling do you do personally? Are you optimistic or pessimistic about the future of the environment?

2 ▶ LOOKING AT LANGUAGE

> 🔍 **Comment adverbs**
> Candida uses a lot of comment adverbs (e.g., *unfortunately*) to clarify how she feels about what she is saying.

Watch some extracts from the interview and write in the missing adverbs.

1 "We ended up _____ filming in 11 countries…"
2 "…but the stories that I've chosen are universal and, _____, I spoke to, to people in communities, um, in more countries, um, than we actually filmed in…"
3 "…and so I sent him the treatment and _____ he, um, he loved it."
4 "…but _____, again, he was very shocked, um, by the film and really wanted to get involved."
5 "…yes and no, um, _____ enough. Obviously I had a wonderful DOP, Director of Photography, so, um, he can pretty much make anything look beautiful…"
6 "I did a lot of research and so, _____, these things were repeatable and, and in every country around the world…"
7 "_____, what's happened with the way that soft plastic degrades in water is that, um, the pieces become so fragmented…"

3 ▶ THE CONVERSATION

Simon   Joanne   Syinat

a Watch the conversation. Circle the correct phrase to sum up their conclusion.

They think being plastic-free is *definitely possible / possible but difficult / impossible*.

b Watch again. Answer with **S** (Simon), **J** (Joanne), or **Sy** (Syinat).

Who…?
1 ▢ gives an example of plastic straws
2 ▢ thinks that consumers need to lead the way
3 ▢ brings up the problem of plastic packaging in supermarkets
4 ▢ mentions that China no longer accepts other countries' recycling
5 ▢ suggests that it might be possible to be plastic free in 20 years' time
6 ▢ says that there is more plastic than fish in the sea
7 ▢ compares the use of plastic today to in the past
8 ▢ tells the others about bacteria that can eat plastic
9 ▢ talks about plastic bottles that you can use and then eat the plastic

c Do you agree with the participants about the possibility of being plastic free? Why (not)?

d Watch some extracts and match some of the different ways that the participants respond to what another person had said.

1 The deepest place on the planet… and they found plastic. ▢▢
2 …there's more plastic in the sea by weight than there are fish… ▢▢
3 …plastic bottles that actually you can then eat the plastic. ▢▢▢

A Yes, isn't that awful?
B Oh wow!
C It's depressing.
D Yes, it's very scary!
E I mean that's just so depressing, isn't it?
F I think that's just so amazing.
G That sounds pretty cool.

e With a partner, say what the function of each response is: responding to something positive or something negative.

f Now have a conversation in groups of three.

1 What kinds of things in everyday life do you think <u>really</u> make a difference to the environment?
2 What do you think the government could do to make people recycle more?

🌐 **Go online** to watch the video, review the lesson, and check your progress

Communication

1A INDIRECT QUESTIONS
Student A

a Make indirect questions starting with the phrase in parentheses and ask them to **B**.

1 What's the time? (Could you tell me…)
2 Where were the last Olympic Games held? (Can you remember…)
3 Is there a good pizza restaurant near here? (Do you know…)
4 How many players are there on a baseball team? (Do you have any idea…)
5 How old are you? (Would you mind telling me…)

b Answer **B**'s questions.

1A TOUGH QUESTIONS
Student A

a You're going to interview **B** for a job as a manager in your company. Ask the tough questions below, and ask him / her to give reasons for his / her answers. Then say if you would give him / her the job and why (not).

1 Which one aspect of your personality would you change if you could, and why?
2 If you could have dinner with anyone from history, who would you choose?
3 If you were an animal, which animal would you be?
4 What kinds of things make you angry?
5 If you had to spend the rest of your life on a desert island (with plenty of food and water), what two things would you want to have with you?
6 Which TV or movie character would you most like to be?
7 What's the best (or worst) decision you've ever made?
8 If I came to your house for dinner, what would you cook for me?

b Now **B** is going to interview you. Answer the questions. Try to think quickly and make a good impression. Give good reasons for your answers.

1B YOU'RE PSYCHIC, AREN'T YOU? Student A

a Imagine you're a psychic. Use your psychic powers to complete the sentences below about **B**.

1 Your favorite color is _____.
2 You were born in _____ (a place).
3 You really like _____ (a sport or hobby).
4 You _____ (an activity) last weekend.
5 You haven't been to _____ (a city or country).
6 You would like to be able to _____.
7 You can't _____ very well.
8 You're very good at _____.

b Now check if your guesses are true. Say the sentences to **B** and check with a tag question. Try to use falling intonation.

Your favorite color is pink, isn't it?

c Now **B** will check his / her guesses about you. Respond with a short answer. If the guess is wrong, tell **B** the real answer.

d Count your correct guesses. Who was the better psychic?

2A MEDICAL MYTHS OR FIRST-AID FACTS?
Student A

a Read the answers carefully to questions 1, 3, and 5. Then look back at the quiz on p.16 and make notes.

b Take turns. Tell your partner the correct facts, and explain why the myths can cause problems.

1 The correct answer is **b**. Run cool or lukewarm water on the burn for between 5 and 20 minutes. This will cool the skin and stop blisters from forming.
a and **c** are **myths**. Putting anything that is oily on a burn can increase the risk of infection, and ice or iced water will make the damage worse.

3 The correct answer is **c**. Remove any wet clothes, wrap the person in something warm and dry like a coat or a blanket, especially their head, and try to protect them from the wind.
a and **b** are **myths**. Rubbing causes a person to lose more heat, and although a hot drink can also help, it should be caffeine-free.

5 The correct answers are **a** and **b**. Pinch the soft part of your nose firmly and tip your head forwards.
c is a **myth**. Tipping your head backwards can be dangerous if the bleeding is severe.

2B THE JOY OF THE AGE-GAP FRIENDSHIP Student A

a   Read what Dave says about John.

Dave (53) on John (34)

I first met John when I gave him a lift to a music festival. It was the first festival I'd been to since I was a teenager. He jumped into my car with a friend of ours. My first impression was that he was a little ignorant because he didn't want to join in our conversation about cars, but he works as a journalist and so I thought he must be an interesting person, which, as I later found out, he is.

We go to the gym together and, mostly, we go out for dinner or a drink. Our friendship was a gradual process. I talked to him a lot and gave him advice when he was getting divorced. I also counseled his ex-wife, because I was also friendly with her – I've learned never to take sides, something I've tried to teach John. He's a pretty private person, so I think it's good to get him to open up more.

I love the fact that he doesn't take himself too seriously. We're just comfortable with each other and can laugh in any situation. We both like being the center of attention, and if one is getting more, the other won't like it. We complain about each other, but he's very loyal. I've never noticed the age difference. Hopefully, he'll be happy to push me around in a wheelchair in my old age.

b   With **B**, compare what they say about each other. Talk about…

- how they met.
- what their first impressions of each other were, and how they changed.
- what they do together.
- what they have in common, and how they are different.
- what they like about each other.

c   Do you think you would get along well with Dave or John?

3A FLIGHT STORIES Student A

a   Read a news article about a flight. What would you have done if you had heard the announcement? How would you have felt?

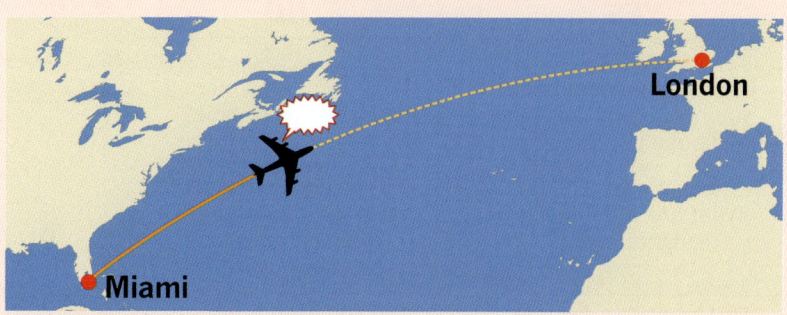

NIGHTMARE OVER THE ATLANTIC

At 6:35 p.m. on January 13, British Airways flight 206 took off from Miami to London. It had been flying for about three hours, and was over the Atlantic, when suddenly a voice came out of the loudspeakers. "This is a passenger announcement. We may shortly have to make an emergency landing on water."

Immediately, panic broke out and passengers were screaming and shouting. Most people thought that the plane was about to crash into the Atlantic. But about 30 seconds later, the cabin crew started to run up and down the aisle saying that the message had been played by accident, and that everything was OK. By this time, a lot of the passengers were crying, and trying to get their life jackets out from under their seats.

Afterwards, many passengers said that they had been traumatized, and that it had been the worst experience of their lives. They complained that the captain hadn't given them any explanation until just before landing, and even then, hadn't told them what had really happened. Later, a British Airways spokesperson apologized to passengers on the flight, and said that a pre-recorded emergency announcement had been activated in error.

b   Imagine that you were one of the passengers on the plane. You are going to tell **B** what happened. Look at the words and phrases in the box and plan what you are going to say.

Setting the scene
Jan. 13   Miami   London   three hours
passenger announcement   emergency landing   water

The main events
panic   scream   shout   crash into the Atlantic
30 seconds later   crew   aisle   by accident   cry   life jackets

What happened in the end
passengers   traumatized   complain   captain
just before landing   spokesperson apologized   error

---

c   Now tell **B** your story.

This happened to me a few years ago, when I was flying from Miami to London…

d   Listen to **B**'s story. Which situation do you think was more scary?

3B READING HABITS Students A+B

a   **B** close your book. **A** ask **B** the questions.

b   Switch roles. How similar are your reading habits?

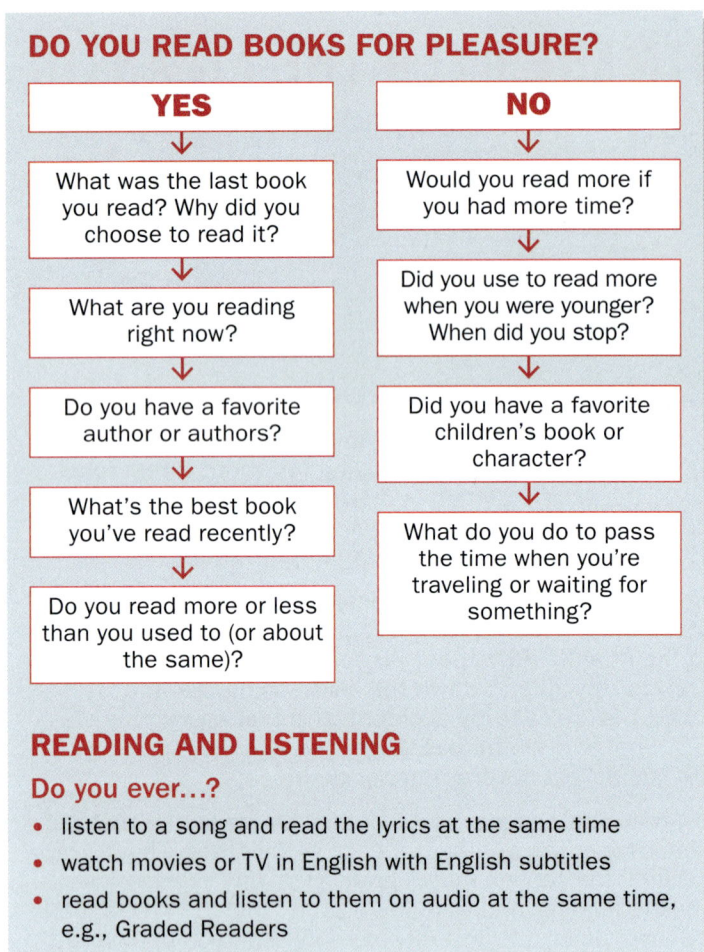

DO YOU READ BOOKS FOR PLEASURE?

YES	NO
↓	↓
What was the last book you read? Why did you choose to read it?	Would you read more if you had more time?
↓	↓
What are you reading right now?	Did you use to read more when you were younger? When did you stop?
↓	↓
Do you have a favorite author or authors?	Did you have a favorite children's book or character?
↓	↓
What's the best book you've read recently?	What do you do to pass the time when you're traveling or waiting for something?
↓	
Do you read more or less than you used to (or about the same)?	

READING AND LISTENING

Do you ever…?

- listen to a song and read the lyrics at the same time
- watch movies or TV in English with English subtitles
- read books and listen to them on audio at the same time, e.g., Graded Readers

4A YOUR SCORE Students A+B

a   Read about what your score means.

b   Do you agree with it? Compare your results with a partner.

> If the final number is zero or minus, you live up to your environmentally friendly intentions. The bigger the difference between the two numbers, the greater your failure to live up to your green values.
>
> Most people are not very successful. When these questions were put to 100,000 people in a survey, it turned out that, although most of us do easy things (like turning off faucets and TVs), few of us make real sacrifices.

4B I'LL TAKE A QUESTION Student A

a   Complete the phrasal verbs or expressions.

1   Who do you take _____ more, your father or your mother?

2   Do you take _____ _____ yourself, or are you very laid-back about your health?

3   Have you ever <u>not</u> taken _____ _____ a good opportunity and then regretted it?

4   Has any big sporting event ever taken _____ in your (nearest big) city? Did you go to it?

5   Do you sometimes get annoyed by little things that people do, or do you take no _____? What kinds of things?

b   Ask **B** your questions.

c   Answer **B**'s questions. Give examples to explain your answers, and then return the question.

> 🔍 **Giving examples**
> We often use *for example* or *for instance*, to give examples.
>
> *I usually get up quickly, but sometimes I take my time, **for example** / **for instance**, on the weekend.*

5A IT'S AN EMERGENCY! Student A

a   Read the answers to survival questions 1 and 2. Make notes under these headings:

You should…   **You shouldn't…**

> 1   However strong you are, it's usually a mistake to confront the intruder. They may have a weapon and react violently. Take your phone and lock yourself (and your family) in your bedroom or bathroom, and move a piece of furniture against the door. Then call the police.

> 2   Whether you're driving an automatic or a manual car, the first thing to do is to put your car in a lower gear. This will slow down the car and will hopefully allow you to put on the emergency brake. Putting the car into neutral won't slow the car down – it will just make the car more unstable and on a hill, it might even make the car go faster.

b   Now use your notes and tell **B** and **C** what you should and shouldn't do.

1A INDIRECT QUESTIONS Student B

a Make indirect questions starting with the phrase in parentheses and ask them to **A**.

1 Where did you buy your bag? (Could you tell me…)
2 What year were the Rio Olympics? (Can you remember…)
3 How long does this class last? (Do you know…)
4 When did Germany last win the World Cup? (Do you have any idea…)
5 Do you have any allergies? (Would you mind telling me…)

b Answer **A**'s questions.

1A TOUGH QUESTIONS Student B

a **A** is going to interview you for a job as a manager in his / her company. Answer the questions. Try to think quickly and make a good impression. Give good reasons for your answers.

b Now interview **A** for a similar job in your company. Ask the tough questions below, and ask him / her to give reasons for his / her answers. Then say if you would give him / her the job and why (not).

1 Which three adjectives describe you best?
2 If you were a car, what type of car would you be?
3 How do you usually treat animals?
4 Who do you admire most, and why?
5 If you could be a superhero, what would your superpowers be?
6 Tell me about something in your life that you're really proud of.
7 If Hollywood made a movie about your life, who would you like to see play the lead role as you?
8 If you could have six months with no obligations or financial limitations, what would you do with the time?

1B YOU'RE PSYCHIC, AREN'T YOU? Student B

a Imagine you're a psychic. Use your psychic powers to complete the sentences below about **A**.

1 You were born in _____ (a month).
2 You don't like _____ (a kind of music).
3 You're going to _____ (an activity) tonight.
4 You've seen _____ (a movie).
5 Your favorite season is _____.
6 You didn't like _____ (a kind of food) when you were a child.
7 You can play _____ (a musical instrument).
8 You wouldn't like to live in _____ (a place).

b **A** is going to make some guesses about you. Respond with a short answer. If the guess is wrong, tell **A** the real answer.

c Now check if your guesses are true. Say the sentences to **A** and check with a tag question. Try to use falling intonation.

You were born in July, weren't you?

d Count your guesses. Who was the better psychic?

2A MEDICAL MYTHS OR FIRST-AID FACTS? Student B

a Read the answers carefully to questions 2, 4, and 6. Then look back at the quiz on p.16 and make notes.

b Take turns. Tell your partner the correct facts, and explain why the myths can cause problems.

2 The correct answers are **b** and **c**. Get the person to sit down and raise their leg by putting it on a chair. Then put an ice pack on the ankle. These two things will help to reduce the swelling.
a is a **myth**. Applying heat to an area increases blood flow, which can increase swelling, so the injury will take longer to get better.

4 The correct answers are **b** and **c**. First check the mouth and encourage them to keep coughing. If this doesn't work, hit the person's back hard five times.
a is not the <u>first</u> thing you should try. Abdominal thrusts (also known as the Heimlich maneuver) won't work if the choking is due to an allergic reaction or throat injury. It should only be used if the person can't talk, cough, or breathe. In this case, stand behind the person and push up with your fists against their stomach suddenly, up to five times.

6 The correct answers are **a** and **b**. After cleaning the cut with soap and water, or just water, put on antibiotic ointment and a bandage to stop the wound from getting infected.
c is a **myth**. An uncovered wound is unprotected, which makes it less likely that it will heal.

2B THE JOY OF THE AGE-GAP FRIENDSHIP
Student B

a Read what John says about Dave.

John (34) on Dave (53)

A group of us had tickets to a music festival and my friend said that a guy named Dave, who was a little older, would give us a lift. He arrived in his BMW. He didn't look his age, but he talked about cars for five hours and I thought he was really boring. However, the next day, he barbecued some great food for us, and I thought, maybe he's not so bad after all.

We live around the corner from each other, so we started meeting at a local restaurant, or watching local bands play. We still go to festivals. The funny thing is, we don't have much in common. He loves cars, I couldn't care less. I love sports, he doesn't understand soccer. But we both like talking to people. We're competitive in our friendship, so for example, we're always trying to be funnier than each other. We argue a lot, mostly about politics, (I'm more left-wing and he's more right-wing), but then we're best friends again.

Being around someone like Dave, who is so full of life, is refreshing. Our friendship is fun, but it goes a lot deeper. I look up to him in some ways. My dad died when I was 19 and Dave is someone I can talk to about that. Maybe he sees me as some sort of weird son. He's not just fun – he's a really kind person. If I were in trouble and could only make one call, it would be to Dave.

b With **A**, compare what they say about each other. Talk about…
- how they met.
- what their first impressions of each other were, and how they changed.
- what they do together.
- what they have in common, and how they are different.
- what they like about each other.

c Do you think you would get along well with Dave or John?

4B I'LL TAKE A QUESTION Student B

a Complete the phrasal verbs or expressions.
1 Do you get up very quickly in the morning or do you take _____ _____?
2 Have you taken _____ a new sport or hobby recently, or is there one you would like to take _____?
3 If you were thinking of buying a new phone, what factors would you take _____ _____?
4 Have you ever taken _____ _____ a charity walk or some other kind of fundraiser that benefited your community?
5 Who takes the trash _____ in your house, you or someone else?

b Answer **A**'s questions. Give examples to explain your answers, and then return the question.

c Ask **A** your questions.

> 🔍 **Giving examples**
> We often use *for example* or *for instance* to give examples.
> *I take after my mother, **for example** / **for instance** we both have the same sense of humor.*

5A IT'S AN EMERGENCY! Student B

a Read the answers to survival questions 3 and 4. Make notes under these headings:

You should…   **You shouldn't…**

3 Look for an area of low ground and make yourself as small a target as possible. Go down on your knees with your feet together and head on the ground. This makes it less likely that lightning will strike you. Lying flat will expose more of your body to the lightning, and sheltering under a tree is very dangerous, because if it gets hit by lightning, a branch may fall and injure you.

4 First, keep your clothes on. They can trap air, which will keep you warm and help you to float. Turn towards the direction where you fell – the ice was strong enough to hold you once – and kick your feet to get your body horizontal. Use your elbows to pull yourself out and then roll off the ice. Don't try to stand and run, as this might cause the ice to break again.

b Now use your notes and tell **A** and **C** what you should and shouldn't do.

3A FLIGHT STORIES Student B

a Read a news article about a flight. What would you have thought if you had heard the bang? How would you have felt?

EXPLODING ENGINE CAUSES EMERGENCY LANDING

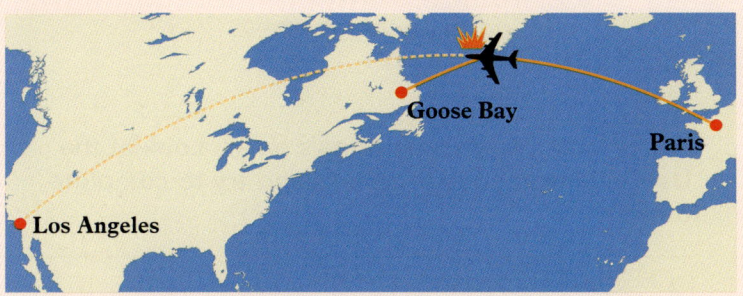

Passengers traveling on an Air France flight from Paris to Los Angeles had been relaxing and enjoying movies and food when, five hours after take-off, just after they had crossed the southern tip of Greenland, they suddenly heard a loud bang.

The cabin started vibrating, some passengers screamed, and everybody knew something was wrong. Passengers nervously joked to each other as they tried to figure out what had happened. Some thought the plane had hit a bird. But passengers sitting in window seats said they had seen one of the engines exploding. The cabin crew walked through the aisles reassuring passengers, and then the captain confirmed that there had been an explosion in one of the engines.

The atmosphere was tense, but about two hours later, the plane landed at a military airfield in Goose Bay on the far northeast edge of Canada, which is used as an emergency landing spot for transatlantic flights. There were no injuries among the 520 passengers. Passengers completed their journeys to Los Angeles on two planes sent by Air France to Goose Bay.

b Imagine that you were one of the passengers on the plane. You are going to tell **A** what happened. Look at the words and phrases in the box and plan what you are going to say.

Setting the scene
Air France   Paris   Los Angeles   relax   movies and food
five hours   Greenland   bang

The main events
cabin   vibrate   scream   joke   bird   window seats   engine
explode   cabin crew   aisles   captain   confirm   explosion

What happened in the end
land   Goose Bay, Canada   no injuries   complete journey
two planes
---

c Now listen to **A**'s story. Then tell **A** your story.

> This happened to me a few years ago, when I was flying from Paris to Los Angeles…

d Which situation do you think was more scary?

5A IT'S AN EMERGENCY! Student C

a Read the answers to survival questions 5 and 6. Make notes under these headings:

You should…   **You shouldn't…**

5 The number one tip is to stay where you are, or find a sheltered space nearby if it's night time, and wait to be rescued (especially if you have told someone where you were going to walk). But make sure you stay in the open during the day, so that you can be seen by a helicopter. Make a fire, or tie a piece of bright clothing to a stick, to attract attention. Never keep walking, as you will only get further lost and make it more difficult for searchers to find you.

6 Abandon any equipment, as it could pull you further down, and use swimming movements to try to get to the surface. Don't try to dig yourself out, as this is almost impossible. If you're covered and can't get to the surface, try to thrust part of your body through the snow, so rescuers can see you. But the best thing to do if you are skiing off the trail is to always carry avalanche safety equipment with you, including a two-way radio.

b Now use your notes and tell **A** and **B** what you should and shouldn't do.

Writing

1 AN INFORMAL EMAIL

From: Anna
To: johnstons586@gmail.com
Subject: News!

Hi Olivia,

Sorry that I havent been in touch for a while, but I've been sick. I got the flu last week and I had a temprature of 102°F, so I've been in bed since four days. I'm feeling a little better today, so I've been catching up on my emails. Luckly my college classes don't start until next week.

How are you? What have you been doing? Anything exciting. Here everyone are fine (apart from me and my flu!). My brother Mike started his new job with a software-company – I think I told you about it when I wrote last time – anyway, so far, he's really been enjoying it. How is your family? I hope their well.

I have some good news – I'm going to a conference in your town in may, from the 16th to the 20th. Could you recomend a hotel where I could stay near the downtown area? It needs to be somewhere not too expensive because my college is paying. I'll have a free half-day for siteseeing. Do you think you'll be able show me around? That would be great.

Well, that's all for now. Please give my regards to your family.

Hope to hear from you soon.

Take care,

Anna

PS Please reply to this email address. I've stopped using the old Yahoo one.

> 🔍 **Beginning an informal email**
> When you are writing an informal email, it is more usual to start with *Hi* than with *Dear*.

a Read the email from Anna. It has 12 highlighted mistakes – four grammar or vocabulary, four punctuation, and four spelling. With a partner, decide what kind of mistake each one is and correct it.

b Read Anna's email again and find phrases that mean…
emailed, messaged, or called
reading and replying to
Have you been doing anything fun?
I don't have anymore news.
send my best wishes to

c You're going to answer Anna's email. Look at the **Useful language** expressions and try to complete them.

> 🔍 **Useful language: an informal email**
> **Opening expressions**
> *Thanks* [1]_____ *your email / letter.*
> *It was great* [2]_____ *hear from you.*
> *Sorry that I haven't been in touch for a while. / Sorry for* [3]_____ *writing earlier.*
> *I* [4]_____ *you and your family are well.*
>
> **Responding to news**
> *Glad to* [5]_____ *that you're all well.*
> *Sorry* [6]_____ *hear about your final grades.*
> *Good* [7]_____ *with the new job.*
> *Hope you* [8]_____ *better soon.*
>
> **Closing expressions**
> *Anyway, / Well, that's all* [9]_____ *now.*
> [10]_____ *my regards (love) to…*
> *Hope to hear from you soon. / Looking* [11]_____ *to hearing from you soon.*
> *Take* [12]_____ */ (Lots of) love*
> [13]_____ *wishes / Regards*
>
> **Something you forgot and want to add**
> [14]_____ *Don't forget to send me the photos you promised.*

d **Plan** the content of your email.
1 Underline the questions in the email that Anna wants you to answer.
2 Underline other places in the email where you think you need to respond, e.g., *I've been sick.*
3 Think about how to respond to each of the things you've underlined.

e **Write** 140–190 words, in two or three paragraphs. Use informal language (contractions, etc.), and expressions from **Useful language**.

f **Check** your email for mistakes (grammar, punctuation, and spelling).

➔ p.19

2 A SHORT STORY

It was only a small mistake, but it changed my life forever. I had been working at J.B. Simpson's for ten years. It was a small ¹ _family-run_ company that exported outdoor furniture. I was ² _____ happy with my job. I got along ³ _____ with the owner, Arthur Simpson, but not with his wife, Linda. She was a loud, ⁴ _____ woman, who ⁵ _____ used to turn up at the office and start criticizing us for no reason. Everyone disliked her.

One afternoon, Mrs. Simpson came in while I was finishing writing a report. She looked at me and said, "If I were you, I wouldn't wear that color. It doesn't suit you at all." I was wearing a ⁶ _____ pink shirt that I was very ⁷ _____ of, and her comment really annoyed me. I typed a ⁸ _____ message to Alan Simmonds in sales. "Watch out! The old witch is here!" and pressed send. A couple of minutes later, I was surprised to receive a message from Mr. Simpson, asking me to come to his office ⁹ _____. When I opened the door, I saw his wife glaring at the computer screen. I realized, to my horror, what I had done. I had clicked on Simpson instead of Simmonds. ¹⁰ _____, I was packing my things. I had been fired!

a Read the story. What was the "small mistake"? What happened in the end?

b Using adverbs and adjectives helps to make a story come alive and makes it more enjoyable to read. Complete the story with an adjective or adverb from the box.

| aggressive | an hour later | ~~family-run~~ | fond |
| frequently | immediately | new | quick | very | well |

c You may want to write some dialogue as part of your story. Rewrite the following with the correct punctuation. Use the dialogue in the story to help you.

> i want to talk to you about an email you sent
>
> Mr. Simpson said coldly

d Look at the highlighted time expressions in **Useful language** and complete them.

> 🔍 **Useful language: time expressions**
> ¹ _____ _that moment_, the door opened.
> ² _As soon_ _____ I saw him, I knew something was wrong.
> ³ _Ten minutes_ _____, I went back to sleep.
> ⁴ _____ _morning in September_, I got to work early.
> We got to the station ⁵ _just_ _____ _time_ to catch the train.

e You are going to write a story beginning with one of the sentences below. With a partner, choose which story to write, and discuss what the plot could be.

1 It was eleven o'clock at night when my phone rang.

2 As soon as I saw my mother's face, I knew something was wrong.

3 We had been driving for four hours when we saw the sign for a small hotel and decided to stop.

f **Plan** the content.

1 Write a quick outline of what happens in the story (50–60 words).
2 Think about what tenses you need for each part of the story, e.g., how to set the scene, what significant events had happened before the story starts.
3 Think about how you could improve your story by adding extra details, and using more adjectives and adverbs. Think also about where you might want to include some dialogue.

g **Write** 140–190 words, organized in two or three paragraphs. Set the scene and then tell the story. Use the time expressions in **Useful language** to make the sequence of events clear.

h **Check** your short story for mistakes (grammar, punctuation, and spelling).

← p.33

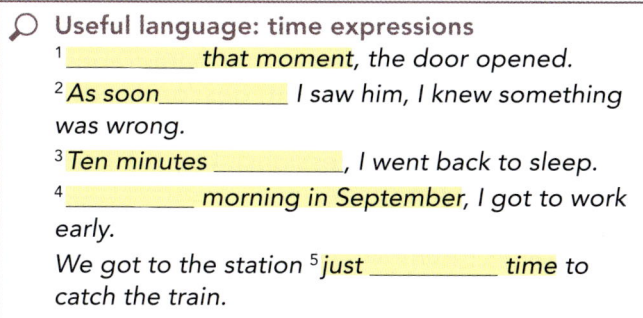

3 FOR AND AGAINST

a Read a post about adventure sports on a blog site called *For and against?* Do you think there are more advantages or more disadvantages?

b Read the blog post again and complete it with the linking expressions from the box (two of them are interchangeable).

> although   another advantage   because of
> for example (x2)   furthermore   in addition
> on the other hand   ~~the main advantage~~
> to sum up

c Put the linking expressions from **b** in the **Useful language** chart below.

> 🔍 **Useful language: linking expressions**
>
> **To list advantages / disadvantages**
> *the main advantage*
> _____
>
> **To add more points to the same topic**
> _____
>
> _____
>
> **To introduce an example**
> *For instance,…*
> _____
>
> **To make contrasting points**
> *However,…*
> *In spite of (the fact that)…*
> _____
>
> _____
>
> **To give a reason**
> *Because (+ clause)…*
> _____ *(+ noun)…*
>
> **To introduce the conclusion**
> *In conclusion,…*
> _____

d You are going to write a post for the site. Choose one of the titles below.

Going to work abroad: an exciting opportunity or a scary one?

Being a celebrity: a dream or a nightmare?

Home	About	Blog	Subscribe

Everything has two sides to it, a positive one and a negative one. Post your opinions on our blog…

Adventure sports – fun or too risky?

Every year, more and more people are tempted by the idea of going on an adventure sports vacation, especially during the summer months.

Spending your vacation being active and enjoying the outdoors has a lot of advantages. [1]*The main advantage* is that adventure sports, like many other physical activities, offer health benefits and help keep your mood positive, [2]_____, when you practice extreme sports your brain releases endorphins because of the adrenalin rush and that makes you feel happy. [3]_____ is the self-confidence that you gain from doing these activities. [4]_____, the lessons learned from facing the difficulties and the risks of these extreme sports may be very valuable in everyday life.

[5]_____, there are also some important disadvantages. [6]_____ they make you feel good, risky sports can be extremely dangerous. The possibility of getting seriously injured while performing these activities is very high, and some adventure sports, [7]_____ skydiving or cliff jumping, can even have fatal consequences. [8]_____ these risks, you need to be in very good shape to practice these sports during a vacation, which means that they are not for everyone. [9]_____, they are likely to be expensive because they require a lot of equipment, safety measures, and well-trained and qualified instructors.

[10]_____, adventure sports vacations have both advantages and disadvantages. Whether they suit you or not depends on your level of fitness, your personality, and how much you can afford.

Like | Share | Comment

e **Plan** the content.

1 Decide what kinds of things you could say to start the post for the topic you chose, for example, why young people choose to go abroad or why people today are so interested in famous people. This will give you material for the introduction.
2 List two or three advantages and disadvantages, and number them in order of importance.
3 Decide if you think there are more advantages than disadvantages.

f **Write** 140–190 words, organized in four paragraphs: introduction, advantages, disadvantages (or disadvantages then advantages), and conclusion. Use a formal style (no contractions or colloquial expressions). Use the linking expressions in **Useful language**.

g **Check** for mistakes (grammar, punctuation, and spelling).

 p.43

How to keep children safe in your home

You probably think that your home is a very safe place. But this may not be true if you have children coming to visit. Here are some tips to prevent accidents. / First, look at the bedroom where the children are going to sleep. Make sure the beds are not under a window, in case a child tries to climb out. If a very small child is going to sleep in the bed, you could put some pillows on the floor next to the bed, in case the child falls out. The next place to check is the bathroom. Many people keep medicines in a drawer or on a shelf above the sink. But this can be dangerous, because children may find them and think they are candy. You should keep them in a locked cabinet. Finally, take a look at the kitchen, which is the most dangerous room in the house for children. Knives should be kept in drawers that children can't reach, and make sure that all cleaning liquids are in high or locked cabinets. If you follow this simple advice, children who come to stay will never be at risk in your home.

16:03 Thursday 2nd May

a Look at the three pictures. What do you think should and shouldn't have been done? Read the advice from a health and safety blog and check.

b This blog post was originally written in five short sections. Mark / where each new section should begin.

c You are going to write a health and safety blog post. With a partner, choose one of the titles below.

How to keep safe if you go hiking in the mountains

How to keep safe on a day at the beach

How to keep safe on a long drive

d **Plan** the content.
 1 Think of at least three useful tips.
 2 Think of a good introductory sentence (or sentences).

e **Write** 140–190 words, organized in paragraphs. Use expressions from **Useful language** below, and write in a neutral or informal style.

> Useful language: giving advice
> *Don't forget to… / Remember to…*
> *Make sure you…*
> *You should…*
> *Never…*
>
> **Reasons**
> *…in case*
> *…so (that)*
> *…because it might…*

f **Check** your blog post for mistakes (grammar, punctuation, and spelling).

 p.49

Listening

🔊 **1.2**

All four journalists Excuse me…, Excuse me…, Cindy…, Cindy…

Journalist 1 Just a few questions…

Actress OK, OK, but you have just one minute.

Journalist 1 What brings you to Toronto?

Actress I'm here to accept an award and do some interviews.

Journalist 2 How long are you going to be in Toronto for?

Actress Just 48 hours, then I'm flying back to the States.

Journalist 3 That's a very short stay. Don't you like Toronto?

Actress I love Toronto, but unfortunately my new movie starts shooting on Monday.

Journalist 4 There've been rumors that you and your husband are having relationship problems. Can you tell us if there's any truth in that?

Actress No, no, no, no. No comment. No more questions.

🔊 **1.9**

1 Dominic

Interviewer Have you ever been asked a strange question in an interview?

Dominic Yes, it was my first interview when I was applying to Sarah Lawrence University in New York – where I'm studying now.

Interviewer What was the question?

Dominic The question was, if you could have dinner with three people from the past, who would you choose and why?

Interviewer And what did you answer?

Dominic It was one of the first questions I was asked, and I said, "I can't answer this right now. Can I answer this at the end?" because I couldn't think of anyone. So they said, "OK," and then they asked me the question again later, and I said something ridiculous like John Lennon, um, Picasso, uh, I can't even remember who the third person was, it was another sort of artist or musician I think.

Interviewer Do you think it was a good question?

Dominic Yes, because it made me think, I mean, it wasn't something I was expecting at all, and all the other ones were more yes / no, direct questions, so this one made me think a little more.

Interviewer And you got in?

Dominic Yes, I did.

2 Heidi

Interviewer Have you ever been asked a strange question in an interview?

Heidi Yes, I have, that was many years ago, it was one of my first job interviews, in London, actually, after I moved to London from Germany. It was for a financial department, and the manager who interviewed me, I can't remember, but I believe he was German, he asked me, "Do you have a boyfriend?", and "Are you planning to get pregnant?"

Interviewer That's illegal now, isn't it?

Heidi Yes, I know, and I believe that was illegal then.

Interviewer And what did you answer?

Heidi I said no, I didn't have a boyfriend, and I had no plans to get pregnant any time soon, but at that point, it was clear to me that I didn't want to work for that company.

3 Sean

Interviewer Have you ever been asked a strange question in an interview?

Sean Yes. I was being interviewed for a job with an advertising agency and the interviewer kept checking information on my résumé and then asking me about it, and he saw that I'd studied philosophy in college, and he said, "Oh, I see that you studied philosophy in college. Do you still practice philosophy?"

Interviewer What did you answer?

Sean I said the first thing that came into my head, I said, "Well, I still think a lot."

Interviewer Was the interviewer impressed?

Sean Well, he obviously liked the answer because I got the job.

4 Alice

Interviewer Have you ever been asked a strange question in an interview?

Alice There's one I can think of, which was when I was being interviewed for a job with a company in Canada.

Interviewer What was it?

Alice Well, the interviewer asked me, "What animal would you like to be reincarnated as?"

Interviewer Weird question!

Alice Totally.

Interviewer What did you say?

Alice So I said a cat, because it was the first thing I thought of and because cats have a good life – well, at least in the US they do. And then the interviewer immediately looked embarrassed and said that he'd been told to ask me that question to see how I would react, but that he thought it was a stupid question.

Interviewer What happened in the end?

Alice I didn't get the job, so maybe the interviewer wasn't very fond of cats!

🔊 **1.10**

On December 4th, 1872, a ship called the *Mary Celeste* was found floating in the Atlantic. There was no one on board. The ship wasn't damaged, and everything was in order, although the lifeboat was missing. None of the crew or passengers were ever seen again.

On March 4th, 1918, a huge ship called the *USS Cyclops* left Barbados with 300 people on board, and sailed into what we now call the Bermuda Triangle. Then it disappeared without a trace. No distress call was made and no bad weather was reported in the region. A huge search for the *Cyclops* was launched – boats and planes scoured the area for wreckage or survivors – but nothing of the enormous ship was ever seen again.

On July 2nd, 1937, Amelia Earhart, the famous American aviator, took off with her navigator from New Guinea, in a small plane, on the last stage of their around-the-world flight. It was the last time they were seen alive. $4 million dollars were spent on the search, but no trace of Amelia or the navigator was ever found.

🔊 **1.12**

An Edinburgh police officer, Robert Muirhead, was sent to the island to solve the mystery. Muirhead was a hard-working, practical investigator, and not at all superstitious. Among other clues, he found equipment lying all over the island, and also a huge rock, much too heavy for any men to carry, lying on the steps leading up to the lighthouse. In the end, the only explanation he could think of was that the men had been carried off by an enormous wave.

Muirhead's explanation was immediately rejected. But more than 100 years later, in 1995, the ship *Queen Elizabeth II* was hit by a 100-foot wave that according to her captain, "came out of the darkness" and "looked like the White Cliffs of Dover."

Then a paper published in a scientific journal recently proved that the "monster wave," which for centuries had been considered a sailors' myth, is a mathematical reality: many smaller waves can suddenly combine in mid-ocean and create a huge wave of devastating force. Most marine scientists now agree that it is a naturally occurring (though rare) event.

So finally, the only explanation that fits the facts is that the three lighthouse men had rushed out to attend to some emergency and had then been swept away by an enormous wave. Inspector Muirhead, it now appears, was almost certainly right. He solved the case back in 1901, but he had to wait another century for the proof.

However, science still cannot answer all the questions surrounding the Flannan Islands mystery. Why did one man leave his rain jacket behind? Why were the bodies of the men never found? Maybe these are things we will never know.

🔊 **1.16**

A walk in the forest

I'm going to describe a situation and ask you some questions. Answer quickly without thinking about it too much, the first thing that comes into your head. Are you ready?

Imagine that you're walking through a beautiful forest. The sun is out, there's a light breeze. It's a really beautiful day. You're walking with one other person.

Question 1 Who are you walking with?

As you walk through the forest, you come across an animal.

Question 2 What kind of animal is it? A big animal or a small one? How do you interact with the animal?

Now you're walking deeper into the forest, and you come to a clearing, where there are no trees. There's a house in the middle of the clearing.

Question 3 How big is the house? Does it have a fence around it or not?

You walk up to the door of the house and it's open. You go in, and you see a table.

Question 4 What is there on the table? Are there any people sitting around it?

You finish looking around the house and you leave out of the back door. There's a huge yard behind the house. You go into the yard, and in the middle you find a cup.

Question 5 What is the cup made of? Is it a ceramic cup? Metal? Plastic? Paper?

As you walk to the end of the yard, you come to some water. You must cross this water in order to get home.

Question 6 What kind of water is it? A lake? A river? A small pond? How do you cross it? How wet do you get?

What you have just done is a psychological test that analyzes how you interact with other people. Now I'm going to tell you what your answers mean.

The person you were walking with is an important person in your life.

The animal represents problems in your life. The bigger the animal, the more problems you have. How you interact with the animal represents how you deal with your problems. If you were aggressive or decisive, that means you confront your problems, try to solve them. If the interaction was peaceful, then you're a more passive person and often wait for problems to go away.

The house represents your ambitions. The bigger the house, the more ambitious you are. If there was no fence around the house, it means you're very open-minded, and welcome new ideas. If it had a fence, then you're more convinced that you're right, and tend to surround yourself by people who agree with you.

The table represents how you're feeling right now. If there was food or there were flowers on the table, and people sitting around it, this suggests that you're feeling happy in your relationships. No food, flowers, or people suggests that someone in your family or a friend is making you unhappy.

The cup represents how strong your relationship is with the person you're walking with, and how long the relationship will last. The harder and more resistant the material of the cup is, the stronger your relationship is.

The water represents your friends. If you saw a large river or lake, you have a big social circle and like to be surrounded by people. If you got very wet when you crossed it, your friends are very important for you. If you hardly got wet at all, it means that you depend less on your friends and are more self-sufficient.

Bettina So, my husband and I were out shopping in our local town, and I saw a man lying on the ground. He was just a stranger, not someone I knew, and his wife was there, standing by him. And I used to be a nurse in the ER, so I went straight up to him to see if I could help. He was a little blue, I felt his pulse and he didn't have a pulse, so I thought he was probably having a heart attack. I felt calm because I knew what to do – um, I started doing cardiac massage, you know, putting your hand on the chest and pressing down fast and at regular intervals, and my husband talked to the man's wife, he took her to one side to calm her down, because obviously she was in shock. I kept going until the ambulance turned up and the man was still alive then, and they took him to the hospital. I was really happy that I could do something.

Umesh So, I was riding my bike to work one morning, and just as I was coming around the corner, an old lady stepped off the sidewalk in front of me and she tripped and fell onto the street. I just managed not to ride my bike into her, and I dropped my bike and I went over to see if she was OK, and it was busy on the street because the stores were just opening and lots of people were around. She'd fallen pretty hard, but she was still conscious and she told us she was sure she'd broken her arm. Somebody stopped the traffic, and I helped move her to the sidewalk, somebody else went and got a chair from one of the stores, and someone else called an ambulance, and we stayed with her until it came. It was obviously an effort for her to sit up, it was very painful, so I let her lean against me. I remember I was kind of worried because I'd left my backpack on the bike with all my things in it and I was worried someone was going to steal it, but I couldn't move because I was holding the woman up.

Later, I went to visit her in the hospital and she'd actually broken her shoulder in two places and had to have an operation. I think though, if I'd just been walking past, I wouldn't necessarily have gone to help, but because it had happened right in front of me, I felt I had to do something, and now I'm, I'm glad I was able to do something – I felt pretty good about it afterwards.

Alison So, I was waiting for the bus at the end of my street to go into work. A very big man, very tall man walked past the bus stop and I noticed him particularly because he was wearing very dirty clothes and he was walking in kind of a strange way, and to be honest, I thought he might be dangerous. Then all of a sudden, he stopped walking and fell backwards, and hit the back of his head on the sidewalk. He fell so hard on the back of his head that it made a really loud noise. And then he just lay still. Some teenagers in line called an ambulance and I stood by the man. I felt completely helpless. He was breathing, but I didn't really know what to do. The ambulance arrived pretty quickly, and the paramedic took the man's hand and talked to him, and then they put him on a stretcher and took him away. Afterwards, I thought I should've done more, I should've maybe turned him on his side, or put a coat under his head – at least, I should have held his hand to show someone was there. I felt kind of ashamed because I think the reason why I didn't help him more was because he was dirty and scruffy, and I was scared of him.

Doctor Hello again, Mr. Payne. What's the problem this time?

Mr. Payne Doctor, I haven't been feeling well for a few days. I've been coughing a lot, and I keep getting headaches. I have a temperature today.

Doctor What have you been taking for the headaches?

Mr. Payne Acetaminophen. But I read on the internet that headaches can be the first symptom of a brain tumor.

Doctor How many tablets have you taken today?

Mr. Payne I took two before breakfast.

Doctor And have you taken your temperature this morning?

Mr. Payne Yes. I've taken it five or six times already. It's high.

Doctor Let me see. Mmm…well, your temperature seems to be perfectly normal now.

Mr. Payne I think I need a blood test. I haven't had one for two months.

Doctor Well Mr. Payne, you know, I think we should wait for a few days and see how your symptoms…um…develop. Take two more acetaminophen and go to bed early tonight.

Mr. Payne But…

Doctor Goodbye, Mr. Payne. Goodbye.

Receptionist Your next patient is Mrs. Morris – here is her file…

Doctor How many times has Mr. Payne been to the Health Center this month?

Receptionist Uh, six times, I think…

Doctor That Mr. Payne! He's a complete pain in the neck…

Host Welcome to today's program. The topic is age and fashion, and the question is, do people these days dress their age, and should they? Our guests are both fashion journalists with well-known magazines. Hello, Liza and Adrian.

Liza, Adrian Hello. Hi!

Host Hi. Let's start with you, Liza.

Liza Well, the first thing I'd like to say to all the young people out there is, next time you give your grandma a warm cardigan and some fur slippers for her birthday, don't be surprised if she asks for the receipt, because she'll probably want to go out and change them for something more exciting.

Host So you think these days older women dress much younger than they used to?

Liza Oh, absolutely. Think of women like Meryl Streep, Catherine Deneuve, Helen Mirren, Jane Fonda… When Jane Fonda was in her seventies, she appeared on a talk show wearing a leather miniskirt – she looked fabulous! But, of course…

Adrian I have to say, I saw that show and I thought Jane Fonda looked awful…

Host Adrian, can you let Liza finish?

Adrian Sorry. Sorry, go ahead.

Liza Well, what I was going to say was that it isn't just famous women who are dressing younger; some recent research says that nine out of ten women say that they try to dress younger than their years.

Adrian What about younger women?

Liza Well, yes, of course it depends on your age. A lot of teenage girls try to dress older than they are, maybe to get into clubs. But I would still say that from 30 onwards, most women try to dress younger than they are.

Host And do you think there's anything wrong with that?

Liza Nothing at all, it's a question of wearing what suits you. And that could be anything, from current trends to classics. I mean, OK, there are a very few things that can look a bit ridiculous on an older woman, like, let's see, very short shorts…but not many.

Adrian I think very short shorts look ridiculous at any age, well, on anyone over 15 or so.

Host Adrian, what about men? Do you think they also try to look younger than their age?

Adrian Well, interestingly, in the research Liza mentioned, only 12% of the men who were questioned said that they had ever thought about dressing to look younger. But actually, I think a lot of them weren't telling the truth. Look at all those middle-aged men you see wearing jeans which are too tight and T-shirts with slogans. I think they look terrible, as if they're trying to pretend they're still in their twenties.

Liza Sorry, but I don't agree. I think Mick Jagger looks great in tight jeans and T-shirts. They suit him!

Adrian True, but Mick Jagger is one in a million. Most men of his age can't carry it off. Personally, I do think that men should take their age into account when they're buying clothes.

Host Let's go back to the idea of dressing older than your age. Do you think that men do that too?

Adrian Yes, definitely, some do. Some men in their twenties look as if they were 20 years older by wearing blazers and chinos, or wearing a suit and a tie to work when these days most men don't dress like that.

Liza Maybe they've just started work and they want their bosses to take them more seriously?

Adrian Well, maybe.

Host I think we're running out of time. So, to sum up, Liza, Adrian, what would your fashion rules be?…

🔊 **2.24**

Host So, to sum up, Liza, Adrian, what would your fashion rules be? Liza?

Liza Wear whatever you think suits you and makes you feel good.

Host And Adrian?

Adrian Dress for the age you are, not for the age you wish you were.

Host Liza, Adrian, thank you very much.

🔊 **3.1**

A Good afternoon. This is your captain speaking. I'd like to welcome you all aboard JetBlue Flight 23 to Los Angeles. We are currently cruising at an altitude of 33,000 feet at an airspeed of 400 miles per hour. The weather along the way looks good and we are expecting to land in Los Angeles approximately 15 minutes ahead of schedule. So, sit back, relax, and enjoy the rest of the flight.

B Attention passengers. This is a track change. The 9:04 New Haven Line train from Grand Central Terminal with service to Waterbury will now depart from track 103. Passengers traveling on the 9:04 New Haven Line train to Waterbury, please go to track 103. The train is boarding.

C Attention please. Hudson Line service from Croton-Harmon to Grand Central Terminal may experience delays of 10 to 15 minutes because of track work. We apologize for any inconvenience.

D Ladies and gentlemen, we ask for your attention for the following safety instructions. Please review the safety information card located in the seat pocket in front of you. There are six emergency exits on this aircraft, all marked with exit signs. Take a minute to locate the exit closest to you. Note that the nearest exit may be behind you.

E This is the final boarding call for passengers Alice and Christopher Carter for Delta Flight 2116 to Las Vegas. Please proceed to Gate three immediately. I repeat. This is the final boarding call for Alice and Christopher Carter. Thank you.

F Ladies and gentlemen, welcome aboard United Flight 78 to San Francisco. We are currently third in line for take-off and are expected to be in the air in approximately seven minutes time. We ask that you please fasten your seatbelts at this time and place all carry-on luggage securely underneath the seat in front of you or in the overhead compartments. We also ask that you make sure your seat backs and tray tables are in their full upright and locked positions for take-off. Please turn off all personal electronic devices at this time.

G The next train arriving on track 3 will be the 10:25 AmTrak Texas Eagle with service to Chicago, making stops at Lincoln, Bloomington-Normal, Pontiac, and Joliet. Please board using all doors. Full meal service is offered in the dining car, which is located at the back of the train.

H This is a Brooklyn-bound F train. The next stop is Delancey Street. Change here for the J, M, and Z trains.

I This is the pre-boarding announcement for AeroMexico Flight 5279 to Mexico City. We're now inviting those passengers with small children, and any passengers requiring special assistance, to begin boarding at this time. Please have your boarding pass and identification ready. Regular boarding will begin in approximately ten minutes time. Thank you.

J We have now landed in London Gatwick. Please disembark by either the front or rear exits. Make sure you have all your personal belongings with you.

🔊 **3.9**

Interviewer With me in the studio today I have Richard, who's a pilot, and he's going to answer some of the most frequently asked questions about flying and air travel. Hello, Richard.

Richard Hello.

Interviewer So, Richard, the first question is, what weather conditions are the most dangerous when flying a plane?

Richard Probably the most dangerous weather conditions are when the wind changes direction very suddenly. Uh… this tends to happen during thunderstorms and tropical storms and it's especially dangerous during take-off and landing. But it's very unusual – I've been flying for 25 years now and I've only experienced this three or four times.

Interviewer What about turbulence? Is that dangerous?

Richard It can be very bumpy and very uncomfortable but it isn't dangerous. Even strong turbulence won't damage the plane. Pilots always try to avoid turbulence, but it can sometimes occur without any warning, which is why we always advise passengers to wear their seat belt all the time during the flight.

Interviewer Which is more dangerous, take-off or landing?

Richard Both take-off and landing can be dangerous. They are the most dangerous moments of a flight. Pilots talk about the "critical eight minutes" – the three minutes after take-off and the five minutes before landing. Most accidents happen in this period. But I would say that take-off is probably slightly more dangerous than landing. There is a critical moment just before take-off when the plane is accelerating, but it hasn't yet reached the speed to be able to fly. If the pilot has a problem with the plane at this point, he has very little time – maybe only a second – to abort the take-off.

Interviewer Why are passengers asked to turn off their electronic devices during take-off and landing?

Richard It's mainly because they don't want passengers to be distracted, in case there's an emergency. It has nothing to do with the devices interfering with aircraft controls, I mean, aircraft control systems are so sophisticated now, that they wouldn't cause any interference. Incidentally, that's also the reason why people have to put their tray tables up. If we had to abandon take-off or have an emergency evacuation a tray table could cause a passenger injury or prevent other passengers from getting out easily.

Interviewer Is it really worth listening to safety demonstrations?

Richard Definitely. I can tell you for a fact that when pilots are passengers during a flight they always identify the nearest emergency exit and count how many rows in front or behind it is.

Interviewer Do you ever get scared?

Richard I've been asked this many times and the answer is no – honest to goodness. I've been flying since I was 16 and there's never been a single occasion where I've felt scared in the air. Bear in mind you've been asking me about dangerous situations, but these are incredibly rare.

Interviewer Thank you very much, Richard.

🔊 **3.21**

Part 2

The day of the party arrived. Mathilde was a success. She was the prettiest of them all, elegant, smiling, and mad with joy. All the men stared at her, asked her name, and asked to be introduced. She danced all night in a cloud of happiness.

They left at about four in the morning. It was a cold night, and her husband could not find a cab.

They walked towards the Seine, shivering and finally found one. When they got home, Mathilde took off her cloak, but as she glanced at the mirror to see herself one last time, she suddenly gave a cry. Her husband, half undressed already, asked –

"What is the matter with you?"

She turned to him, in terror.

"The necklace. I have lost Madame Forestier's diamond necklace!"

He jumped up, frightened –

"What? How? It is not possible!"

They searched everywhere, but they did not find it. They had no way of contacting the cab driver. Her husband rushed out, and retraced their steps from the Ministry to where they had caught the cab. He came back at about seven o'clock in the morning. He had found nothing. He went to the police, to the newspapers, and to the cab companies to offer a reward, hoping against hope that it would be found.

"You must write to your friend," he said, "that you have broken the clasp of her necklace and that you are having it repaired. That will give us time to decide what to do."

By the end of the week they had lost all hope. The next day they went from jeweler's to jeweler's, looking for a necklace like the one Mathilde had borrowed.

In a shop in the Palais Royal, they found a diamond necklace that seemed to them absolutely identical. The price was thirty-six thousand francs.

Monsieur Loisel had eighteen thousand francs which he had inherited from his father. He borrowed the rest, asking a thousand francs from one friend, five hundred from another, doing business with money lenders, and signing promises to pay which he was not sure he would be able to keep. Finally, he was able to raise the eighteen thousand more that they needed. When Mathilde took the necklace back to Madame Forestier, she said, coldly,

"You should have brought it back sooner. I might have needed it."

🔊 **4.7**

Host And moving on to our next guest… We all know that one of our favorite topics of conversation here in the US is the weather, especially after this summer's scorching temperatures in the Southwest, along with the unusual below-average temperatures in the Northeast. Now, we have with us in the studio meteorologist Matt Wallace, and earlier in the show we asked listeners to tweet us any questions they had about the weather, and now Matt's going to answer some of them for us. Welcome to the show, Matt.

Matt Thanks, Jennie.

Host So, the first question for you from our listeners is: What's the difference between a meteorologist and a TV weatherman?

Matt Well basically, a meteorologist collects all the data, whereas a TV weatherman, well, is given the information and presents it on the radio or on TV or wherever. Keep in mind, a few TV weathermen are also trained meteorologists, but not many.

Host How far ahead can you accurately predict the weather?

Matt I think typically, we can forecast about five to seven days ahead on average. But some weather is more predictable than others. If there's high pressure, with not much changing, we could forecast, maybe, seven to ten days ahead. On other occasions, it can be very uncertain, we don't know even over just a few hours, so for example, if there's a lot of low cloud at airports, it will be very difficult for us to know when the cloud is going to clear enough for aircraft to take off or land.

Host Are long-term forecasts ever accurate?

Matt In terms of forecasting as far ahead as next summer or winter, there's a very new system where we can see how what's happening in one part of the world might affect another weather system somewhere else, so, like, weather in the Arctic, the Gulf of Mexico, the Caribbean, and even the Pacific Ocean all make a difference to the weather in the US. So we can't get real detail that far ahead, but we can get a general trend.

Host What's your favorite kind of weather?

Matt Thunderstorms, especially at night, because they're very exciting. You can see things like the lightning moving around inside the clouds, especially when the lightning really highlights the shape of the clouds. You never quite know what weather might come out of a thunderstorm, it's a kind of "weather factory" really. It can generate large amounts of rain of tremendous intensity, it can bring very strong winds, large hail, snow sometimes… there's just incredible power and majesty in thunderstorms.

Host In what ways have you noticed that the weather has changed in the last ten years?

Matt Well, in fact, over the last ten years, I don't think the weather has changed an awful lot. This year we've had an intense heatwave in Texas with over 30 days of 100-degree temperatures, while in Alaska—typically one of the wettest places in the US—there's been a drought, it's unusual, yes, these are quite extreme for the US, I guess, but it's not unprecedented, both have happened before, and both will happen again. There's evidence to show that maybe extreme weather is happening a little bit more frequently; certainly globally, looking at the science, it tends to have gotten more extreme than it has been in the past, and it's obviously becoming a little warmer as well, so yeah, but I haven't necessarily noticed it myself day to day.

Host Are you optimistic or pessimistic about climate change?

Matt I'm pretty pessimistic about it. I think in the US, it will probably lead to more frequent, more extreme heat waves in the South and in Southern California, potentially colder and longer winters in the Northeast, and some more extreme weather as well, more intense rainfall, and a greater risk of extreme flooding in the Midwest and in the Pacific Northwest.

Host Matt, thank you very much for coming and answering our questions…

 4.8

1 Holly

Interviewer Are you a risk-taker?

Holly Generally definitely not, and I think that started early in life when I was little. I hated getting hurt, so I thought, if I don't take any risks, I won't get hurt, and so I think even to this day I'm not really a risk-taker.

Interviewer Can you give me an example of a risk you have taken?

Holly Well, as I said I don't usually take risks, for example, I hate flying. I only fly if there's no alternative, and I drive safely, carefully, because I don't want to put myself or my family in any danger. But once, someone persuaded me to try scuba-diving. I was very worried in the beginning, until I knew what I was doing. My mom was absolutely horrified that I was going to try it, so maybe it's a personality thing. In my family, my children are the same way, but anyway, in the end I was pretty happy I tried scuba-diving, it's one of the best things I've ever done! That's so interesting, isn't it, so even for me, I can see that sometimes taking a risk has a positive outcome.

2 Natalie

Interviewer Are you a risk-taker?

Natalie I'd say that, on the whole, that I am, yes.

Interviewer Can you give me an example of a risk you've taken?

Natalie Well, something I do a lot is buy things on eBay. And there, you're buying something you, you've never seen, you're relying on what the seller says about it, but you're going to calculate the risk based on their description, and how much you're paying, so if it only costs $10.00, it's not a great risk, however, if it's an expensive item, you might lose some money. But I guess that's something that most people take a risk on now.

3 Tom

Interviewer Are you a risk-taker?

Tom I am in some ways, I mean I've done some things that were physically dangerous – but when it comes to things like money, then I think I'm much more conservative.

Interviewer Can you give me an example of a risk you've taken?

Tom Well, when I finished college, my mom and dad just wanted me to apply for a normal kind of job, like, working for a company, but I decided that I wanted a little more fun while I was that age, so I decided to spend some time working as a restaurant manager, and I worked at lots of different food and drink festivals all over the world. I knew it would affect my résumé, because employers are always asking you questions about why you chose to do that, how was that useful to you, and just saying it seemed like a fun idea isn't a very good answer. After two or three years, I realized that it was going to be pretty hard for me to keep on doing the job past the age of about 30. But now I'm glad I did it, and actually maybe it gave me what they call soft skills, like being flexible and dealing with people, which are really useful in my job now – I work in sales in a computer software company – so yeah, I think the risk was worth it in the end.

4 Jeanie

Interviewer Are you a risk-taker?

Jeanie Um, not really, no, I don't think I am. Though once I took a really big risk.

Interviewer What was it?

Jeanie When I graduated from college I went right into a really well-paid job straightaway, um, and after about two years I was doing really well and enjoying it a lot. And then, through some friends, I met this guy, Marco, and we fell in love immediately, I know people think love at first sight doesn't really happen, but it did. Anyway, um, he was – is – a scientist, a marine biologist, um, and after we'd been going out for maybe two months or so he was offered a job working in Australia and he said, "Come with me." I did think about it for a little bit, but not much, and I left my well-paid job to follow a man I'd known less than three months to the other side of the world. My parents were horrified. I was horrified myself, actually. But I married him and we're still together. So it was definitely worth it, but on the other hand, um, I haven't really had a career as such, and if I hadn't gone with him then, maybe I would've had a different kind of life. Who knows?

 4.14

1 Skiing was the first extreme sport that I did. I started when I was six and I haven't really stopped since. I take after my dad – we're both sports-crazy. He got me into skiing so he could take me on winter vacations.

2 I've done a lot of extreme sports in the mountains, such as mountain biking, and rock climbing, and ice-walking across glaciers. I've also done white-water rafting recently. It's very hard work, but really worth the energy.

3 I think it's because I love taking risks, I love the adrenaline rush.

4 I don't really think about getting injured or killed. I've never had a bad accident, but I've had some scary moments, where I knew if I made a mistake, I could get seriously hurt. But I've never really thought there was a chance I could die.

5 I think more and more people are taking part in extreme sports because they're becoming more accessible, and there's much more exposure than before on TV and on social media. Like I said before, it's the adrenaline rush that people really enjoy – you can't always get that in your everyday life.

6 A few years ago, I would have said men were much more associated with extreme sports. However, I think it's becoming a little more equal between men and women. Extreme sportswomen are really appreciated, because they're going against the gender stereotype, but, men do still seem to dominate, maybe because they were more involved when the sports were first recognized.

 5.2

Interviewer What was the most difficult or challenging part of your experience?

Ali Well, because you're, um, put on the island with just the clothes on your back and a few basic tools, it means that anything you eat you have to find, catch, and kill, if necessary. So for the first week, we didn't eat anything at all except a few coconuts. Um, so I lost four kilos in just a week. Um, after that most of what we ate was yucca, which is like a potato, grows in the ground. But you have to walk a lot to find it, um, and even then it would only be the equivalent of having a small potato each, um, every day. So we were still hungry. We were able to catch some fish, um, and then we did manage to kill a wild boar. And also because of the lack of food we became really weak, so it was hard you, hard even to go out for a stroll along the beach. That became really difficult. It was also difficult being dirty all the time, because the water we had to wash in, uh, was the ocean. So you're obviously salty and covered in sand and you never really feel clean. Um, when it rained, which was all the time, the ground would become really muddy and everything would just get absolutely filthy. We had a couple of weeks where the weather was really bad, so we were completely soaked, really freezing cold, wet, miserable, and hungry. Um, and the other thing that was really difficult was the tension between the groups and also within our group, because everyone was very stressed and hungry and tired, it didn't take much for arguments to occur. And there's nowhere to escape from on the desert island.

Interviewer What were the highlights?

Ali So at first, even just landing on the island was a highlight, um, because we were so excited and we were meeting all these new people, um, we'd never met before, and we were full of enthusiasm and energy. Um, and we just had lunch, so we weren't hungry. Um, so when Bear Grylls picked us up on his boat and drove us round the island, um, and then he stopped in the middle of the ocean and threw us out of the boat and told us to swim to the island, um, which was so exciting. Um, and the last week was also a real highlight for me because the two groups came together and we built a communal shelter in the middle of the beach so everyone – for everyone to sleep in and to enjoy, and we had a really good time. The weather at this point, um, had turned really good and so, we had a sports day and we had a talent show, and even a wedding! It was a really fun week. Um, but I think probably leaving the island was the real highlight – best day of my life, even. Um, it was so good to know that we'd survived for 35 days. And seeing Bear pull up on his boat, uh, to come and collect us was just an amazing feeling. I felt both really proud and super relieved.

Interviewer Out of the 16 people that landed on the island, 13, including Ali, managed to last the whole five weeks. Two participants decided to leave before the end, and unfortunately, one had to go to the hospital with an eye injury. By the last week, the participants had all realized that they were much more effective working together as one big team than trying to survive in separate groups. How much money they earned or what their background was turned out to be completely irrelevant. Both teams worked hard, kept their moral high, and survived.

🔊 **5.8**

Yossi and Kevin soon realized that going by river was a big mistake. The river got faster and faster, and soon they were in rapids.
The raft was swept down the river at an incredible speed until it hit a rock. Both men were thrown into the water. Kevin was a strong swimmer and he managed to swim to land, but Yossi was swept away by the rapids.
But Yossi didn't drown. He was carried several miles downriver by the rapids, but he eventually managed to swim to the river bank. He was totally exhausted. By an incredible piece of luck, he found their backpack floating in the river. The backpack contained a little food, insect repellent, a lighter, and most important of all…the map. But the two friends were now separated by a canyon and three or four miles of jungle.

🔊 **5.9**

Kevin was feeling desperate. He didn't know if Yossi was alive or dead, but he started walking downriver to look for him. He felt responsible for what had happened to his friend because he had persuaded him to go with him on the river.
Yossi, however, was feeling very optimistic. He was sure that Kevin would look for him, so he started walking upriver, calling his friend's name. But nobody answered.
At night Yossi tried to sleep, but he felt terrified. The jungle was full of noises. Suddenly, he woke up because he heard a branch breaking. He turned on his flashlight. There was a jaguar staring at him…
Yossi was trembling with fear. But then he remembered something that he had once seen in a movie. He used the cigarette lighter to set fire to the insect repellent spray and he managed to scare the jaguar away.

🔊 **5.10**

After five days alone, Yossi was exhausted and starving. Suddenly, as he was walking, he saw a footprint on the trail – it was a hiking boot. It had to be Kevin's footprint! He followed the trail until he discovered another footprint and then another. But suddenly he realized that the footprints weren't Kevin's footprints. They were his own. He had been walking around in a circle. At that moment Yossi realized that he would never find Kevin. In fact, he felt sure that Kevin must be dead. He felt totally depressed and at the point of giving up.

🔊 **5.11**

But Kevin wasn't dead. He was still looking for Yossi. But after nearly a week, he was also weak and exhausted from lack of food and lack of sleep. He decided that it was time to forget Yossi and try to save himself. He had just enough strength left to hold onto a log and let himself float down the river.
Kevin was incredibly lucky – he was rescued by two Bolivian hunters who were traveling downriver in a canoe. The men only hunted in that part of the rainforest once a year, so if they had passed by a short time earlier or later, they wouldn't have seen Kevin. They took him back to the town of San José, where he spent two days recovering.

🔊 **5.12**

As soon as Kevin felt well enough, he went to a Bolivian army base and asked them to look for Yossi. ("*My friend is lost in the jungle. You must look for him.*") The army officer he spoke to was sure that Yossi must be dead, but in the end Kevin persuaded them to take him up in a plane and fly over the part of the rainforest where Yossi might be. But the plane had to fly too high over the rainforest and the forest was too dense. They couldn't see anything at all. It was a hopeless search. Kevin felt terribly guilty. He was convinced that it was all his fault that Yossi was going to die in the jungle. Kevin's last hope was to pay a local man with a boat to take him up the river to look for his friend.

🔊 **5.13**

By now, Yossi had been on his own in the jungle for nearly three weeks. He hadn't eaten for days. He was starving, exhausted, and slowly losing his mind. It was evening. He lay down by the side of the river ready for another night alone in the jungle.
Suddenly he heard the sound of a bee buzzing in his ear. He thought a bee had got inside his mosquito net. But when he opened his eyes, he saw that the buzzing noise wasn't a bee…
It was a boat. Yossi was too weak to shout, but Kevin had already seen him. It was a one-in-a-million chance that Kevin would find his friend. But he did. Yossi was saved.
When Yossi had recovered, he and Kevin flew to the city of La Paz and they went directly to the hotel where they had agreed to meet Marcus and Karl.
But Marcus and Karl were not at the hotel. The two men had never arrived back in the town of Apolo. The Bolivian army organized a search of the rainforest, but Marcus and Karl were never seen again.

🔊 **5.20**

1 One thing I really regret is not being brave enough to ask out a girl who I met at a party last summer. I really liked her but I was just too scared to invite her on a date in case she said no. I wish I'd tried. I'm absolutely sure we would have gotten along. Now it's too late – she's engaged to another guy!
2 Um, I wish I'd had more time with my grandmother. She died when I was 12, and since then I've discovered that she must have been a really fascinating person, and there are so many things I'd love to have been able to talk to her about. She was Polish, but she was in Russia, in St. Petersburg, during the Russian Revolution and she knew all sorts of interesting people at the time: painters, writers, people like that. I was only a kid, so I never asked her much about her own life. Now, I'm discovering all about her through reading her old letters and papers, but I wish she'd lived longer so that I could have talked to her about those times face-to-face.

3 When I was in college, I had the chance to earn two degrees at the same time—a four-year degree in aeronautical engineering and a Master's degree in mechanical engineering. My parents were eager for me to study for both degrees because they thought I'd probably get better job offers when I graduated. But I was totally against the idea because my engineering classes were hard, and I spent a lot of my time studying. Plus, I wanted to hang out with my friends every now and then and have some fun. So, I ended up graduating with one degree, and I have a good job. But now I wish I'd listened to my parents because if I want to advance my career at my current job, I have to go back to school and get my Master's degree in … mechanical engineering.

question formation

> 1 How long **have you** been waiting?   How many children 1.3 **does your sister** have?   **Should we** buy her a present?
> 2 Why **didn't you** like the movie?   **Isn't this** a beautiful place? **Don't you** have to be at school today?
> 3 **What** are you talking **about**?   **Who** does this bag belong **to**?
> 4 **Who lives** in that house? **How many people follow** you on Twitter?

1 We make questions with tenses where there is an auxiliary verb (*be, have,* etc.) and with modal verbs (*should, must,* etc.) by inverting the subject and the auxiliary / modal verb. With the simple present and past, we add the auxiliary verb *do / does* or *did* before the subject.

2 We often use negative questions to show surprise when we expect somebody to agree with us, or to check whether something is true.

3 If a verb is usually followed by a preposition, e.g., *talk about something*, the preposition comes at the end of the question, not at the beginning. **NOT** *About what are you talking?*

- We often just use the question word and the preposition, e.g., **A** *I'm thinking.* **B** *What about?*

4 When *who / what / which*, etc., is the **subject** of questions in the simple present or past, we <u>don't</u> use *do / did*, e.g., *Who wrote this?* **NOT** *Who did write this?*

indirect questions

> Could you tell me **what time the store next door opens**? 1.4
> Do you know **if (whether) Mark's coming to the meeting**?

- We use indirect questions when we want to ask a question in a more polite way. We begin with a phrase such as *Can / Could you tell me…? Do you know…? Do you think…? Do you remember…? Would you mind telling me…? Do you have any idea…?*
- Compare: *What time does the post office open?* (direct question) and *Could you tell me what time the post office opens?* (indirect question)
- In indirect questions, the order is subject + verb. *Can you tell me where* ***it is***? **NOT** *Can you tell me where* ***is it***?
- We don't use *do / did* in the second part of the question. *Do you know where he lives?* **NOT** *…where does he live?*
- You can use *if* or *whether* in questions <u>without</u> a question word and after: *Can you tell me, Do you know,* etc.

🔍 **Other expressions followed by the word order of indirect questions**

The word order of indirect questions is used after:
I wonder…, e.g., **I wonder** *why they didn't come.*
I'm not sure…, e.g., **I'm not sure** *what time it starts.*
I can't remember…, e.g., **I can't remember** *where I left my phone.*
I'd like to know…, e.g., **I'd like to know** *what time you're coming home.*

---

a Order the words to make questions.

tomorrow can't Why come you ?
Why can't you come tomorrow?
1 I Should her tell I feel how ?
2 friend known long best have How you your ?
3 tell when you train next leaves the Could me ?
4 are What about you thinking ?
5 on do weekend you What doing the like ?
6 music to does What Junko kind like listening of ?
7 you time movie know finishes Do what the ?
8 class students yesterday to many came How ?
9 you remember is where Do the restaurant ?
10 housework family in Who your the does ?

b Complete the questions with the words in parentheses.

Where *did you go* on vacation last year? (you / go)
1 How often _____ ? (you / usually exercise)
2 Who _____ *The Great Gatsby*? (write)
3 Could you tell me how much _____? (this book / cost)
4 I can't remember where _____ my car this morning. (I / park)
5 _____ your trip to Paris last weekend? (you / enjoy)
6 What kind of work _____? (your sister / do)
7 Who _____ the last cookie? (eat)
8 Do you know what time _____ on Saturdays? (the swimming pool / open)
9 Why _____ the present you gave her? (your sister / not like)
10 _____ play your music so loud? I can't concentrate. (you / have to)   ⬅ p.7

1B

auxiliary verbs

1 I like cats, but my husband **doesn't**. 🔊1.14
Sally's coming tonight, but Angela **isn't**.

2 A I loved his latest movie.
B **So did I.**
A I haven't finished the book yet.
B **Neither have I.**
Andrew's a doctor and **so is his wife**.

3 A I don't like shopping online.
B I **do**. I buy a lot of my clothes online.

4 A I went to a psychic yesterday.
B **You did?**
A I'll make dinner tonight.
B **You will?** That's great!

5 A You didn't lock the door!
B I **did** lock it; I know I **did**.
A Silvia isn't coming.
B She **is** coming. I just spoke to her.

6 You won't forget, **will** you?
She can speak Italian, **can't** she?

• We use auxiliary verbs (*do, have,* etc.) or modal verbs (*can, must,* etc.):

1 to avoid repeating the main verb / verb phrase, e.g., **NOT** ~~I like cats, but my husband doesn't~~ **like cats**.

2 with *so* and *neither* to say that someone or something is the same. Use *so* + auxiliary + subject to respond to a statement with an affirmative verb, and *neither* + auxiliary + subject to respond to a statement with a negative verb.

• We use an affirmative auxiliary verb after *neither*, e.g., *Neither did I.* **NOT** ~~Neither didn't I.~~

3 to respond to a statement and say that you (or someone or something) are different.

4 to make "reply questions." These often show interest or surprise.

5 to show emphasis in an affirmative sentence, often when you want to contradict what somebody says. With the simple present and simple past, we add *do / does / did* before the main verb. With other auxiliaries, e.g., *be, have, will,* the auxiliary verb is stressed and not contracted.

6 to make tag questions, we use an affirmative auxiliary with a negative verb, and a negative auxiliary with an affirmative verb.

• Tag questions are often used simply to ask another person to agree with you, e.g., *It's a nice day, isn't it?* In this case, the tag question is said with falling intonation, i.e., the voice goes down.

• Tag questions can also be used to check something you think is true, e.g., *She's a painter, isn't she?* In this case, the tag question is said with rising intonation, as in a normal *yes / no* question.

---

a Complete the mini-dialogues with an auxiliary or modal verb.

A You didn't remember to buy coffee.
B I *did* remember. It's in the cabinet.

1 A He's booked the flights, _____ he?
B Yes, I think so.

2 A It's hot today, _____ it?
B Yes, it's boiling.

3 A Why don't you like classical music?
B I _____ like it, but it isn't my favorite.

4 A I wouldn't like to be a celebrity.
B Neither _____ I.

5 A Mike's arriving tomorrow!
B He _____? I thought he was arriving today.

6 A What did you think of the movie?
B Tom liked it, but I _____. I thought it was awful.

7 A Emma doesn't like me.
B She _____ like you. She just doesn't want to go out with you.

8 A Are you a vegetarian?
B Yes, I am, and so _____ my boyfriend.

9 A You'll remember to call me, _____ you?
B Yes, of course!

10 I really want to go to Thailand, but my wife _____. She hates the heat.

b Complete the conversation with a suitable auxiliary verb.

A You're Tom's sister, *aren't* you?
B Yes, I'm Carla.
A It's a great club, [1]_____ it?
B Well, it's OK. But I don't like the music much.
A You [2]_____? I love it! I've never been here before.
B Neither [3]_____ I. I don't go clubbing very often.
A Oh, you [4]_____? I [5]_____. In fact, I usually go most weekends.
B You [6]_____? I can't afford to go out every weekend.
A I didn't see you at Tom's birthday party last Saturday. Why [7]_____ you go?
B I [8]_____ go, but I got there really late because my car broke down.
A Oh, that's why I didn't see you. I left early.
B I'd like something to drink. I'm really thirsty after all that dancing.
A So [9]_____ I.

 p.11

2A

present perfect simple and continuous

present perfect simple: *have / has* + past participle

> 1 **Have** you ever **broken** a bone? 🔊 2.12
>   I**'ve** never **seen** him before.
> 2 I**'ve called** for an ambulance, but it **hasn't arrived** yet.
>   I**'ve** already **told** you three times.
> 3 It's the best book I**'ve** ever **read**.
> 4 I**'ve known** Keiko since I was a child.
>   My sister **has been** sick for ten days now.
> 5 How many Patricia Cornwell novels **have you read**?
>   They**'ve seen** each other twice this week.

- We use the present perfect simple:
1 to talk about past experiences when you don't say when something happened, often with *ever* or *never*.
2 with *yet* and *already*.
3 with superlatives and *the first, second, last time*, etc.
4 with nonaction verbs (= verbs not usually used in the continuous form, e.g., *be, need, know, like*, etc.) to say that something started in the past and is still true now.
- This use is common with time expressions like *How long...?, for* or *since, all day / evening*, etc.
- Don't use the simple present in this situation. **NOT** ~~I know Keiko since I was a child.~~
5 when we say or ask *how much / many* we have done or *how often* we have done something up to now.

present perfect continuous: *have / has + been* + verb + *-ing*

> 1 How long **have** you **been waiting** to see the doctor? 🔊 2.13
>   He**'s been messaging** his girlfriend all evening.
> 2 I **haven't been sleeping** well recently.
>   It**'s been raining** all day.
> 3 I**'ve been shopping** all morning. I'm exhausted.
>   My shoes are filthy. I**'ve been working** in the yard.

- We use the present perfect continuous:
1 with action verbs (e.g., *run, listen, study, cook*) to say that an action started in the past and is still happening now (unfinished actions).
- This use is common with time expressions like *How long...?, for* or *since, all day / evening*, etc.
- Don't use the present continuous in this situation. **NOT** ~~I'm living here for the last three years.~~
2 for repeated actions, especially with a time expression, e.g., *all day, recently*.
3 for continuous actions that have just finished (but that have present results).

present perfect simple or continuous?

> 1 I**'ve been feeling terrible** for days. 🔊 2.14
>   He**'s liked** classical music since he was a teenager.
> 2 She**'s been having** a good time at school.
>   They**'ve had** that car for at least ten years.
> 3 We**'ve lived** in this town since 2010.
>   We**'ve been living** in a rented house for the last two months.
> 4 I**'ve painted** the kitchen. I**'ve been painting** the kitchen.

1 To talk about an unfinished action, we usually use the present perfect continuous with action verbs (e.g., *run, listen, study, cook*) and the present perfect simple with nonaction verbs (e.g., *be, need, know, like*, etc.).
2 Some verbs can be action or nonaction, depending on their meaning, e.g., *have a good time* = action, *have a car* = nonaction.
3 With the verbs *live* or *work*, you can often use the present perfect simple or continuous. However, we usually use the present perfect continuous for more temporary actions.
4 The present perfect simple emphasizes the completion of an action (= the kitchen has been painted). The present perfect continuous emphasizes the duration of an action (= the painting of the kitchen may not be finished yet).

---

a Circle the correct form. Check (✓) if both are possible.

Have you ever ~~tried~~ / *been trying* caviar?

1 She's *worked* / *been working* here since July.
2 Your mother has *called* / *been calling* three times this morning!
3 The kids are exhausted because they've *run* / *been running* around all day.
4 Tim and Lucy haven't *seen* / *been seeing* our new house yet.
5 I've never *met* / *been meeting* her boyfriend. Have you?
6 It's *snowed* / *been snowing* all morning.
7 My brother has *lived* / *been living* alone since his divorce.
8 I've *read* / *been reading* all morning. I've now *read* / *been reading* 100 pages.

b Complete the sentence with the present perfect simple or continuous of the verb in parentheses.

I*'ve bought* a new car. Do you like it? (buy)

1 We _____ Jack and Ann for years. (know)
2 You look really sweaty. _____ at the gym? (you / work out)
3 Emily _____ her homework yet, so I'm afraid she can't go out. (not do)
4 They don't live in Toronto. They _____. (move)
5 I hope they're getting along OK. They _____ a lot recently. (argue)
6 We _____ for hours. Is this the right way? (walk)
7 Why is my laptop on? _____ it? (you / use)
8 Oh, no! I _____ my finger on this knife. (cut)

⬅ p.18

> 🔵 **Go online** to review the grammar for each lesson

using adjectives as nouns, adjective order

adjectives as nouns

1 In most African countries, **the young** still look up to **the old**. 🔊 2.15
  The poor are getting poorer, and **the rich** are getting richer.
  The government needs to create more jobs for **the unemployed**.
2 **The English** are famous for drinking tea.
  The Chinese invented paper.
  The Dutch make wonderful cheeses.

- You can use *the* + some adjectives to talk about groups of people, e.g.,
1 specific groups in society, such as *the young*, *the old* (or *the elderly*), *the sick* (= people who are ill), *the blind*, *the deaf*, *the homeless*, *the dead*.
2 some nationalities that end in *-ch*, *-sh*, *-ese*, and *-ss*, such as *the French*, *the Spanish*, *the British*, *the Japanese*, *the Irish*, *the Swiss*, etc. (most other nationality words are nouns and are used in the plural, e.g., *the Brazilians*, *the Peruvians*, *the Turks*, *the South Koreans*, *the Argentinians*, etc.).
- You can also use adjective + *people* to talk about a group of people, e.g., *poor people*, *homeless people*, *old people*, *Thai people*.
- To talk about one person, use, e.g., *a Japanese woman*, *a rich man*, etc., **NOT** ~~a Japanese~~, ~~a rich~~.

adjective order

We have a **charming old** house near the lake. 🔊 2.16
She has **long brown** hair.
I bought a **beautiful Italian leather** belt.

- You can put more than one adjective before a noun (often two and occasionally three). These adjectives go in a particular order, e.g., **NOT** ~~an old charming house~~.
- Opinion adjectives, e.g., *beautiful*, *nice*, *charming*, always go <u>before</u> descriptive adjectives, e.g., *big*, *old*, *round*.
- If there is more than one descriptive adjective, they go in this order:

OPINION	SIZE	AGE	SHAPE	COLOR	PATTERN	ORIGIN / PLACE	MATERIAL	NOUN
expensive	little	brand new	long	purple	striped	French	silk	scarf
beautiful						Japanese		car

---

a Rewrite the <u>underlined</u> phrase using *the* + an adjective.

> <u>People from Vietnam</u> enjoy spicy food.
> *The Vietnamese*

1 <u>People from the Netherlands</u> tend to be good at languages.
2 Clara Barton took care of <u>the people who weren't well</u> during the American Civil War.
3 The system of reading for <u>people who can't see</u> is called Braille.
4 <u>People from China</u> have a fascinating history.
5 Ambulances arrived to take <u>the people who had been injured</u> to the hospital.
6 <u>People from Switzerland</u> are usually very punctual.
7 The worst season for <u>people without a home</u> is winter.
8 There is a discount for <u>people without a job</u>.
9 The World War II monument was erected to honor <u>the people who died</u>.
10 There are special TV shows for <u>people who can't hear</u>, that use sign language.

b Write the adjectives in parentheses in the correct place. Change *a* to *an* where necessary.

> a big parking lot (empty)   *a big empty parking lot*

1 a man (young / attractive)
2 shoes (old / dirty)
3 a velvet jacket (black / beautiful)
4 a girl (teenage / tall / American)
5 a beach (sandy / long)
6 a log cabin (charming / old)
7 a leather bag (Italian / stylish)
8 eyes (huge / dark)
9 a dog (black / friendly / old)
10 a T-shirt (striped / cotton)

← p.21

narrative tenses: simple past, past continuous, past perfect, past perfect continuous

narrative tenses

> 1 We **arrived** at the airport and **checked in**. 🔊 3.10
> 2 We **were having** dinner when the plane hit some turbulence. At nine o'clock most people on the plane **were reading** or **were trying** to sleep.
> 3 When we arrived at the airport, we suddenly realized that we**'d left** one of the suitcases in the taxi.
> 4 We**'d been flying** for about two hours when suddenly the captain told us to fasten our seat belts because we were flying into some very bad weather.

1 We use the **simple past** to talk about consecutive actions or situations in the past, i.e., for the main events in a story.

2 We use the **past continuous** (*was / were* + verb + *-ing*) to describe a longer continuous past action or situation that was in progress when another action happened, or to describe an action or situation that was not complete at a past time.

3 We use the **past perfect** (*had* + past participle) to talk about the "earlier past," i.e., things that happened <u>before</u> the main event(s).

4 We use the **past perfect continuous** (*had been* + verb + *-ing*) with action verbs (*go, play, watch,* etc.) to talk about longer continuous actions or situations that started before the main events happened and continued up to that point. Nonaction verbs (e.g., *be, have, know, like,* etc.) are not usually used in the past continuous or past perfect continuous.

past perfect simple or continuous?

> Lina was crying because she**'d been reading** a very sad book. 🔊 3.11
> Lina didn't want to see the movie, because she**'d** already **read** the book.

- The past perfect continuous emphasizes the <u>continuation</u> of an activity. The past perfect simple emphasizes the <u>completion</u> of an activity.

---

a Circle the correct verb form.

Ava and Ryan Miller (got) / *were getting* a nasty surprise when they [1] *had checked in / were checking in* at Calgary International Airport yesterday with their baby, Alec. They [2] *had won / won* three free plane tickets to Mexico in a competition, and they [3] *were looking forward to / had been looking forward to* their trip for months. But, unfortunately, they [4] *had been forgetting / had forgotten* to get a passport for their son, so Alec couldn't fly. Luckily, they [5] *had arrived / were arriving* very early for their flight, so they still had time to do something about it. They [6] *had run / ran* to the police station in the airport to apply for an emergency passport. Ava [7] *was going / went* with Alec to the photo booth, while Ryan [8] *had filled out / was filling out* the forms. The passport was ready in an hour, so they [9] *hurried / were hurrying* to the gate and [10] *got / had got* on the plane just in time.

b Put the verb in parentheses in the past perfect simple (*had done*) or continuous (*had been doing*). If you think both are possible, use the continuous form.

His English was very good. He*'d been learning* it for five years. (learn)

1 I was really fed up because we _____ for hours. (wait)
2 She went to the police to report that someone _____ her bag. (steal)
3 It _____ all morning. The streets were wet, and there were puddles everywhere. (rain)
4 She got to work late because she _____ her phone at home and _____ go back and get it. (leave, have to)
5 I almost didn't recognize Tony at the party. He _____ a lot since I last saw him. (change)
6 The tourists' faces were very red. They _____ in the sun all morning and they _____ any sunscreen. (sit, not put on)
7 I could see from their expressions that my parents _____. (argue)
8 Jamilla had a bandage on her arm because she _____ off her bike that morning. (fall)
9 I was amazed because I _____ such an enormous plane before. (never see)
10 How long _____ you _____ before you realized that you were lost? (walk)

⬅ p.28

3B

the position of adverbs and adverbial phrases

1 He walks very **slowly**.
  I speak five languages **fluently**.
  The driver was **seriously** injured in the accident.
2 I **hardly ever** have time for breakfast.
  Liam's **always** late for work.
  I would **never** have thought you were 40.
3 It rained **all day yesterday**.
  My parents will be **here in half an hour**.

4 I'm **nearly** finished.
  We're **incredibly** tired.
  My husband works **a lot**, but he doesn't earn **much**.
5 **Unfortunately**, the package never arrived.
  Ideally, we should leave here at 10:00.

• Adverbs can describe an action (e.g., *he walks **slowly***) or modify adjectives or other adverbs (e.g., *it's **incredibly** expensive, he works **very** hard*). They can either be one word (e.g., *often*) or a phrase (e.g., *once a week*).
1 **Adverbs of manner** describe how somebody does something. They usually go after the verb or verb phrase, however, with passive verbs they usually go in mid-position (before the main verb but after an auxiliary verb).

2 **Adverbs of frequency** go before the main verb but after the verb *to be*.
• *sometimes*, *usually*, and *normally* can also be put at the beginning of the phrase or sentence for emphasis, e.g., *Sometimes the weather can be very wet, but not today.*
• If there are two auxiliary verbs, the adverb goes after the first one.
3 **Adverbs of time and place** usually go at the end of a sentence or clause. Place adverbs usually go before time adverbs. **NOT** *My parents will be in half an hour here.*
• Adverbs of time can also go at the beginning for emphasis, e.g., **Soon** *it will be my birthday!* **OR** *It will be my birthday* **soon**!
4 **Adverbs of degree** describe how much something is done, or modify an adjective.
• *nearly* and *almost* are used before a verb or verb phrase.
• *extremely*, *incredibly*, *very*, etc., are used with adjectives and adverbs, and go before them.
• *a lot* and *much* are often used with verbs and go after the verb or verb phrase.
• *a little / a little bit (of)* can be used with adjectives or verbs, e.g., *I'm a little tired. We rested a little bit after the flight.*
5 **Comment adverbs** (which give the speaker's opinion) usually go at the beginning of a sentence or clause. Other common comment adverbs are: *luckily, basically, clearly, obviously, apparently, eventually*, etc.

> 🔍 **Other adverbs**
> Most other adverbs go in mid-position, e.g., *I **just** need ten more minutes. I didn't speak to Kelly at the party – I didn't **even** see her. She'll **probably** come in the end.*

---

a Underline the adverbs or adverbial phrases in each sentence. Correct the word order if it's wrong.

> We're going to be <u>unfortunately</u> late. ✗
> *Unfortunately, we're going to be late.*
> He can speak Turkish <u>fluently</u>. ✓

1 She liked a lot the present.
2 Mark came last night very late home.
3 The ambulance arrived at the scene of the accident after a few minutes.
4 A young man was hurt badly and was taken to the hospital.
5 I was incredibly tired last night.
6 She's lazy a little bit about doing her homework.
7 I forgot your birthday almost, but my sister fortunately reminded me.
8 We luckily had taken an umbrella, because it started to rain right away.
9 Mary doesn't always eat healthily – she often has snacks between meals.
10 Yadier has been apparently fired.

b Put the adverbs in parentheses in the normal position in these sentences.

> *seriously*
> I'm _∧considering resigning from my job. (seriously)

1 Their house was damaged in the fire. (badly, last week)
2 Ben is at his friend's house. (often, in the evening)
3 My father takes a nap. (usually, in the afternoon)
4 Julia left and she didn't say goodbye. (early, even)
5 Martin eats quickly. (always, incredibly)
6 His brother died in a skiing accident. (apparently, nearly)
7 We're going to the movies. (probably, tonight)
8 I send emails. (rarely, nowadays)
9 I bought a beautiful new coat. (just, really)
10 Maya realized that she was going to learn to drive. (eventually, never)

◀ p.31

4A

future perfect and future continuous

future perfect: *will have* + past participle

> The rain **will have stopped** by this afternoon. 🔊4.1
> Some people think that sea levels **will have risen** by as much as 3 feet in 50 years.
> Laura **won't have arrived** before dinner, so I'll leave some food on the stove for her.
> When **will they have learned** enough English to be able to communicate fluently?

- We use the future perfect (*will have* + past participle) to say something will be finished before a certain time in the future.
- This tense is frequently used with the time expressions **by** *Saturday / March / 2030*, etc., or *in two weeks / months*, etc.
- *by* + a time expression = at the latest. With *in*, you can say *in six months*.
- We form the negative with *won't have* + past participle, and make questions by inverting the subject and *will / won't*.

future continuous: *will be* + verb + *-ing*

> 1 Don't call between 7:00 and 8:30 because we**'ll be** 🔊4.2
> **having** dinner then.
> Good luck with your test tomorrow. I**'ll be thinking** of you.
> **Will** you **be waiting** for me when I get off the train?
> This time tomorrow, I**'ll be sitting** on the beach **watching** the sunset.
> 2 You don't need to get up early. We **won't be leaving** until about 9:30.
> I**'ll be going** to the supermarket later. Do you want anything?

1 We use the future continuous (*will be* + verb + *-ing*) to say that an action will be in progress at a certain time in the future.

Compare:
Come at around 7:30. **We'll have** dinner at 8:00. (= we will start dinner at 8:00)
and
Don't call between 7:00 and 8:30 because **we'll be having** dinner. (= at 8:00 we will already have started having dinner)

- We form the negative with *won't be* + verb + *-ing* and make questions by inverting the subject and *will / won't*.

2 We sometimes use the future continuous, like the present continuous, to talk about things that are already planned or decided.

---

a Complete the sentence using the future perfect or future continuous.

> The movie starts at 7:00, but I won't arrive until 7:15. When I arrive at the movie theater, the movie *will have started*. (start)

1 The flight to Miami takes off at 9:00 and lands at 10:30.
At 10:00 they _____ to Miami. (fly)
2 I usually save $200 a month.
By the end of the year, I _____ $2,400. (save)
3 Rebecca leaves at 6:30. It takes her an hour to get to work.
At 7:00 tomorrow, she _____ to work. (drive)
4 The meeting starts at 2:00 and finishes at 3:30.
Don't call me at 2:30, because we _____ a meeting. (have)
5 Sam is paying for his car. The last payment is in May.
By June, he _____ for his car. (pay)
6 Their last test is on May 31st.
By the end of May, they _____ their tests. (finish)
7 She writes a chapter of her novel a week. This week she's on chapter five.
By the end of this week, she _____ five chapters. (write)
8 Sonia is usually at the gym between 6:30 and 7:30.
There's no point calling Sonia now. It's 7:00 and she _____ at the gym. (work out)

b Complete the conversation with the verbs in parentheses in the future perfect or continuous.

> A Well, it looks like we*'ll be having* very different weather in the future if climate change continues. (have)
> B What do you mean?
> A Well, they say *we'll be having* much higher temperatures here in New York, as high as 96°. And remember, we
> 1_____ on the beach – we (not lie)
> 2_____ in 96°, which is very (work)
> different. And islands like Puerto Rico
> 3_____ by 2100 because (disappear)
> of the rise in sea levels. They say the number of storms and tsunamis
> 4_____ by the middle of (double)
> the century, too, so even more people
> 5_____ to the cities by (move)
> then, looking for work. Big cities
> 6_____ even bigger by (grow)
> then. Can you imagine the traffic?
> B I don't think there will be a problem with the traffic. Gas 7_____ (run out)
> completely by then anyway, so nobody will have a car. Someone
> 8_____ a new method of (invent)
> transportation, so we 9_____ (get)
> around in flying taxis or something.

 p.37

Go online to review the grammar for each lesson

138

zero and first conditionals, future time clauses (with all present and future forms)

zero conditional

> If you **want** to be in shape, you **need to** exercise every day. 🔊 4.9
> If people **are wearing** headphones while walking, they often **don't notice** other people.
> If you **haven't been** to New York, you **haven't lived**.

- We use zero conditionals to talk about something that is always true or always happens as a result of something else. We use *if* + simple present, and the simple present in the other clause.
- You can also use the present continuous or present perfect in either clause.

first conditional

> If the photos **are** good, I'**ll send** them to you. 🔊 4.10
> If you'**re not going** to Jason's party, I'**m not going to go** either.
> If I **haven't come back** by 9:00, **start** dinner without me.
> I'**ll have finished** in an hour **if** you **don't** disturb me.

- We use first conditionals to talk about something that will probably happen in the future as a result of something else. We use *if* + a present tense, and a future tense in the other clause.
- You can use any present form in the *if*-clause (simple present, continuous, or perfect) and any future form (*will*, *going to*, future perfect, future continuous) or an imperative in the other clause.

future time clauses

> I'll be ready **as soon as** I'**ve had** a cup of coffee. 🔊 4.11
> Text me **when** your train'**s coming into** the station.
> I'm not going to buy the new model **until** the price **has gone down** a little.
> I'm not going to work overtime this weekend **unless** I **get** paid for it.
> Take your umbrella **in case** it'**s raining** when you leave work.

- Future time clauses are similar to the *if*-clause in first conditional sentences, but instead of *if*, we use expressions like: *as soon as, when, until, unless, before, after,* and *in case* followed by a present (not a future) tense. This can be any present form, e.g., simple present, present continuous, present perfect. We can use any future form or imperative in the other clause.
- We use *in case* when we do something in order to be ready for future situations / problems. Compare the use of *if* and *in case*:
- *I'll take an umbrella if it's raining.* = I'll only take an umbrella if it's raining.
- *I'll take an umbrella in case it rains.* = I'll take an umbrella anyway because it might rain.

---

a (Circle) the correct form.

> If Rob (*has studied*) / *had studied* enough, he'll easily pass the exam.

1 If you *aren't feeling* / *won't be feeling* better tomorrow, you should go to the doctor.
2 If we're lucky, we *have sold* / *'ll have sold* our house by New Year's.
3 I'll pay for dinner – if I *have* / *'ll have* enough money!
4 If we continue playing like this, we *'ll have scored* / *have scored* ten goals by halftime.
5 Don't call Sophie now. If it's eight o'clock, she *'ll bath* / *'ll be bathing* the baby.
6 If you don't hurry up, you *don't get* / *won't get* to school on time.
7 You can be fined if you *aren't wearing* / *won't be wearing* a seat belt in your car.
8 If you go out with wet hair, you *'ll catch* / *'ll be catching* a cold.
9 My suitcase *always gets* / *will always get* lost if I have a connecting flight.
10 I *won't go* / *don't go* to work on Monday if my daughter is still sick.

b Complete the sentence with a time expression from the box.

---

after   as soon as (x2)   before   if   in case (x2)
unless (x2)   until   when

> I'll call you _as soon as_ my plane lands.

1 I'm going to pack my suitcase _____ I go to bed.
2 Take your phone with you _____ you get lost.
3 I'll be leaving work early tomorrow _____ there's a last-minute crisis.
4 Let's meet _____ I'm in Toronto next week.
5 There's a crisis! Please call me _____ you possibly can.
6 _____ I'm late tomorrow, start the meeting without me.
7 Mei Ting will have packed some sandwiches _____ we get hungry.
8 Dan will be playing soccer in the park _____ it gets dark. Then he'll go home.
9 Lunch is ready now. Then, _____ we've eaten, we could go for a walk.
10 Don't call 911 _____ it's a real emergency.

🔵 p.41

5A

unreal conditionals

second conditional sentences: *if* + simple past, *would /*
wouldn't + base form

> 1 If there **was** a fire in this hotel, it **would be** very   🔊 **5.14**
>   difficult to escape.
>   I **wouldn't have** a car if I **didn't live** in the suburbs.
> 2 If it **wasn't raining** so hard, we **could get** to the top of the
>   mountain.
> 3 If I **were** you, I**'d make** Jimmy wear a helmet when he's riding
>   a bike.

1 We use second conditional sentences to talk about a
  hypothetical or imaginary situation in the present or future
  and its consequences.

2 In the *if*-clause you can also use the past continuous. In the
  other clause you can use *could* or *might* instead of *would*.

3 With the verb *be* you can use *was* or *were* for *I*, *he*, and *she*
  in the *if*-clause, e.g., *If Dan was / were here, he would know*
  what to do. However, in conditionals beginning *If I were*
  you… to give advice, we always use *were*.

third conditional sentences: *if* + past perfect, *would /*
wouldn't have + past participle

> 1 If they **had found** the river sooner, they **would** all   🔊 **5.15**
>   **have survived**.
>   I **wouldn't have gotten lost** if I **hadn't taken** the wrong path.
> 2 He **would have died** if he **hadn't been wearing** a helmet.
>   If the weather **had been** better, I **might have arrived** earlier.

1 We use third conditional sentences to talk about a
  hypothetical past situation and its consequences.

2 You can also use the past perfect continuous in the
  if-clause. You can also use *could have* or *might have* instead
  of *would have* in the other clause.

• In the past perfect simple and continuous, *had* can be
  contracted to *'d*, e.g., *If they'd found the river sooner…*

second or third conditional?

> 1 If you **came** to class more often, you **would** probably   🔊 **5.16**
>   **pass** the exam.
> 2 If you **had come** to class more often, you **would** probably
>   **have passed** the exam.

• Compare the two conditionals:
  1 = You don't come to class enough. You need to come
  more often if you want to pass the exam.
  2 = You didn't come to class enough, so you failed.

> 🔍 **Mixed conditionals**
>
> We sometimes mix second and third conditionals if a
> hypothetical situation in the past has a present / future
> consequence, e.g., *You wouldn't be so tired if you had gone*
> *to bed earlier last night.*
> *If he really loved you, he would have asked you to marry him.*

a Complete the sentence with the correct form of
the verb in parentheses, using a second or third
conditional.

> If Tim *hadn't gotten injured,* he would have played in
> the championship game. (not get injured)

1 I _____ so much food if you'd told me you
  weren't hungry. (not make)

2 If I were you, I _____ money to members
  of your family. (not lend)

3 If Jack were here, I _____ him to help me.
  (ask)

4 Joe _____ an accident if he hadn't been
  driving so fast. (not have)

5 I'd run a half-marathon if I _____ in better
  shape. (be)

6 If you _____ where you were going, you
  wouldn't have fallen. (look)

7 I'm sure you _____ dancing if you came to
  the classes with me. (enjoy)

8 We'd go to the local restaurant more often if they
  _____ the menu from time to time. (change)

9 Nina wouldn't have gone abroad if she
  _____ to find a job here. (be able)

10 If you _____ for a discount in the store,
  they might have given you one. (ask)

b Complete the sentence using a second or third
conditional.

> You didn't wait ten minutes. You didn't see Jim.
> If *you'd waited ten minutes, you would have seen Jim.*

1 Luke missed the train. He was late for the interview.
  If Luke _____ the train, he _____
  late for the interview.

2 Maxie didn't buy the top. She didn't have enough money.
  Maxie _____ the top if she _____
  enough money.

3 It started snowing. We didn't reach the top.
  If it _____ snowing, we _____
  the top.

4 Rebecca drinks too much coffee. She sleeps badly.
  If Rebecca _____ so much coffee, she
  _____ badly.

5 I don't drive to work. There's so much traffic.
  I _____ to work if _____ so
  much traffic.

6 Matt doesn't work very hard. He won't get promoted.
  If Matt _____ harder, he _____
  promoted.

7 We ran for the bus. We caught it.
  If we _____ for the bus, we _____ it.

⟲ p.49

🔘 **Go online** to review the grammar for each lesson

wish for present / future

wish + simple past

> I wish I **was** ten years younger!   5.17
> I wish I **could** understand what they're saying.
> I wish we **didn't live** so far from my parents.

- We use *wish* + person / thing + simple past to talk about things we would like to be different in the present / future (but that are impossible or unlikely).
- After *wish*, you can use *was* or *were* with *I*, *he*, *she*, and *it*, e.g., *I wish I was / were taller.*

wish + would / wouldn't

> I wish the bus **would come**. I'm freezing.   5.18
> I wish you**'d spend** more time with the children.
> I wish you **wouldn't leave** your shoes there. I almost tripped over them.
> I wish bike riders **wouldn't ride** on the sidewalk!

- We use *wish* + person / thing + *would / wouldn't* to talk about things we want to happen, or stop happening, because they annoy us.
- You can't use *wish* + *would* for a wish about yourself, i.e., **NOT** ~~I wish I would…~~, ~~I wish we would….~~

wish for past regrets

wish + past perfect

> I wish I**'d worked** harder in school.   5.21
> I wish I **hadn't spoken** to him like that!
> I wish she**'d told** me her true feelings.

- We use *wish* + past perfect to talk about things that happened or didn't happen in the past and that we now regret.

> 🔍 **if only…**
> *if only* is sometimes used instead of *I wish* in certain situations, to express deep regret, e.g., *If only I had worked harder in school (I wouldn't have such a boring job now).*

---

a Write sentences with *I wish* + simple past for 1–5, and *I wish…would / wouldn't* for 6–10.

> I'd like to be taller.   *I wish I was taller.*
> It annoys me that you don't put away your clothes.
> *I wish you'd put away your clothes!*

I'd like these things to be different

1 I'd like to be in better shape.
  _____

2 I'd like my sister not to share a room with me.
  _____

3 I'd like to be able to dance.
  _____

4 I'd like my grandmother not to be dead.
  _____

5 I'd like to live in a country with a better climate.
  _____

It annoys me that…

6 salespeople aren't more polite.
  _____

7 you turn the heat up all the time.
  _____

8 my brother doesn't clean our room.
  _____

9 the neighbor's dog barks at night.
  _____

10 it doesn't stop raining.
  _____

 p.51

b Rewrite the sentence beginning with *I wish* + past perfect.

> I regret having written that email.
> I wish *I hadn't written that email.*

1 I regret not seeing Prince live.
  I wish _____.

2 He regrets not learning to cook at school.
  He wishes _____.

3 Do you regret buying a used car?
  Do you wish _____?

4 Jenny regrets marrying her first husband.
  Jenny wishes _____.

5 My parents regret moving to the city.
  My parents wish _____.

6 Does Tom regret not studying law?
  Does Tom wish _____?

7 I regret having my hair cut so short.
  I wish _____.

8 They regret not going to the wedding.
  They wish _____.

↩ p.53

Illnesses and injuries

1 MINOR ILLNESSES AND CONDITIONS

a Match the sentences with the pictures.

She has / She's got…

☐ a **cough** /kɔf/

☐ a **headache** /ˈhɛdeɪk/ (<u>back</u>ache, <u>ear</u>ache, <u>stom</u>achache, <u>tooth</u>ache)

☐ *1* a **rash** /ræʃ/

☐ a **temperature** /ˈtɛmprətʃər/

☐ **sunburn** /ˈsʌnbərn/

☐ She's **sick**. / She's **vomiting**. /ˈvɑmətɪŋ/.

☐ She's **sneezing**. /ˈsnizɪŋ/

☐ Her **ankle's swollen**. /ˈswoʊlən/

☐ Her back **hurts**. /hərts/ / Her back **aches**. /eɪks/

☐ Her <u>finger's</u> **bleeding**. /ˈblidɪŋ/

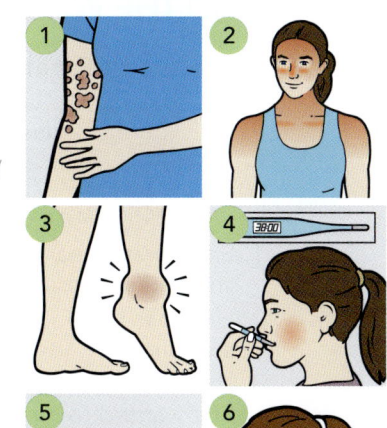
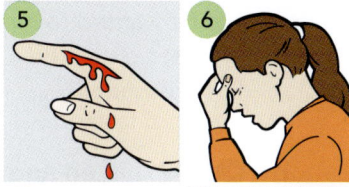

b 🔊 **2.1** Listen and check.

c Match the illnesses and conditions with their cause or symptoms.

1 *B* He has **a sore throat**. /sɔr θroʊt/
2 ☐ He has **diarrhea**. /daɪəˈriə/
3 ☐ He **feels sick**. /ˈfilz sɪk/
4 ☐ He's **fainted**. /ˈfeɪntəd/
5 ☐ He has a **blister** on his foot. /ˈblɪstər/
6 ☐ He has **a cold**. /ə ˈkoʊld/
7 ☐ He has **the flu**. /flu/
8 ☐ He feels **dizzy**. /ˈdɪzi/
9 ☐ He's **cut himself**. /ˈkʌt hɪmˈsɛlf/

A He has a temperature and he aches all over.
B ~~It hurts when he talks or swallows food.~~
C It's so hot in the room that he's lost consciousness.
D He's been to the bathroom five times this morning.
E He feels like he's going to vomit.
F He's sneezing a lot and he has a cough.
G He feels like everything is spinning around.
H He's been walking in uncomfortable shoes.
I He's bleeding.

d 🔊 **2.2** Listen and check.

2 INJURIES AND MORE SERIOUS CONDITIONS

a Match the injuries with their causes or symptoms.

1 *C* He's **unconscious**. /ʌnˈkɑnʃəs/
2 ☐ He's had an **allergic reaction**. /əlɜrdʒɪk riˈækʃn/
3 ☐ He's **sprained** his ankle. /spreɪnd/
4 ☐ He has **high** (low) **blood pressure**. /ˈblʌd prɛʃər/
5 ☐ He has **food poisoning**. /ˈfud pɔɪzənɪŋ/
6 ☐ He's **choking**. /ˈtʃoʊkɪŋ/
7 ☐ He's **burned** his hand. /bərnd/

A He spilled some boiling water on himself.
B He fell badly and now it's swollen.
C ~~He's breathing, but his eyes are closed and he can't hear or feel anything.~~
D It's 180 over 140.
E He ate some chicken that wasn't fully cooked.
F He was eating a steak and a piece got stuck in his throat.
G He was stung by a wasp and now he has a rash and has difficulty breathing.

> 🔍 **Common treatments for…**
> **a cut** minor: put a bandage on it and antibiotic ointment, major: get stitches
> **headaches** take <u>pain</u>killers
> **an infection** take anti<u>bio</u>tics
> **a sprained ankle** put ice on it and <u>ban</u>dage it
> **an allergic reaction** take anti<u>his</u>tamine <u>ta</u>blets / pills or apply cream

b 🔊 **2.3** Listen and check.

ACTIVATION Cover the illnesses, injuries, and conditions in **1a/c** (1–9) and **2a** (1–7). Look at the pictures, or causes and symptoms, and say the sentences.

3 PHRASAL VERBS CONNECTED WITH ILLNESS

a Match the **bold** phrasal verbs to their meanings.

Please **lie down** on the table. I'm going to examine you.
I'd been standing for such a long time that I **passed out**, and when I **came around** I was lying on the floor.
It often takes a long time to **get over** the flu.
A few minutes after drinking the liquid I had to run to the bathroom to **throw up**.

1 _____ faint
2 _____ put your body in a horizontal position
3 _____ vomit, be sick
4 _____ get better / recover from something
5 _____ become conscious again

b 🔊 **2.4** Listen and check. ⟵ p.16

⟵ p.16

🔵 **Go online** to review the vocabulary for each lesson

Clothes and fashion

1 DESCRIBING CLOTHES

a Match the adjectives and pictures.

Fit
- [ ] loose /lus/
- [1] tight /taɪt/

Style
- [ ] hooded /'hʊdəd/
- [ ] long-sleeved /lɔŋ slivd/ (*also* short-sleeved)
- [ ] sleeveless /'slivləs/
- [ ] turtleneck /'tɜrtl,nɛk/
- [ ] V-neck /'vi nɛk/

Pattern
- [ ] dotted /'dɑtəd/
- [ ] patterned /'pætərnd/
- [ ] plaid /plæd/
- [ ] plain /pleɪn/
- [ ] striped /straɪpt/

b 🔊 **2.17** Listen and check.

c Match the phrases and pictures.

Materials
- [ ] a cotton undershirt /'kɑtn 'ʌndər,ʃɜrt/
- [ ] a denim vest /'dɛnəm vɛst/
- [ ] a fur collar /fər 'kɑlər/
- [ ] a lace top /leɪs tɑp/
- [1] a linen suit /'lɪnən sut/
- [ ] a Lycra swimsuit /'laɪkrə 'swɪmsut/
- [ ] a silk scarf /sɪlk skɑrf/
- [ ] a velvet bow tie /'vɛlvət boʊ taɪ/
- [ ] a wool cardigan /wʊl 'kɑrdɪgən/
- [ ] leather sandals /'lɛðər 'sændlz/
- [ ] suede boots /sweɪd buts/

d 🔊 **2.18** Listen and check.

ACTIVATION Cover the words and phrases. Look at the photos and describe the items.

2 ADJECTIVES TO DESCRIBE CLOTHES AND THE WAY PEOPLE DRESS

a Complete the sentences with an adjective.

casual /'kæʒuəl/   classic /'klæsɪk/
fashionable /'fæʃənəbl/   old-fashioned /oʊld 'fæʃnd/
scruffy /'skrʌfi/

1 She always wears _____ clothes to work – she hates dressing formally.
2 He looks really _____. His clothes are old and dirty.
3 Jane looked very _____ in her new suit. She wanted to make a good impression.
4 That tie's a little _____! Is it your dad's?
5 I like wearing _____ clothes that don't go out of fashion.

b 🔊 **2.19** Listen and check.

ACTIVATION Say one item you own for each adjective in the box.

3 VERBS AND VERB PHRASES

a Match the sentences.
1 [C] I'm going to dress up tonight.
2 [ ] Please hang up your coat.
3 [ ] These jeans don't fit me.
4 [ ] That skirt really suits you.
5 [ ] Your bag matches your shoes.
6 [ ] I need to get changed.
7 [ ] Hurry up and get undressed.
8 [ ] Get up and get dressed.
9 [ ] That tie doesn't really go with your shirt.

A Don't leave it on the chair.
B I just spilled coffee on my shirt.
C I'm going to a party.
D They don't look good together.
E It's bath time.
F They're too small.
G They're almost the same color.
H You look great in it.
I Breakfast is on the table.

b 🔊 **2.20** Listen and check.

ACTIVATION Cover 1–9. Look at A–I and remember the matching sentences.

← p.22

Air travel

1 AT THE AIRPORT

a Match the words and definitions.

1	*A* **Airport terminal**	6	**Departures board**
2	**Bag(gage) drop**	7	**Gate**
3	**Baggage claim**	8	**Runway**
4	**Check-in desk**	9	**Security**
5	**Customs**	10	**(airline) Lounge**

A ~~a building at an airport divided into Arrivals and Departures~~

B an electronic display showing **flight times** and if the flight is **on time**, **boarding**, **closed**, or **delayed**

C where you hand in any checked **baggage** (bags, suitcases, etc.) and are given a **boarding pass if you don't already have one**

D where you take your luggage to check it in if you already have your boarding pass

E where they check that you are not trying to take prohibited items (e.g., **liquids** or **sharp objects**) onto the plane, by **scanning** your **carry-on luggage** and making you walk through a metal detector

F where passengers who are traveling **business** or **first class** can wait for their flight

G where you show your boarding pass and ID and **board** your flight

H where planes **take off** and **land**

I where you **collect** your luggage on arrival, and where there are usually **carts** for carrying heavy suitcases

J where your luggage may be **checked** to see if you are bringing **illegal goods** into the country

b 🔊 **3.5** Listen and check.

ACTIVATION Cover the words and look at the definitions. Say the words.

2 ON BOARD

a Complete the text with the words in the box.

---
aisle /aɪl/   cabin crew /ˈkæbən kru/   connecting flight /kəˈnɛktɪŋ flaɪt/   direct flights /dəˈrɛkt flaɪts/   jet lag /ˈdʒɛt læg/   long-haul flights /lɒŋ hɔl ˈflaɪts/   row /roʊ/   seat belts /ˈsit bɛlts/   turbulence /ˈtɜrbyələns/

I often fly to Chile on business. I always choose an ¹*aisle* seat, so that I can get up and walk around more easily. My favorite place to sit is the emergency exit ²_____ so I have more legroom. Sometimes there's ³_____ when the plane flies over the Andes, which I don't enjoy, and the ⁴_____ tells the passengers to put their ⁵_____ on.
There aren't any ⁶_____ to Santiago from Calgary, so I usually have to get a ⁷_____ in Toronto. Whenever I take ⁸_____, I always suffer from ⁹_____ because of the time difference and I feel tired for several days.

b 🔊 **3.6** Listen and check.

ACTIVATION Cover the words in the box. Read the text aloud with the correct words in the blanks.

3 *TRAVEL, TRIP, OR JOURNEY?*

a Complete the sentences with *travel*, *trip*, or *journey*.

1 Have a good *trip*! Hope the weather's great!
2 **A** How long was your _____ across China?
   B It was about two months long, and it was amazing.
3 Do you have to _____ much for your job?
4 Have a good _____! See you when you get back.

b 🔊 **3.7** Listen and check. Which word…?

1 is usually used as a verb
2 just refers to going from one place to another
3 covers going somewhere, staying there, and coming back.

4 PHRASAL VERBS RELATED TO AIR TRAVEL

a Complete the sentences with a phrasal verb from the box in the past tense.

---
check in   ~~drop off~~   fill out   get off
get on   pick up (x2)   take off
---

1 My husband *dropped* me *off* at the airport two hours before the flight.
2 I _____ _____ online the day before I was going to fly.
3 As soon as I _____ _____ the plane, I put my bag in the overhead compartment.
4 The plane _____ _____ late because of the bad weather.
5 When I _____ _____ my luggage at the baggage claim, I bumped into an old friend who had been on the same flight.
6 I _____ _____ the immigration form for the US, which the cabin crew gave me shortly before landing.
7 When I _____ _____ the plane, I felt exhausted after the long flight.
8 My flight arrived really late at night, but luckily, a friend _____ me _____ at the airport.

b 🔊 **3.8** Listen and check.

🌱 **Go online** to review the vocabulary for each lesson   154

Adverbs and adverbial phrases VOCABULARY BANK

1 CONFUSING ADVERBS AND ADVERBIAL PHRASES

a Match each pair of adverbs with a pair of sentences. Then decide which adverb goes where and write it in the **Adverbs** column.

☐ right now / <u>actually</u>	☐ 1 hard / <u>hardly</u>	☐ near / <u>nearly</u>
☐ especially / <u>s</u>pecially	☐ in the end / at the end	☐ still / yet
☐ ever / <u>e</u>ven	☐ late / <u>lately</u>	

Adverbs

1 He trains very ☐ – at least three hours a day.   *hard* _____
It's incredibly foggy. I can ☐ see anything.   *hardly* _____
2 I hate it when people arrive ☐ for meetings.   _____
I haven't heard from Mike ☐. He must be very busy.   _____
3 ☐ of a movie, I always stay and watch the credits roll.   _____
I didn't want to go, but ☐ they persuaded me.   _____
4 I love most kinds of music, but ☐ jazz.   _____
My wedding dress was ☐ made for me by a dressmaker.   _____
5 She looks younger than me, but ☐ she's two years older.   _____
☐ they're renting a house, but they're hoping to buy one soon. _____
6 I'm ☐ finished with my book. I'm on the last chapter.   _____
Excuse me, is there a bank ☐ here?   _____
7 Have you found a job ☐?   _____
He's 35, but he ☐ lives with his parents.   _____
8 Have you ☐ been to the US?   _____
I've been all over the US – I've ☐ been to Alaska!   _____

b 🔊 3.16 Listen and check.

ACTIVATION Cover the **Adverbs** column and look at sentences 1–8. Say the adverbs.

2 COMMENT ADVERBS

a Read the sentences. Then match the **bold** adverbs with definitions 1–8.

I thought the job was going to be difficult, but **in fact** it's very easy. /ɪn ˈfækt/

It took us over five hours to get there, but **eventually** we were able to relax. /ɪˈvɛntʃəli/

Ideally, we'd go to Australia if we could afford it. /aɪˈdiəli/

Basically, it's a pretty simple idea. /ˈbeɪsɪkli/

I thought they'd broken up, but **apparently**, they're back together again. /əˈpɛrəntli/

…so you can tell it was a really awful weekend. **Anyway**, let's forget about it and talk about something else. /ˈɛniˌweɪ/

He's only 14, so **obviously** he can't stay at home on his own. /ˈɑbviəsli/

She's been sick for weeks, but **gradually** she's beginning to feel better. /ˈgrædʒuəli/

1	_____	in a perfect world
2	*in fact*	the truth is; actually (used to emphasize something, especially the opposite of what was previously said)
3	_____	in the main and most important way
4	_____	clearly (used to give information you expect other people to know or agree with)
5	_____	little by little
6	_____	according to what you have heard or read
7	_____	in any case (used to change or finish a conversation)
8	_____	in the end; after a series of events or difficulties

b 🔊 3.17 Listen and check.

ACTIVATION Cover the definitions and look at the sentences. Say what the adverbs mean.

🔙 p.31

Weather

1 WHAT'S THE WEATHER LIKE?

a Put the words or phrases in the correct place in the chart.

below zero /bɪˈloʊ ˈzɪroʊ/   boiling /ˈbɔɪlɪŋ/   breeze /briz/   chilly /ˈtʃɪli/   cool /kul/   damp /dæmp/   drizzling /ˈdrɪzlɪŋ/
freezing /ˈfrizɪŋ/   humid /ˈhyuməd/   mild /maɪld/   pouring /ˈpɔrɪŋ/ (rain)   showers /ˈʃaʊərz/   warm /wɔrm/

1 It's _cool_. (a little cold) 2 It's _____. (unpleasantly cold)	5 It's _____. (pleasant and not cold) 6 It's _____. (a pleasantly high temperature)	8 It's _____. (warm and wet but not raining) 9 It's _____. (cold and slightly wet) 10 It's _____. (raining lightly)	13 There's a _____. (a light wind)
It's cold. ❄️	**It's hot.** ☀️	**It's raining / wet.** 💧	**It's windy.** 🌬️
3 It's _____. (very cold) 4 It's _____. (−10°)	7 It's _____ / It's scorching. (unpleasantly hot)	11 There are _____. (raining intermittently) 12 It's _____. (raining a lot)	

b Complete the sentences with *fog*, *mist*, and *smog*.

When the weather's foggy or misty, or there's _smog_, it is difficult to see.
1 _____ isn't usually very thick, and often occurs in the mountains or near the ocean.
2 _____ is thicker, and can be found in towns and in the country.
3 _____ is caused by pollution and usually occurs in big cities.

c 🔊**4.3** Listen and check **a** and **b**.

2 EXTREME WEATHER

a Match the words and definitions.

blizzard /ˈblɪzərd/   drought /draʊt/   flood /flʌd/
hail /heɪl/   heat wave /ˈhit weɪv/   hurricane /ˈhərəkeɪn/
lightning /ˈlaɪtnɪŋ/   monsoon /mɑnˈsun/   thunder /ˈθʌndər/

1 _heat wave_ (*noun*) a period of unusually hot weather
2 _____ (*noun*) a long, usually hot, dry period when
there is little or no rain
3 _____ (*noun* and *verb*) small balls of ice that fall like
rain
4 _____ (*noun*) a flash of very bright light in the sky
caused by electricity
5 _____ (*noun* and *verb*) the loud noise that you hear
during a storm
6 _____ (*noun*) a snow storm with very strong winds
7 _____ (*verb* and *noun*) when everything becomes
covered with water
8 _____ (*noun*) a violent storm with very strong winds
(also *cyclone*, *tornado*, *typhoon*)
9 _____ (*noun*) the season when it rains a lot in
southern Asia

b 🔊**4.4** Listen and check.

ACTIVATION Cover the weather words and look at the
definitions. Say the weather words.

3 ADJECTIVES TO DESCRIBE WEATHER

a Complete the weather forecast with these
adjectives.

bright /braɪt/   changeable /ˈtʃeɪndʒəbl/   clear /klɪr/
heavy /ˈhɛvi/   icy /ˈaɪsi/
settled /ˈsɛtld/ (= not likely to change)
strong /strɔŋ/   sunny /ˈsʌni/   thick /θɪk/

In the western part of New York it will be very cold,
with ¹_strong_ winds and ²_____ rain. There will
also be ³_____ fog in the hills and valleys,
though it should clear by midday. Driving will be
dangerous because the roads will be ⁴_____.
However, the Hudson Valley and the Tri-state area
will have ⁵_____ skies and it will be
⁶_____ and sunny, though the temperature will
still be low. Over the next few days the weather will
be ⁷_____, with some showers, but occasional
⁸_____ periods. It should become more ⁹_____
over the weekend.

b 🔊**4.5** Listen and check.

ACTIVATION What kind of weather do you associate
with the different seasons where you live?

⬅ p.38

 Go online to review the vocabulary for each lesson

Feelings

1 ADJECTIVES

a Match the feelings and the situations.

1 **B** "I feel really **miserable**." /ˈmɪzrəbl/
2 **F** "I feel a little **homesick**." /ˈhoʊmsɪk/
3 ☐ "I'm a little **disappointed**." /dɪsəˈpɔɪntəd/
4 ☐ "I'm very **lonely**." /ˈloʊnli/

5 ☐ "I'm incredibly **proud**." /praʊd/
6 ☐ "I'm really **fed up**." /fɛd ˈʌp/
7 ☐ "I'm very **grateful**." /ˈgreɪtfl/
8 ☐ "I'm very **upset**." /ʌpˈsɛt/
9 ☐ "I'm so **relieved**." /rɪˈlivd/
10 ☐ "I'm very **offended**." /əˈfɛndəd/

A You discover that your beloved dog has disappeared.
B ~~You've been stuck at home all weekend and it's been raining.~~
C A stranger gives you a lot of help with a problem.
D You are abroad and you think someone has stolen your passport, but then you find it.
E You don't get a job you were hoping to get.
F ~~You go to study abroad and you're missing your family and friends.~~
G You move to a new town and don't have any friends.
H You've been doing the same job for a long time and it's really boring.
I Someone in your family wins an important prize.
J A friend doesn't invite you to his wedding.

b 🔊 **5.4** Listen and check.

2 STRONG ADJECTIVES

a Match the strong adjectives describing feelings with their definitions.

a<u>sto</u>nished /əˈstɑnɪʃt/	be<u>wil</u>dered /bɪˈwɪldrd/	de<u>ligh</u>ted /dɪˈlaɪtəd/
<u>des</u>perate /ˈdɛspərət/	<u>dev</u>astated /ˈdɛvəsteɪtəd/	<u>hor</u>rified /ˈhɔrəfaɪd/
over<u>whelmed</u> /oʊvərˈwɛlmd/	~~<u>stunned</u> /stʌnd/~~	thrilled /θrɪld/

1 _stunned_ very surprised and unable to move or react
2 _____ extremely upset
3 _____ very happy and excited
4 _____ incredibly happy
5 _____ (SYN *amazed*) very surprised
6 _____ with little hope, and ready to do anything to improve the situation
7 _____ feeling such strong emotions that you don't know how to react
8 _____ extremely confused
9 _____ extremely shocked or disgusted

b 🔊 **5.5** Listen and check.

ACTIVATION Make true sentences for five of the adjectives in **1a** and **2a**.

3 INFORMAL OR SLANG WORDS AND EXPRESSIONS

a Look at the ==highlighted== words and phrases and try to figure out their meaning.

1 **B** I was ==scared stiff== when I heard the bedroom door opening. /skɛrd ˈstɪf/
2 ☐ You look a little ==down==. What's the problem? /daʊn/
3 ☐ I'm absolutely ==worn out==. I want to relax and put my feet up. /wɔrn aʊt/
4 ☐ When I saw her, ==I couldn't believe my eyes==. She looked ten years younger.
5 ☐ I'm ==sick and tired of== listening to you complain about your job.
6 ☐ He finally passed his driver's test. He's ==jumping for joy==!

b Match the words and phrases in **a** to the feelings.

A sad or depressed   D exhausted
B ~~terrified~~   E fed up or irritated
C extremely happy   F astonished

c 🔊 **5.6** Listen and check.

ACTIVATION Cover the sentences in **a**. Look at the feelings in **b**. Remember the informal words and expressions.

⬅ p.47

Irregular verbs

Infinitive	Past simple	Past participle
be /bi/	was/were /wʌz/ /wər/	been /bin/
beat /bit/	beat	beaten /'bitn/
become /bɪ'kʌm/	became /bɪ'keɪm/	become
begin /bɪ'gɪn/	began /bɪ'gæn/	begun /bɪ'gʌn/
bite /baɪt/	bit /bɪt/	bitten /'bɪtn/
break /breɪk/	broke /broʊk/	broken /'broʊkən/
bring /brɪŋ/	brought /brɔt/	brought
build /bɪld/	built /bɪlt/	built
burn /bərn/	burned /bərnd/ (burnt) /bərnt/	burned (burnt)
buy /baɪ/	bought /bɔt/	bought
can /kæn/	could /kʊd/	–
catch /kætʃ/	caught /kɔt/	caught
choose /tʃuz/	chose /tʃoʊz/	chosen /'tʃoʊzn/
come /kʌm/	came /keɪm/	come
cost /kɔst/	cost	cost
cut /kʌt/	cut	cut
deal /dil/	dealt /dɛlt/	dealt
do /du/	did /dɪd/	done /dʌn/
draw /drɔ/	drew /dru/	drawn /drɔn/
dream /drim/	dreamed /drimd/ (dreamt) /drɛmt/	dreamed (dreamt)
drink /drɪŋk/	drank /dræŋk/	drunk /drʌŋk/
drive /draɪv/	drove /droʊv/	driven /'drɪvn/
eat /it/	ate /eɪt/	eaten /'itn/
fall /fɔl/	fell /fɛl/	fallen /'fɔlən/
feel /fil/	felt /fɛlt/	felt
find /faɪnd/	found /faʊnd/	found
fly /flaɪ/	flew /flu/	flown /floʊn/
forget /fər'gɛt/	forgot /fər'gɑt/	forgotten /fər'gɑtn/
get /gɛt/	got /gɑt/	gotten /'gɑtn/
give /gɪv/	gave /geɪv/	given /'gɪvn/
go /goʊ/	went /wɛnt/	gone /gɔn/
grow /groʊ/	grew /gru/	grown /groʊn/
hang /hæŋ/	hung /hʌŋ/	hung
have /hæv/	had /hæd/	had
hear /hɪr/	heard /hərd/	heard
hit /hɪt/	hit	hit
hurt /hərt/	hurt	hurt
keep /kip/	kept /kɛpt/	kept
kneel /nil/	knelt /nɛlt/	knelt
know /noʊ/	knew /nu/	known /noʊn/
lay /leɪ/	laid /leɪd/	laid
learn /lərn/	learned /lərnd/	learned

Infinitive	Past simple	Past participle
leave /liv/	left /lɛft/	left
lend /lɛnd/	lent /lɛnt/	lent
let /lɛt/	let	let
lie /laɪ/	lay /leɪ/	lain /leɪn/
lose /luz/	lost /lɔst/	lost
make /meɪk/	made /meɪd/	made
mean /min/	meant /mɛnt/	meant
meet /mit/	met /mɛt/	met
pay /peɪ/	paid /peɪd/	paid
put /pʊt/	put	put
read /rid/	read /rɛd/	read /rɛd/
ride /raɪd/	rode /roʊd/	ridden /'rɪdn/
ring /rɪŋ/	rang /ræŋ/	rung /rʌŋ/
rise /raɪz/	rose /roʊz/	risen /'rɪzn/
run /rʌn/	ran /ræn/	run
say /seɪ/	said /sɛd/	said
see /si/	saw /sɔ/	seen /sin/
sell /sɛl/	sold /soʊld/	sold
send /sɛnd/	sent /sɛnt/	sent
set /sɛt/	set	set
shake /ʃeɪk/	shook /ʃʊk/	shaken /'ʃeɪkən/
shine /ʃaɪn/	shone /ʃoʊn/	shone
shut /ʃʌt/	shut	shut
sing /sɪŋ/	sang /sæŋ/	sung /sʌŋ/
sit /sɪt/	sat /sæt/	sat
sleep /slip/	slept /slɛpt/	slept
speak /spik/	spoke /spoʊk/	spoken /'spoʊkən/
spend /spɛnd/	spent /spɛnt/	spent
stand /stænd/	stood /stʊd/	stood
steal /stil/	stole /stoʊl/	stolen /'stoʊlən/
swell /swɛl/	swelled /swɛld/	swelled swollen /'swoʊlən/
swim /swɪm/	swam /swæm/	swum /swʌm/
take /teɪk/	took /tʊk/	taken /'teɪkən/
teach /titʃ/	taught /tɔt/	taught
tell /tɛl/	told /toʊld/	told
think /θɪŋk/	thought /θɔt/	thought
throw /θroʊ/	threw /θru/	thrown /θroʊn/
understand /ʌndər'stænd/	understood /ʌndər'stʊd/	understood
wake /weɪk/	woke /woʊk/	woken /'woʊkən/
wear /wɛr/	wore /wɔr/	worn /wɔrn/
win /wɪn/	won /wʌn/	won
write /raɪt/	wrote /roʊt/	written /'rɪtn/

Vowel sounds

		usual spelling		! but also
	tree	ee	bleed sneeze	people thief
		ea	beat steal	key relieved
		e	even medium	receipt
	fish	i	linen silk	pretty women
			trip fit	guilty decided
			fill pick	village physics
	ear	eer	career	seriously zero
			volunteer	weird
		ere	here we're	
		ear	nearly clear	
	cat	a	pack campus	
			active cash	
			balance stand	
	egg	e	denim dress	friendly leather
			trendy belt	deaf threaten
			ever yet	anybody said
	chair	air	airport stairs	their there
			fair hair	wear
		are	scared stare	area
	clock	o	cotton top	watch want
			drop shot	calm
			cottage off	
	saw	a	bald wall	thought caught
		aw	yawn draw	exhausted
		al	stalker talk	launch
	horse	(o)or	sore floor	warm course
			outdoor	board
		ore	bore score	
	boot	oo	loose cool	suit recruit
		u*	argue refuse	shoe prove
		ew	chew news	through

* especially before consonant + e

		usual spelling		! but also
	bull	u	full put	could should
		oo	hooded	would woman
			woolen	
			stood good	
	tourist	A very unusual sound.		
		jury sure plural		
	up	u	cut scruffy	money someone
			lungs	enough touch
			stunned	flood blood
			upset discuss	
	computer	Many different spellings. /ə/ is always		
		unstressed.		
		collar patterned advise complain		
		information sandals		
	bird	er	verdict prefer	research worker
		ir	dirty skirt	worth worse
		ur	hurt burn	journey
	owl	ou	hour mouth	drought
			proud around	
		ow	showers frown	
	phone	o*	choke chose	throw elbow
			froze fold	below although
		oa	toast	shoulders
			approach	
	car	ar	scarf smart	heart
			sharp hardly	
	train	a*	ache lace	break steak
		ai	faint plain	great weight
		ay	may lay	suede obey
	boy	oi	boiling avoid	
			point noise	
		oy	enjoy	
			employer	
	bike	i*	striped ice	buy eyes
		y	Lycra stylish	height aisle
		igh	tight flight	

☐ vowels   ☐ vowels followed by /r/   ☐ diphthongs

Consonant sounds

		usual spelling	! but also
	parrot	**p** postpone polluted hope damp **pp** disappointed kidnapping	
	bag	**b** brain bribe objective biased **bb** robbery hobby	
	key	**c** court critic **k** kidneys shake **ck** shocked homesick	choir orchestra stomachache question expect accuse
	girl	**g** regret grateful colleague forget **gg** hugged mugging	
	flower	**f** fist theft **ph** physicist symphony **ff** offended staff	enough laugh tough
	vase	**v** velvet vandalism nervous prevent evidence review	of
	tie	**t** taste tend stand chest **tt** matter bottom	produced passed
	dog	**d** deny murder editor confident **dd** addictive suddenly	failed bored
	snake	**s** stops sick **ss** witness loss **ce/ci** notice censored	science scenery fancy
	zebra	**z** breeze freezing **zz** dizzy blizzard **s** nose raise spends agrees	
	shower	**sh** shrug brush wish clash **ti (+ vowel)** ambitious sensational **ci (+ vowel)** special sociable	sugar sure chic
	television	An unusual sound. decision conclusion usually genre	

		usual spelling	! but also
	thumb	**th** thunder thick healthy thigh death teeth	
	mother	**th** the that with further rather	
	chess	**ch** change chilly **tch** scratch stretch **t (+ure)** departure temperature	
	jazz	**j** jet-lag hijack **g** generous manager **dge** knowledge judge	
	leg	**l** lie liver heel lonely **ll** colleague pillow	
	right	**r** rise ride risky pretend **rr** terrorism arrested	written wrong
	witch	**w** win waste waist wave **wh** while wherever	one once
	yacht	**y** yet year youth yourself before **u** university argue	
	monkey	**m** mild remind seem remember **mm** commit commentator	comb
	nose	**n** nails honest **nn** announce beginning	kneel knew
	singer	**ng** length belongings hang bring before **g/k** wink sink	
	house	**h** humid hail behavior inhabit inherit perhaps	who whose whole

☐ voiced   ☐ unvoiced

Go online to watch the Sound Bank videos

American English File

Third Edition

4

MULTI-PACK A
Student Book | Workbook

Christina Latham-Koenig
Clive Oxenden
Kate Chomacki

with Jane Hudson

Paul Seligson and Clive Oxenden
are the original co-authors of
English File 1 and *English File 2*

OXFORD
UNIVERSITY PRESS

Contents

How to use your Workbook and Online Practice

American English File
Third Edition

Student Book
Use your Student Book in class with your teacher.

IN CLASS

ACTIVITIES   AUDIO   VIDEO   RESOURCES

AT HOME

Sold separately

Christina Latham-Koenig
Clive Oxenden

ONLINE

Go to
americanenglishfileonline.com
and use your **Digital Materials
Access Code** to log into
the Online Practice.

Workbook

Practice **Grammar**, **Vocabulary**, and **Pronunciation**
for every lesson.

Practice the **Colloquial English**.

Do the **Can you remember...?** exercises
to check that you remember the Grammar,
Vocabulary, and Pronunciation every two Files.

Online Practice

Look again at the Grammar, Vocabulary, and
Pronunciation from the Student Book before you do
the Workbook exercises.

Listen to the audio for the Pronunciation exercises.

Use the Sound Bank video to practice
English sounds.

Watch the Colloquial English video before you
do the exercises.

Use the interactive video for more Colloquial
English practice.

Look again at the Grammar, Vocabulary, and
Pronunciation if you have any problems.

Practice Reading, Listening, Speaking, and Writing.

1A Questions and answers

Judge a man by his questions rather than by his answers.
Voltaire, 18th-century French author, humanist, rationalist, and satirist

G question formation **V** figuring out meaning from context **P** intonation: showing interest

1 GRAMMAR question formation

a Right (✓) or wrong (✗)? Correct the mistakes in the highlighted phrases.

1 A You have ever been to Thailand?
✗ *Have you ever been*
B Yes, a couple of times.

2 A Why didn't you tell me the truth?
✓ _____
B Because I thought you'd be angry.

3 A Where you usually go on vacation?
_____
B We usually go to Mexico.

4 A Haven't you done the homework?
_____
B No, I haven't. I'm sorry.

5 A What did happen at the meeting yesterday?
_____
B We discussed the sales figures. It was kind of boring.

6 A Who's Jack going out with?
_____
B He's going out with his best friend's sister.

7 A Who fixed your car for you?
_____
B My brother.

8 A Whose jacket you did borrow for the wedding?
_____
B My dad's. It was a little big for me.

9 A It's late. We should go now?
_____
B Yes, we have to get up early tomorrow morning.

10 A For who are you waiting?
_____
B I'm waiting for my brother.

b Complete the indirect questions and sentences.

1 "Would Michael like this wallet?"
Do you think *Michael would like this wallet* ?

2 "Where is the elevator?"
Could you tell me _____ ?

3 "Where did we park the car?"
I can't remember _____ .

4 "Are there any tickets left for the concert tonight?"
Do you know _____ ?

5 "What time does the game start?"
Can you tell me _____ ?

6 "When's Anna's birthday?"
Do you remember _____ ?

7 "What does Jamie do for a living?"
Do you have any idea _____ ?

8 "Where does Natalie live?"
I wonder _____ .

9 "What's Ava's boyfriend's name?"
I'm not sure _____ .

10 "How much did you pay for your new car?"
Would you mind telling me _____ ?

c Write the questions.

1 how long / you / spend / in Brazil last summer
   How long did you spend in Brazil last summer ?
2 who / cook / in your family
   _____?
3 when / your brother / pass / his driver's test
   _____
   _____?
4 you know / who / go / to the party tonight
   _____
   _____?
5 who / the manager / talk to / now
   _____
   _____?
6 who / drink / the milk / I / leave / in the refrigerator
   _____
   _____?
7 why / you / not come / to school yesterday
   _____
   _____?
8 you remember / what time / the meeting / be
   _____
   _____?

d Write questions to ask at a job interview. Use a different phrase to begin each question.

1 salary
   _____?
2 vacation
   _____?
3 working hours
   _____?
4 overtime
   _____?
5 travel
   _____?
6 uniform
   _____?
7 parking space
   _____?
8 lunch
   _____?

2 PRONUNCIATION intonation: showing interest

a ◀) 1.1 Listen to the questions. Check (✓) if the speaker sounds interested.

1 Which university did you go to?   ✓
2 What don't you like about your job?   ☐
3 How's your family?   ☐
4 Would you like to work abroad?   ☐
5 How many languages do you speak?   ☐
6 Why did you leave your last job?   ☐

b ◀) 1.2 Listen and repeat the questions with interested intonation.

c Complete the table with the expressions and questions in the list.

~~How interesting!~~   I'm sorry.   Me too!   Oh, really?
What a shame!   Why (not)?   Why do you say that?
Why's that?   Wow!

Expressions showing interest
How interesting!
Expressions showing sympathy
Follow-up questions

d ◀) 1.3 Listen and check. Then listen again and repeat the expressions.

e ◀) 1.4 Now listen to the questions from **a** in conversations. Complete the phrases or questions that people use to react to the answers.

1 *Me too!* _____ When were you there?
2 _____ How long have you been there?
3 _____ I hope it's nothing serious.
4 _____ What's keeping you here?
5 _____ That's a lot of languages.
6 _____ I'm sorry to hear that.

f ◀) 1.5 Listen and repeat the responses. Copy the intonation.

Go online for more practice

3 READING & VOCABULARY figuring out meaning from context

a Complete the sentences with the words and phrases in the list.

foolproof ~~geek~~ good-natured rivalry
gut feeling job-seekers light-hearted response
the point of work–life balance

1 Josh is a computer _geek_____, so he's been applying for jobs in IT.
2 If someone tries to annoy me, I prefer to give a _____ rather than get angry.
3 My colleague and I enjoy a _____ over who meets our monthly targets first.
4 Great news for _____: more than 50% of US companies intend to hire new staff this year.
5 I have a _____ that this interview will go very badly.
6 I don't see _____ some interview questions – they seem ridiculous.
7 It can be difficult to get the right _____, especially if you have a position of responsibility in a company.
8 This article gives five _____ tips on how to be successful at a job interview.

b Read the article quickly. Match the **bold** words in the highlighted phrases to definitions 1–8.

1 (adj.) extremely useful
   _invaluable_____

2 (adj.) done very carefully, with attention to detail
   _____

3 (adj.) possible
   _____

4 (phrasal verb) be noticeable because of being different
   _____

5 (verb) sit in a lazy way, with your shoulders bent forwards
   _____

6 (phrase) avoid
   _____

7 (adj.) real; true
   _____

8 (verb) keep touching something because you are nervous
   _____

Important interview tips

Your résumé got you in the door; now it's time to convince the interviewer you're the best person for the job.

Research the company
Do your homework so you don't give the impression you're looking for any old job. Search the Internet and read not only the company's website, but also any news stories that come up. Make a list of points you could discuss at the interview and questions you could ask. You want your **potential** future **employer** to believe that you have a **genuine** interest in working for the organization.

Look the part
The company's dress code should give you an idea of what to wear at the interview, but in most cases, you will be expected to look professional. However, it is not only your clothes you must watch. Think about your body language: do you usually **slouch** or sit up straight in a chair, or do you sometimes **fiddle** with a pen? Practice before the day so that you have time to replace any bad habits with positive body language.

Mind your manners
When you get to the interview venue, make sure you greet everyone you meet, including the people in the elevator. Offer the interviewer a warm greeting and say "please" and "thank you" when appropriate. Not only do you want to show that you would be an **invaluable** team member, but you also want the interviewer to choose you over another candidate who may be equally qualified for the job.

Give real examples
You won't be the first candidate the interviewer has met, so you need to **stand out** from the competition. When you are asked about your abilities and experience, **steer clear** of typical answers such as "I have great communication skills" or "I'm a people person." Instead give real examples of situations where you have demonstrated these qualities and brought about a positive result.

Ask the right questions
Towards the end of the interview, you will be invited to ask your own questions about the job. You'll have that list you made beforehand, but the points on it may already have been covered. Even if the interviewer has been very **thorough**, you must ask a few questions. This is where your initial research about the company will come in handy.

🔵 **Go online** for more practice

G auxiliary verbs, *the...*, *the...* + comparatives **V** compound adjectives, modifiers **P** intonation and sentence rhythm

1 GRAMMAR auxiliary verbs

a Cross out the unnecessary words.

1 My mom can drive, but my dad can't ~~drive~~.
2 I loved that book, but my wife didn't love that book.
3 You weren't listening to the instructions, but I was listening to the instructions.
4 Some people believe in ghosts, but others don't believe in ghosts.
5 Gina's going to the party, but Robbie isn't going to the party.
6 I always lock the front door, but my partner doesn't always lock the front door.
7 I've never been to a fortune-teller, but my sister has visited a fortune-teller.
8 My friends had already heard the story, but I hadn't already heard the story.

b **Complete the conversations with a tag question or an auxiliary.**

1 A I texted you last night, but you didn't reply.
  B I *did*_____ reply. I texted you right away.

2 A I don't feel like cooking tonight.
  B Neither _____ I. Let's go out for dinner. I'd love some Mexican food.
  A So _____ I. Come on. Let's go.

3 A I've seen this movie before.
  B Well, I _____.
  A Do you mind if I change channels?
  B Yes, I _____ mind! I want to see the end.

4 A You're going to Sam's party, _____ you?
  B No, I'm not.
  A Why not? You haven't argued with him again, _____ you?
  B Yes. We aren't going out together anymore.

5 A I'll be back a little bit late tonight.
  B You _____ ? Where are you going?
  A To a concert with some friends.
  B Oh, OK. You'll be back before 12, _____ you?
  A Of course.

6 A You couldn't lend me some money, _____ you?
  B No, sorry. Why?
  A I spent my entire salary already this month.
  B So _____ I!

7 A I didn't go out last night.
  B Neither _____ I. I was too tired.
  A So _____ I!

8 A You aren't from around here, _____ you?
  B No, I'm from Australia.
  A I don't suppose you like this cold weather.
  B Actually, I _____ like it. I prefer cool weather to hot weather.

c **Respond to the statements with *So do I, Neither do I, I do, I don't*, etc., and say why.**

1 I didn't go out yesterday.
_____

2 I love the ocean.
_____

3 I've never been to Canada.
_____

4 I'd like to go on a safari.
_____

5 I wasn't interested in history in school.
_____

6 I'm good at languages.
_____

7 I can swim well.
_____

8 I don't exercise at all.
_____

2 PRONUNCIATION intonation and sentence rhythm

a 🔊 1.6 Listen and complete the conversations.

1 A You *don't* _____ like the soup, *do* _____ you?

B I *do* _____ like it. It's just that it's very hot.

2 A We _____ invited to their wedding.

B You _____ ? Neither _____ we.

3 A I _____ enjoy that movie.

B You _____ ? I _____ .

4 A I _____ always very well behaved as a child.

B You _____ ? I _____ .

5 A You _____ forget to call me, _____ you?

B Of course I _____ .

6 A I _____ play tennis well.

B You _____ ? I _____ .

b 🔊 1.6 Listen again and repeat the conversations. Copy the rhythm and intonation.

3 GRAMMAR IN CONTEXT *the...*, *the... + comparatives*

Complete the sentences with the comparative form of the adjectives in the list.

---
big cold difficult ~~early~~ far ~~good~~ high
interesting late likely long qualified

---

1 The *earlier* _____ we set off, the *better* _____ chance we'll have of avoiding the rush hour traffic.
2 The _____ the class, the _____ the students are to learn something.
3 The _____ you go to bed, the _____ it is to get up in the morning.
4 The _____ north you travel in Canada, the _____ it gets.
5 The _____ the person is for the job, the _____ the salary.
6 The _____ your house, the _____ it takes you to clean it.

4 VOCABULARY compound adjectives, modifiers

a Match the definitions to the compound adjectives in the list.

---
absentminded ~~bad-tempered~~ big-headed
easygoing good-tempered laid-back narrow-minded
open-minded self-centered strong-willed tight-fisted
two-faced well-balanced well-behaved

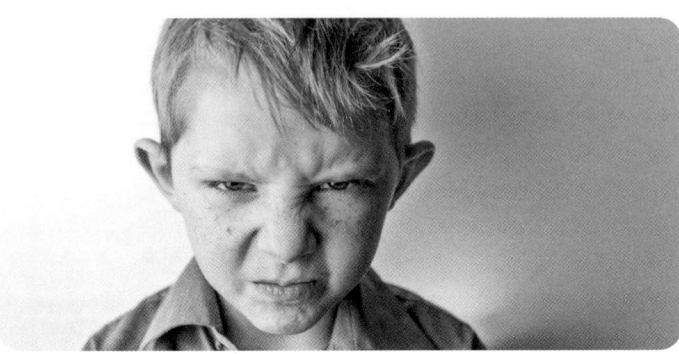

1 easily made angry or annoyed
   bad-tempered _____
2 ready to consider new ideas and opinions
   _____
3 not willing to spend money
   _____
4 often forgetting or not noticing things
   _____
5 determined to do what you want to do, even if other people advise you not to
   _____
6 relaxed; not easily worried by things
   _____
7 sensible and emotionally in control
   _____
8 having a very high opinion of how important and smart you are
   _____
9 not willing to listen to ideas different from your own
   _____
10 dishonest about your feelings; telling people what you think will please them
   _____
11 cheerful and not easily made angry
   _____
12 thinking only about yourself and not about other people
   _____
13 calm; not easily upset by what other people do
   _____
14 behaving in a way that people think is polite and correct
   _____

🔘 **Go online** for more practice

b Complete the sentences with the compound adjectives in **a**.

1 My parents are very _easygoing_____ . They accept most things I do, without getting upset.
2 Tom's wife is very _____. She doesn't seem to let anything worry her.
3 Oliver's new girlfriend isn't as crazy as he is. She seems very _____.
4 My partner is really _____. He won't listen to other people's ideas.
5 Grace never thinks of anyone else because she's so _____.
6 My sister-in-law is very _____. She's nice to me, and then speaks badly of me to other people.
7 Since he went to work abroad for a while, Leo has become more _____ about other cultures.
8 She's very _____, and if she's decided to become a vegetarian, nothing will stop her.
9 When we go out, my friend Jack never offers to pay for gas. I wish he wasn't so _____.
10 The new manager seems very _____. He spent most of the meeting telling us how successful he was.
11 My grandmother never remembers where she's put her keys. She's very _____.
12 I've never seen your children being bad. They're really _____.
13 Our English teacher never seems to get angry. She's extremely _____.
14 It's best not to talk to my brother when he first gets up. He's usually very _____.

c Circle the correct answer. Check (✓) if both answers are possible.

1 Tony's new girlfriend is good for him – she seems *rather* / *really* well-balanced.
2 I don't trust my neighbor – she's *extremely* / *incredibly* two-faced. ✓
3 Some people complain about my kids, but I think they're *pretty* / *a little* well-behaved.
4 My cousin Olivia is *very* / *really* tight-fisted – she doesn't want to give any money towards our grandfather's 80th birthday present.
5 I'm not that sure about my new colleague. I find him *really* / *rather* big-headed.
6 I get along well with my boss. He's *very* / *rather* easygoing.
7 If I have a problem, I usually talk to my aunt. She's *a kind of* / *incredibly* open-minded.
8 I don't spend much time with my roommate – she's *a kind of* / *pretty* self-centered.

d Choose eight of the compound adjectives in **a** and write sentences about yourself. Use a suitable modifier from the list. Explain your answers.

_____
a little   extremely   incredibly   kind of   pretty   rather   really   very
_____

1 _____
   _____
2 _____
   _____
3 _____
   _____
4 _____
   _____
5 _____
   _____
6 _____
   _____
7 _____
   _____
8 _____
   _____

5 VOCABULARY FROM READING

Complete the missing letters in the words.

1 Detectives are searching for clues to help them s _o_ l _v_ _e_ last night's murder.
2 She told reporters the ex _ _ _ _ _ r _ _ n _ _ _ _ story of how she survived the plane crash.
3 It takes six days to reach the r _ m _ _ _ _ island of Tristan da Cunha by boat.
4 The search party found no tr _ _ _ _ of the missing climbers.
5 The strange geology of the planet Mars continues to b _ f _ _ _ _ scientists.

1 LOOKING AT LANGUAGE

Complete the sentences with the right form of *make* or *do*.

1 Remember to *make* eye contact when you meet your new manager.
2 Let's _____ a Google search on each of the top five candidates who applied for the job.
3 I _____ a huge mistake on my résumé when I included every job I've had in the past ten years.
4 Did you _____ sure your cell phone was turned off during your job interview?
5 Most employers don't care about what you _____ 20 or 30 years ago.
6 I'm _____ a three-column table in the document so the information is easy to read.

2 VOCABULARY FROM THE INTERVIEW

Match the **bold** word or phrase with the correct definition.

1 ...as an employer, I'm thinking this has no **relevancy** to me
   a agreements
   b connection
2 Dress **appropriately** for an interview.
   a in a suitable way
   b in a stylish, formal suit
3 You can often **stake out** the front door, ...
   a watch secretly
   b watch illegally
4 You don't want to have any **interruptions**.
   a times when an activity is stopped
   b times when an activity begins
5 I can deliver enough **value** for this position...
   a how expensive something is
   b how much something is worth compared with its price

3 THE CONVERSATION

Complete the sentences with one word, using repetition or an adverb to add emphasis.

1 It's a terrible, *terrible* idea to go to an interview when you're feeling hungry.
2 I've _____ told you this before more than once.
3 I felt really, _____ silly when I realized I'd locked my keys in the house.
4 You _____ told me you would be here by 11:00.
5 Can you make me a cup of tea? I've had a _____ bad day.
6 It's a wonderful _____ movie. You really should go and see it.

4 VOCABULARY FROM THE CONVERSATION

Complete the sentences with a word from the list.

caught   potentially   ~~slightly~~   white   willing

1 I sometimes *slightly* exaggerate when I talk about my experience.
2 You might find yourself in a _____ difficult situation.
3 Nobody will worry if you tell a couple of _____ lies.
4 You could get _____ out if they ask you questions about something on your résumé.
5 You need to show that you are _____ to learn.

GRAMMAR & VOCABULARY

a Complete the second sentence so that it means the same as the first sentence. Use the word in parentheses. Contractions are one word.

1 My husband and I both love animals. (so)
I love animals and _so_ _does_ _my_ _husband_ .

2 I'm sure I sent you a message last night. (did)
I _did_ _send_ _you_ _a_ _message_ last night.

3 Whose is this phone? (belong)
Who _____ _____ _____ _____ to?

4 What was wrong with the hotel you stayed in? (like)
Why _____ _____ _____ the hotel you stayed in?

5 Where did you get that book from? (gave)
_____ _____ _____ that book?

6 How much is gas in your country? (costs)
Do you know _____ _____ _____ _____ in your country?

7 Do you have any vacancies right now? (whether)
Can you _____ _____ _____ _____ _____ any vacancies right now?

8 I'm just checking that you'll pick me up from work tonight. (you)
You will pick me up from work tonight, _____ _____?

9 My friends and I can't afford to go on vacation this year. (neither)
I can't afford to go on vacation this year and _____ _____ _____ _____.

10 I'm sure Tom knows about the meeting – he mentioned it yesterday. (does)
Tom _____ _____ _____ _____ _____ – he mentioned it yesterday.

b Read the text. Circle a, b, or c.

FACT OR FICTION?

The Bermuda Triangle

During the 1960s and 70s, many stories were told of ships and aircraft disappearing mysteriously in a region of the Atlantic Ocean known as the Bermuda Triangle. People asked, "[1]____ is causing these boats and planes to disappear?", and several [2]____ reasons were given to explain the mystery. Some writers wondered [3]____ aliens had established an underwater base and were hijacking aircraft to study their crew. Others said that enormous waves might be hitting vessels, causing them to sink without a [4]____. However, nobody asked the question of whether there really [5]____ any mystery to explain.

Journalist Larry Kusche was the first person to do this. He asked questions about the mysterious disappearances that previous writers [6]____. These writers had simply collected stories that had already been written and repeated them in their own way. Kusche found many mistakes in their stories: in some cases, there was no record of the ships and planes that were said to have been lost, and in others, they had disappeared during [7]____ bad storms. Kusche pointed out that it was logical that more accidents would occur in the busy Bermuda Triangle than in more [8]____ areas such as the South Pacific because the more ships there are in an area, the [9]____ it is for one of them to sink.

In the end, Kusche concluded that the explanation for the Bermuda Triangle [10]____ was neither aliens nor massive waves, but the lack of research done by writers in search of a sensational story.

1 a How   b What   c Which
2 a foreign   b extraordinary   c absentminded
3 a how   b whether   c where
4 a mark   b sign   c trace
5 a is   b has   c was
6 a didn't   b hadn't   c weren't
7 a rather   b pretty   c extremely
8 a crowded   b far   c remote
9 a likely   b more likely   c most likely
10 a puzzle   b quiz   c story

✓ **Go online** to check your progress

11

Doctors are great – as long as you don't need them.
Edward E. Rosenbaum, doctor, professor, and author

G present perfect simple and continuous | **V** illnesses and injuries | **P** /ʃ/, /dʒ/, /tʃ/, and /k/

1 VOCABULARY illnesses and injuries

a Complete the minor illnesses and injuries.

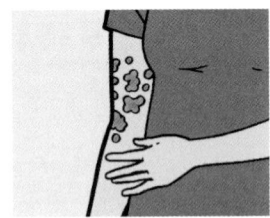

1 She has a r _a_ s _h_.

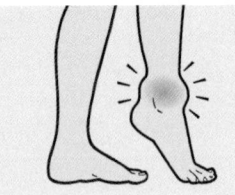

2 Her ankle is
s _ _ l _ _ n.

3 She's
v _ _ _ t _ _ _ _.

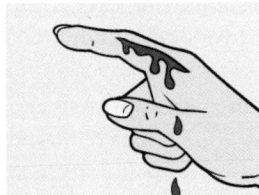

4 Her finger is
bl _ _ d _ _ _ _.

5 She has
s _ _ b _ _ _ _.

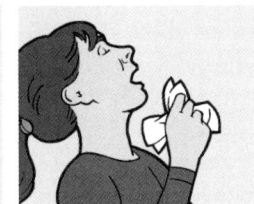

6 She's
sn _ _ z _ _ _ _.

7 She has a
c _ _ g _.

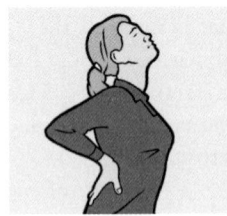

8 Her back
h _ _ t _.

9 She has a
h _ _ d _ c _ _ _.

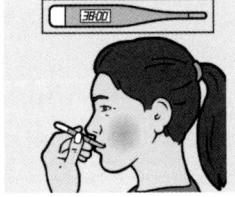

10 She has a
t _ _ p _ r _ t _ _ _.

b Complete the sentences.

1 Alex has d_iarrhea_____. He's been to the bathroom six times this morning.
2 I think I have the fl_____. I have a temperature and I ache all over.
3 That knife is very sharp. Please don't c_____ y_____.
4 Matt f_____ in the art gallery. It was so hot that he lost consciousness.
5 These shoes aren't very comfortable. I think I have a bl_____.
6 I have a s_____ thr_____. It hurts when I talk.
7 Rachel f_____ s_____. She thinks she's going to vomit.
8 You're coughing and sneezing a lot. Do you have a c_____?
9 I feel d_____. Everything is spinning around.

c Complete the conversations with a word from the list.

~~allergic reaction~~ blood pressure burned choking
food poisoning sprained unconscious

1 **P** There's a rash all over my body.
  D You might have had an _allergic reaction_____ to something.

2 **P** Where am I?
  D In the hospital. You had an accident and you've been _____ for an hour.

3 **P** I fell and hurt my wrist playing tennis – now it's very swollen.
  D I think you've _____ it.

4 **P** I sometimes feel a little dizzy when I first get up.
  D It sounds like you have low _____.

5 **P** I've been sick and I have diarrhea.
  D You might have _____. Didn't you say you thought the shrimp you had for lunch weren't fully cooked?

6 **P** What should I do if one of my children starts _____?
  D Tell them not to panic and to keep coughing – they need to move the food.

7 **P** I dropped a pan of boiling water on my hand.
  D Yes, you've _____ yourself very badly.

d Match conditions 1–6 to treatments a–f.

1 an allergic reaction   <u> e </u>
2 a headache   <u>   </u>
3 an infection   <u>   </u>
4 a major cut   <u>   </u>
5 a minor cut   <u>   </u>
6 a sprained ankle   <u>   </u>

a get stitches
b put antibiotic ointment and a Band-Aid™ on it
c put ice on it and bandage it
d take antibiotics
e ~~take antihistamine tablets or cream~~
f take painkillers

e Complete the sentences with a word from the list.

~~down~~   out   over   around   up

1 You should go and lie <u>*down*</u> if you aren't feeling well.
2 If you stand for too long in this heat, you might pass _____.
3 You shouldn't go out until you get _____ the flu completely.
4 If you think you're going to throw _____, tell me and I'll stop the car.
5 I must have fainted. When I came _____ I was lying on the floor.

f Complete the medical advice with the words in the list.

bandage   damp cloth   ~~pinch~~   press   rub running water   tip

1 You can stop a nosebleed if you *pinch* the soft part of your nose and _____ your head forward.
2 If you put cool _____ on a burn, it will stop blisters from forming.
3 You shouldn't put a hot _____ on a sprained ankle because the heat will make the ankle more swollen.
4 Don't _____ the arms and legs of someone with hypothermia because you will make them lose more heat.
5 You should only stand behind someone who's choking and _____ their stomach inwards if they can't talk, cough, or breathe.
6 If you put antibiotic ointment and a _____ on a bad cut, you will stop the wound from getting infected.

g Write a short paragraph about your last illness / injury. Include…

- when you were ill / injured and what the illness / injury was.
- what the symptoms were.
- what the treatment was.
- how long it took you to get over it.

2 VOCABULARY FROM READING

Complete the sentences with a phrase from the list.

heart rate   life-threatening illness   ~~miracle cures~~ open-heart surgery   scare stories   under the weather worst-case scenario

1 Most stories about <u>*miracle cures*</u> are fake news.
2 Ethan is concerned because his _____ gets very high when he exercises.
3 Most people want to know about the _____ when they are diagnosed with an illness, but it's unlikely things will get that bad.
4 It isn't easy for doctors to tell patients that they are suffering from a _____.
5 I've been feeling _____ recently, so I've made an appointment with my doctor.
6 My uncle is very sick in the hospital, and he's going to have _____ tomorrow.
7 Newspapers are full of _____ about what will happen if we eat certain foods.

3 PRONUNCIATION /ʃ/, /dʒ/, /tʃ/, and /k/

a Circle the word with a different sound.

1	ʃ **sh**ower	1 (**ch**est) infe**c**tion pre**ss**ure ra**sh**
2	k **k**eys	2 a**ch**e **ch**olesterol si**ck** spe**c**ialist
3	dʒ **j**azz	3 aller**g**ic emer**g**ency fin**g**er in**j**ury
4	tʃ **ch**ess	4 **ch**oke sti**tch**es stoma**ch** tempera**t**ure
5	ʃ **sh**ower	5 cou**ch** opera**t**ion **sh**ock unsons**ci**ous
6	dʒ **j**azz	6 banda**g**e in**j**ection ne**g**ative sur**ge**on

b ◖2.1 Listen and check. Then listen again and repeat the words.

4 GRAMMAR present perfect simple and continuous

a Right (✓) or wrong (✗)? Correct the mistakes in the highlighted phrases.

1 You don't need to call the doctor – I've already made an appointment for you.
   _✓_____

2 This is the first time I've been spraining my ankle – I didn't know it hurt so much!
   _✗ I've sprained my ankle_____

3 Mia isn't going to school today because she's been throwing up all night.
   _____

4 I've fallen lots of times playing soccer, but I've never broken a bone.
   _____

5 I can't take anything for my headache because we've been running out of painkillers.
   _____

6 You've been complaining about your back for weeks – why don't you go to the doctor?
   _____

7 How long have you been knowing about your grandfather's illness?
   _____

8 Sasha's coughed all day, and now he has a sore throat.
   _____

9 My sister has a skin problem – she's been going to a doctor for treatment for over two years.
   _____

10 How many times have you been fainting recently?
   _____

b Complete the sentences using the words in parentheses. Use the present perfect simple or continuous form of the verb. Put the adverbs in the correct position.

1 Jess is a little nervous – _she's never ridden_ a horse before. (she / ride / never)
2 How many cookies _____? (you / eat)
3 My brother's really stressed about work, so _____ very well recently. (he / not sleep)
4 _____ my hand on the oven – it really hurts! (I / burn / just)
5 _____ problems with my shoulder for several months now. (I / have)
6 Ed is one of the nicest people _____. (I / meet / ever)

7 _____ to the gym for long – just a few weeks. (Georgia / not go)
8 _____ a sore throat for more than a week now. (Jamie / have)
9 How long _____ a job? (your girlfriend / look for)
10 I bought that book last month, but _____ it yet. (I / not read)

c Complete the email with the correct form of the verbs in parentheses. Use the present perfect simple or continuous.

> ✉
>
> Hi Junko,
>
> Thanks for your email – it was great to hear from you!
>
> Sorry I ¹_haven't replied_ (not reply) until now, but I ²_____ (not feel) very well recently. I ³_____ (have) the flu, and I'm only just getting over it now. I ⁴_____ (not go) to work for a week; I ⁵_____ (lie) on the sofa at home all day. My mom ⁶_____ (take care of) me all week, and I'm almost better now. I'll probably go back to work the day after tomorrow.
>
> Anyway, I'm so glad you're planning on coming to visit next summer – it will be great to see you! While I've been sick, I ⁷_____ (think) about what we can do while you're here, and I ⁸_____ (come up with) a few ideas. I know how much you love music, so for the last few days I ⁹_____ (try) to get some tickets for a music festival, but I ¹⁰_____ (not manage) to get any yet. Is there anything else you'd like to do during your visit? I'm really looking forward to seeing you, and I know that we'll have a fantastic time.
>
> Write back soon!
>
> Love,
>
> Aria

d Answer Aria's email. Write 140–190 words. Use the present perfect simple and continuous. Include the following:
- thank Aria for her email
- explain why you haven't written until now
- answer Aria's question
- ask Aria a question

🔄 **Go online** for more practice

> If you speak three languages, you are trilingual.
> If you speak two, you are bilingual.
> If you speak one, you are English.
> *German joke*

G using adjectives as nouns, adjective order   **V** clothes and fashion   **P** vowel sounds

1 GRAMMAR using adjectives as nouns, adjective order

a Complete the sentences with the noun form of the adjectives in the list.

blind   deaf   disabled   ~~elderly~~   injured   rich
unemployed   young

1 Should the family or the state look after *the elderly*?
2 The government is offering courses to help _____ to find jobs.
3 After the accident, _____ were taken to the hospital.
4 The building has easy access for _____.
5 Do you think _____ should pay higher taxes than the poor?
6 In some countries, _____ use special dogs to help them find their way around.
7 _____ always think that they know better than their parents.
8 _____ usually communicate with each other using sign language.

b Complete the sentences with *the* + adjective.

1 *The Vietnamese* usually celebrate Tet in January or February.
2 _____ eat a lot of fish. (Japan)
3 _____ export a lot of electrical products to the rest of the world. (China)
4 _____ have a good standard of living. (Switzerland)
5 _____ are very kind and friendly to visitors. (Portugal)
6 _____ have a reputation for being polite. (England)
7 _____ enjoy spending time outdoors. (Scotland)
8 _____ are extremely fond of bike riding. (France)

c Right (✓) or wrong (✗)? Correct the mistakes in the highlighted phrases.

1 Sarah's wearing a denim short skirt.
   ✗ *a short denim skirt*
2 I'm looking for a sleeveless cotton T-shirt.
   ✓ _____
3 I want to buy some leather white pants.
   _____
4 You can't wear those old scruffy jeans to the wedding.
   _____
5 He gave his mother a patterned silk scarf for her birthday.
   _____
6 He looks very fashionable in his gray new Armani suit.
   _____
7 She was wearing a bright red wool scarf.
   _____
8 My sister bought some purple trendy glasses.
   _____

15

d Write each pair of sentences as one sentence.

1 My grandparents live in an old brick house. It's big.
   My grandparents live in a big old brick house.

2 I met a Brazilian woman at the party. She was interesting.
   _____

3 My sister has pretty black hair. It's long.
   _____

4 Ava bought an expensive silk top. It's striped.
   _____

5 There's a round wooden table in my friend's kitchen. It's beautiful.
   _____

6 Max gave his girlfriend an unusual ring for her birthday. It's gold.
   _____

7 My boss drives a powerful Italian sports car. It's red.
   _____

8 We've been having some wet weather recently. It's been awful.
   _____

2 VOCABULARY clothes and fashion

a Complete the crossword with the adjectives.

ACROSS →

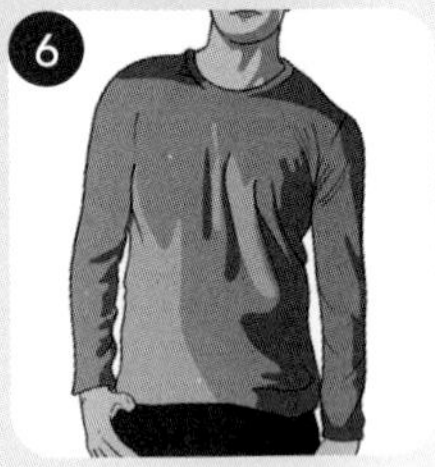

1. 6. 8. 11. 12.

DOWN ↓

2. 3. 4. 5. 7. 9. 10.

1 P L A I N

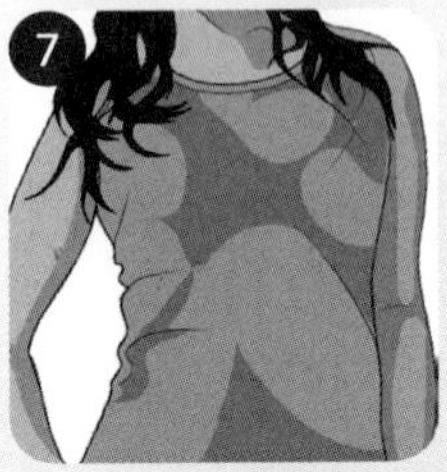

Go online for more practice

b Order the letters in parentheses to make a material. Then complete the sentences.

1 Jack was wearing a blue *denim* jacket. (NIMED)
2 I prefer to wear light _____ shirts in the summer. (TTNCOO)
3 I gave my mom a blouse with a _____ collar for her birthday. (CEAL)
4 Are you sure those boots are made of _____? (HTRELEA)
5 I never buy _____ clothes because they take so long to iron. (NINLE)
6 They gave me a very expensive _____ tie as a going-away present. (LIKS)
7 Don't wear your _____ jacket out – it's raining. (SEDUE)
8 I really like your new _____ jacket. It looks very soft. (VVTEEL)
9 My aunt often wears a _____ coat, but it isn't real. (URF)
10 I always wear a _____ top in the gym – it's the most comfortable. (CRALY)
11 My grandfather wears an old _____ cardigan around the house in the winter. (OLOW)

c Complete the sentences.

1 You don't have to spend a lot of money to look f*ashionable*.
2 Alice enjoys wearing cl_____ clothes that will never go out of fashion.
3 It isn't a formal dinner, so I'm going to wear something c_____.
4 Zach looked very scr_____ when I saw him: his T-shirt was dirty, and he hadn't combed his hair.
5 You look like my dad in those pants – they're really o_____-f_____.

d Match 1–8 to a–h to make questions.

1 How often do you dress _____f_____
2 How many clothes do you have _____
3 Do you get _____
4 When do you get dressed _____
5 Do you always hang _____
6 What color do you think _____
7 Is it important for you that your shoes _____
8 Do you have any clothes that go _____

a suits you best?
b in the morning?
c match your clothes? Why / Why not?
d that don't fit you?
e with everything? What?
f ~~up to go out for a special occasion?~~
g changed as soon as you get home from work / school? Why / Why not?
h up your clothes before you go to bed?

e Answer the questions in **d**.

1 _____
2 _____
3 _____
4 _____
5 _____
6 _____
7 _____
8 _____

3 PRONUNCIATION vowel sounds

a Circle the word with a different sound.

u 1 boot	🐟 2 fish	ɜr 3 bird	aɪ 4 bike	eɪ 5 train
loose	linen	fur	fit	lace
(scruffy)	slippers	shirt	Lycra	leather
shoes	silk	shorts	stylish	plain
suit	striped	skirt	tight	suede

b 🔊 2.2 Listen and check. Then listen again and repeat the words.

*I don't have a fear of flying;
I have a fear of crashing.
Billy Bob Thornton, American actor*

G narrative tenses, past perfect continuous, *so / such...that...* **V** air travel **P** irregular past forms, sentence rhythm

1 VOCABULARY air travel

a Replace the **bold** words with a formal word or phrase from the list.

approximately   disembark   locate
~~personal electronic devices~~   place
proceed to   rear   requiring

1 **Cell phones, tablets, and laptops** may be used in flight mode during the flight. *personal electronic devices*

2 There are bathrooms at the front and at the **back** of the plane. _____

3 Our flight time today is **about** two and a half hours. _____

4 The crew will be passing through the cabin with ear phones for any passengers **needing** them. _____

5 Passengers to New York are asked to **go to** Gate 36 immediately. _____

6 Please check that you have all your belongings with you before you **leave the plane.** _____

7 We ask that you **put** bags and jackets under the seat in front of you. _____

8 Please take some time now to **find** your nearest emergency exit. _____

b (Circle) the correct word.

1 They booked first-class tickets, so they could use the *airport terminal /*(airline lounge)while waiting for their flight.

2 It didn't take long for me to check in my suitcase at the *baggage drop / security*.

3 The passengers were stopped at *customs / the check-in desk* for their bags to be checked.

4 I showed my boarding pass and ID at the *baggage claim / gate* and went to board my flight.

5 I didn't have a boarding pass, so I had to stand in line at the *check-in desk / customs* to get one.

6 We could see our plane on the *runway / gate* while we were waiting to board.

7 We parked as close as possible to the *airport terminal / airline lounge* because we were late.

8 The quickest way to find your flight is to look at the *departures board / runway*.

9 I was wearing boots, so I had to take them off at *security / the baggage drop*.

10 When I went to the *baggage claim / flight times*, I found that my suitcase hadn't arrived.

c Complete the sentences with a word from the list.

arrivals   ~~business class~~   cart   collect
delayed   first class   illegal goods   luggage

1 Companies usually pay for employees to travel *business class* .

2 If your suitcase has wheels, you don't need to use a _____.

3 There's usually a line of taxis waiting outside _____.

4 Passengers who are traveling _____ sit in the most comfortable seats on the plane.

5 You should always keep your _____ with you when you're in an airport.

6 Customs officers check travelers' bags to make sure they are not trying to bring _____ into the country.

7 It can sometimes take a long time to get out of the airport if you have to wait to _____ your bags from the baggage claim.

8 The departures board informs passengers whether a flight is on time, boarding, or _____.

d Complete the text.

Last year, I wanted to travel from Calgary to San Diego to visit a friend. I had booked an [1] int*ernational* fl*ight* from Calgary to Los Angeles and a [2] c_____ fl_____ from Los Angeles to San Diego. I printed my [3] b_____ p_____ the day before my flight, and I took it with me to the airport. I was able to go right to security in [4] D_____ because I only had a [5] c_____ b_____ – a small backpack. After [6] sc_____ my bag, they opened it and [7] ch_____ it to make sure I wasn't carrying any [8] l_____ or [9] sh_____ ob_____, like scissors. When I finally got my bag back, I looked at the [10] d_____ b_____ to see if my flight was already [11] b_____. I shouldn't have worried, because the flight was [12] d_____. The plane didn't [13] t_____ o_____ until two hours later. When I eventually arrived in Los Angeles, I was happy to see that my next flight was [14] o_____ t_____. However, just before we were due to [15] b_____, we were informed that the flight had been canceled – apparently, planes couldn't [16] l_____ in San Diego because of fog. In the end, I finished my journey by train, and I arrived in San Diego eight hours late!

e Complete the crossword.

Crossword grid:
- 1 Across: A I S L E (with L at position 2 down)
- 4 Across: S _ _ T _ B _ _ T
- 5 Across: C _ _ N _ C _ _ W
- 6 Across: T _ _ _ E
- 8 Across: J _ T _ L G
- 9 Across: D _ _ _ T _ C _ F _ _ T
- Down letters shown: 2 L, 3 D, 7 R, and various letters (L, F, T, F, W, E, W)

ACROSS →

1 the passage between the rows of seats on a plane

4 a thing that you fasten around your body to hold you in your seat

5 the people whose job it is to take care of passengers on a plane

6 a series of sudden and violent changes in the direction that air is moving

8 the tired feeling that people often have after a long journey on a plane to a place where the local time is different

9 a flight between places within the same country

DOWN ↓

2 a flight that transports people over long distances, e.g., between two continents

3 a flight that goes from one place to another without stopping

7 a line of seats on a plane

f Circle a, b, or c.

1 I _____ abroad five or six times a year.
  a journey **b** travel **c** trip

2 I had a terrible _____ here – the flight was delayed, and then we had a lot of turbulence.
  a journey **b** travel **c** trip

3 Is Hannah back from her _____ to South America?
  a journey **b** travel **c** trip

4 We have to _____ 250 miles if we want to see my grandparents.
  a journey **b** travel **c** trip

5 My sister wants to go on a _____ around the world after she graduates from college.
  a journey **b** travel **c** trip

6 I went on a long train _____ across Canada last year.
  a journey **b** travel **c** trip

g Complete the phrasal verbs in the questions with a particle from the list.

in   off (x3)   on   out   up (x2)

1 Who **picked** you *up* from the airport the last time you traveled?

2 When do you usually **check** _____ for a flight?

3 Who usually **drops** you _____ at the airport?

4 Have you ever **filled** _____ an immigration form? If so, when?

5 What's the first thing you do when you **get** _____ a plane?

6 Have you ever **picked** _____ the wrong bag at the baggage claim?

7 Are you usually in a hurry to **get** _____ the plane? Why / Why not?

8 Do you ever feel nervous when a plane **takes** _____?

h Answer the questions in **g**.

1 _____

2 _____

3 _____

4 _____

5 _____

6 _____

7 _____

8 _____

Go online for more practice

2 GRAMMAR IN CONTEXT
so / such...that...

Circle the correct word.

1 Her suitcase was *so* / *so much* / *such* heavy that she couldn't pick it up.
2 We had *so* / *such* / *such a* long delay that we missed our connecting flight.
3 There were *so* / *so much* / *so many* people at the airport that there weren't any carts left.
4 We flew over *so* / *such* / *such a* beautiful countryside that I took some photos from the plane.
5 There was *so* / *so much* / *so many* rain that the road to the airport was flooded.
6 We were sitting in *so* / *so much* / *such* narrow seats on the plane that it was very uncomfortable.
7 The flight attendant spoke *so* / *so much* / *such* softly that I couldn't hear what she was saying.

3 GRAMMAR narrative tenses, past perfect continuous

a Circle the correct verb form. Check (✓) if both are correct.

1 Tim couldn't close his suitcase because he *had put* / *had been putting* too many clothes in it.
2 She *had worked* / *had been working* for the same airline for eight years before she was promoted. ✓
3 I was delighted when I found my passport. I *had looked* / *had been looking* for it for hours.
4 After I *had picked up* / *had been picking up* my luggage, I took a taxi to my hotel.
5 I *had sat* / *had been sitting* in departures for 20 minutes when I saw that my flight was boarding at a different gate.
6 They *had lived* / *had been living* in Brooklyn before they moved to Boston.
7 The passengers were angry because the airline *had canceled* / *had been canceling* their flight.
8 I was surprised when I was told that my suitcase was too big: I *had taken* / *had been taking* it for years without having to pay for it.

b Complete the text with the correct form of the verbs in parentheses.

My parents [1] *had never flown* (never fly) before, so they were very nervous when we [2] _____ (arrive) at Logan Airport to take our flight to Mexico. It [3] _____ (rain), so I [4] _____ (leave) them at the terminal building with instructions to get in line at the check-in desk while I [5] _____ (go) to park my car in the long-term parking lot. However, when I [6] _____ (get) to the check-in desk myself, they were nowhere in sight. I [7] _____ (look) for them everywhere until it suddenly occurred to me that it was possible they [8] _____ (already / check in) and they [9] _____ (wait) for me in the departure lounge. This was a real problem for me because I [10] _____ (give) my passport to my mother, so I couldn't check in. I [11] _____ (call) my parents on their cell phone and, fortunately, my mother answered. They [12] _____ (already / go) through to the departure lounge, and they [13] _____ (wait) for me for almost half an hour at the gate. Apparently, my mom [14] _____ (read) her book and my dad [15] _____ (do) a crossword. After we hung up, my mom found an understanding staff member who met me at the information desk with my passport!

c Write a paragraph about an air travel experience you have had. Use several different narrative tenses.

4 PRONUNCIATION irregular past forms, sentence rhythm

a Write the simple past of the verbs in the list next to the simple past verb that has the same pronunciation of the vowel sound.

~~catch~~ cut fly meet pay say sing stand tell wake

1 bought	*caught*	6 spoke	_____
2 rang	_____	7 sold	_____
3 made	_____	8 knew	_____
4 let	_____	9 could	_____
5 shut	_____	10 read	_____

b 🔊 3.1 Listen and check. Then listen again and repeat the simple past forms.

c 🔊 3.2 Listen and fill in the blanks in the anecdote.

We were on a [1] *flight* to **Tokyo**, and we'd been [2] _____ for about [3] _____ **hours**. I was **listening** to [4] _____, and my [5] _____ was **sleeping**, when [6] _____ we **heard** a **very loud** [7] _____. It [8] _____ as if an **engine** had **exploded**. The [9] _____ **didn't tell** us what had [10] _____ until **half** an **hour later**.

d 🔊 3.2 Listen again and practice reading the anecdote aloud with the right rhythm.

🔵 **Go online** for more practice

Wanting to meet a writer because you like their books is like wanting to meet a duck because you like paté.
Margaret Atwood, Canadian author

1 GRAMMAR the position of adverbs and adverbial phrases

a Circle the adverb or adverbial phrase that is different.

1 **time** all day (indoors) soon tonight
2 **place** here in fact in the park outside
3 **manner** absolutely fluently rudely slowly
4 **degree** a little almost hard very
5 **comment** clearly fortunately obviously sometimes
6 **frequency** always hardly ever usually right away

b Re-order the words to make sentences. Put the adverb in its usual position.

1 I / umbrella / an / had / luckily / taken
Luckily, I had taken an umbrella.
2 sick / hardly ever / daughter / is / my
_____.
3 parents / next year / are / his / retiring
_____.
4 boy / rude / teacher / was / to / the / extremely / his
_____.
5 dresses / my / stylishly / very / sister
_____.
6 is / Omar / apparently / divorced / getting
_____.
7 were / would / you / never / thought / I / have / 30
_____.
8 bandaged / was / by a nurse / his ankle / carefully
_____.
9 be / in five minutes / I'll / there
_____.
10 go / much / the / to / later / in / I / summer / bed
_____.

c In each sentence one of the highlighted adverbs or adverbial phrases is in the wrong position. Rewrite the sentences.

1 He usually immediately gets up when his alarm rings.
He usually gets up immediately when his alarm rings.
2 Although she studies a lot, she goes rarely to the library.
_____
_____
3 I crashed my new car unfortunately last week.
_____
_____
4 Ideally, we should leave tomorrow early.
_____
_____
5 I can understand a word hardly when people speak English quickly.
_____
_____
6 Hiro almost forgot yesterday his doctor's appointment.
_____
_____
7 She's angry incredibly because her husband came home late last night.
_____
_____
8 It surprisingly didn't rain at all while we were in London.
_____
_____

2 VOCABULARY adverbs and adverbial phrases

a (Circle) the correct word.

1 Ellie ate all her lunch, *ever* / (*even*) the vegetables!
2 I haven't seen Tyler *late* / *lately*, have you?
3 I can't stand most TV shows, *specially* / *especially* reality shows.
4 Dave *near* / *nearly* crashed his car, but he braked just in time.
5 Please don't tell me what happens because I haven't read the book *still* / *yet*.
6 I'm not going to Sam's party. I *hard* / *hardly* know him! He's your friend, not mine.
7 Do you *ever* / *even* wear jeans to work?
8 My grandparents don't live *near* / *nearly* here; they live about 30 miles away.
9 My father worked very *hard* / *hardly* all his life.
10 Alan's feet are so big that his shoes are *especially* / *specially* made for him.
11 My cousin is a doctor, and *right now* / *actually* she's working in Africa.
12 I can't wait to find out what happens *at the end* / *in the end* of this book.
13 I missed my bus because I got up *late* / *lately*.
14 We were thinking of going to the movies, but *at the end* / *in the end* we just went out for some coffee.
15 I thought the movie was going to be boring, but *actually* / *right now* I really enjoyed it.
16 I didn't finish the exam – I was *still* / *yet* writing when the teacher told us to stop.

b Complete the sentences with an adverb from the list that matches the definition in brackets.

apparently   ~~basically~~   certainly   eventually
gradually   ideally   in fact   obviously

1 *Basically* (the main reason is), we don't have enough money to buy our own house.
2 _____ (in a perfect world), we'd each have our own room in the house, but that isn't possible.
3 That's _____ (without a doubt) the best lobster that I've ever eaten – it was delicious!
4 My sister is _____ (little by little) building a new life for herself after her divorce.
5 If you keep applying for jobs, you'll find one _____ (in the end).
6 I thought the meal was going to be expensive, but _____ (the truth is) it was very reasonable.
7 _____ (clearly), her son will move out when he gets a job, but for now he's living with her.
8 _____ (according to what I've heard), a lot of flights have been canceled because of the bad weather.

c Complete the stories with the correct adverbs from the lists.

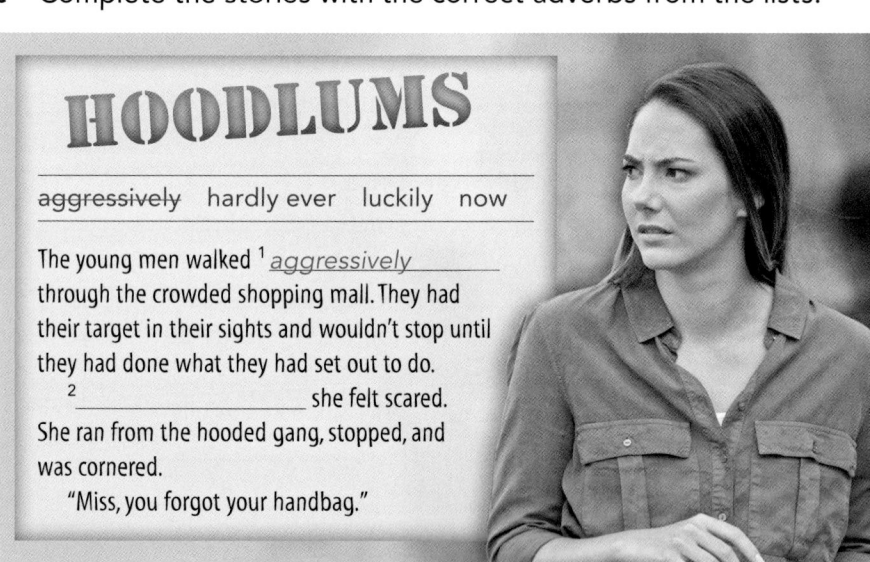

HOODLUMS

~~aggressively~~   hardly ever   luckily   now

The young men walked [1] *aggressively* through the crowded shopping mall. They had their target in their sights and wouldn't stop until they had done what they had set out to do.
[2] _____ she felt scared. She ran from the hooded gang, stopped, and was cornered.
"Miss, you forgot your handbag."

Revenge is sweet

all day   bitterly   suddenly   very

They had been arguing [3] _____ the night before. He had come in from the garage with oil on his shoes. Fed up, desperate, she hit him. Horrified by what she had done, she drove away from the house along the mountain road.
[4] _____, she realized that the brakes weren't working.

Go online for more practice

Generation **gap**

always   angrily   extremely   unfortunately

He was worried. ⁵_____, since his wife's death, his teenage daughter had become ⁶_____ difficult. They had agreed 2:00 a.m. as the latest return time from clubs. Now it was 3:30. He prepared himself for confrontation as the door opened. "Dad," she shouted ⁷_____. "I've been frantic. You're late again."

The story of my life

actually   last week   normally   slightly

Stage one: Feel fat. Go on diet. Lose weight. Feel fabulous. Buy new clothes.

Stage two: Eat ⁸_____ but controlling intake. Look fabulous. New clothes ⁹_____ tight.

Stage three: Eat and drink normally (potatoes, bread, dessert, and soda). New clothes don't fit. Old clothes thrown away.

Back to stage one.

d Choose six adverbs or adverbial phrases from the list and write sentences that are true for you.

| a lot   apparently   fluently   here   ideally   incredibly |
| slowly   sometimes   tonight   usually |

1 _____
2 _____
3 _____
4 _____
5 _____
6 _____

3 PRONUNCIATION word stress and intonation

a <u>Underline</u> the stressed syllable in the adverbs in the list. Then put them in the correct column.

~~ab|so|lute|ly~~   ac|tu|a|lly   a|ppar|ent|ly   ba|si|ca|lly   de|fi|nite|ly
e|ven|tual|ly   e|spe|cia|lly   fortu|nate|ly   gra|dua|lly   i|de|a|lly
in|cre|di|bly   lu|cki|ly   ob|vi|ous|ly   un|fortu|nate|ly

Stress on first syllable	Stress on second syllable
absolutely	

b 🔊 3.3 Listen and check. Then listen again and repeat the adverbs.

c 🔊 3.4 Listen and complete the sentences.
1 I *absolutely* love Japanese food, *especially* sushi.
2 I thought Brad was single, but _____ he's _____.
3 We paid a lot for the tickets, but _____, the play was _____ boring.
4 That movie is _____ – even my husband cried at the end!
5 I _____ want to change my job, _____ for something better paid.
6 _____, Tina has been downsized, so she's moving back in with her _____.

d 🔊 3.4 Listen again and repeat the sentences. <u>C</u>opy the stress and intonation of the adverbs.

🔵 **Go online** for more practice   ✅ **Go online** to check your progress

1 LOOKING AT LANGUAGE

Fill in the blanks to complete the conversations.

1 A Which book have you enjoyed reading recently?
   B *The Hunger Games*. A*lright*_____, it was written for teenagers, but I really liked it.

2 A How do you like that e-reader I gave you?
   B I was worried I wouldn't use it but, a_____, it's very handy.

3 A Do you know anything about Ken Follett's books?
   B I think they're s_____ o_____ thrillers, aren't they?

4 A Have you ever read a Charles Dickens novel in English?
   B No way! I m_____, it would be too hard, wouldn't it?

5 A Did you enjoy *Crime and Punishment*?
   B Yes, although it was a little bit, y_____ kn_____, depressing in places.

6 A What do you think of the writer Dan Brown?
   B W_____, he's not a great writer, but I enjoy his books.

2 VOCABULARY FROM THE INTERVIEW

Complete the sentences from the interview with Marion Pomeranc with a verb from the list.

brought	~~flow~~	go	rules	take

1 The words, the made-up words, the way the words *flow*_____ together and sound.
2 It just _____ me to a different place.
3 Kids like to _____ back, they like to become familiar with a character in the story.
4 _____ a trip to a publishing house.
5 Youth dominates, and kind of _____ the world a little bit.

3 THE CONVERSATION

Complete the sentences with two possible words or phrases from the list.

I mean	kind of (x2)	like	sort of (x2)	stuff	things

1 You can just *kind of*_____ / *sort of*_____ lose yourself in this imaginary world.
2 I like science fiction and fantasy and _____ / _____ like that.
3 It's just something I _____ / _____ grew up with.
4 _____ / _____, it's something that I would recommend to my friends and family.

4 VOCABULARY FROM THE CONVERSATION

Replace the *italic* words with a word or phrase from the list.

a clue	huge	key to	out of it	~~tough~~

1 It's really *difficult*. *tough*_____
2 I don't have *any idea*. _____
3 I feel a little *bit disconnected*. _____
4 It's *so big*. _____
5 That's the *critical thing about* any good book. _____

GRAMMAR & VOCABULARY

a Complete the sentences with the correct form of the **bold** word.

1 I don't agree with my brother's _____ views. He refuses to listen to other people's opinions. **MIND**

2 Your wrist is very _____ – I think you might have sprained it. **SWELL**

3 Andrea is taking antibiotics because she has a nasty throat _____. **INFECT**

4 Matt was _____ relieved when he found out he'd passed his driver's test. **INCREDIBLE**

5 My shoulders got sunburned because I was wearing a _____ dress. **SLEEVE**

6 She tends to wear clothes that are practical rather than _____. **FASHION**

7 There was a long line at _____ because only one of the scanning machines was working. **SECURE**

8 My dad's picking me up from the airport – he said he'd wait for me in _____. **ARRIVE**

9 We had some shelves _____ made for the space between the cabinet and the window. **SPECIAL**

10 Living on my own felt strange at first, but I'm _____ getting used to it. **GRADUAL**

b Read the article. Circle a, b, or c.

LUCKY ESCAPE AT TRABZON AIRPORT

Can you imagine how ¹____ if you were on a plane that slid off the runway when it landed? This is exactly what happened on a domestic flight in Turkey one evening in January 2019. The plane had ²____ without incident from the capital, Ankara, and the flight had continued as usual. However, the pilot had difficulties as he ³____ in Trabzon, in the northeastern part of the country. Freezing temperatures in the area ⁴____ a thick layer of ice to form on the runway. The ice was ⁵____ slippery that when the Boeing 737-800 landed, the wheels began to slide. The pilot tried to correct the mistake, but he ⁶____. The plane slid off the tarmac and started going towards the cliffs above the Black Sea. ⁷____, the wheels got stuck in the mud on the side of the cliffs, and the plane stopped before it reached the water. At the time, there were 168 people on board: 162 passengers, two pilots, and four cabin ⁸____. Fortunately, they only had to wait 20 minutes for emergency services to arrive and help them get off. ⁹____ were taken directly to the hospital, but they were all sent home within a very short time. Psychologists say it may take time for some of the passengers to ¹⁰____ the shock.

	a	**b**	**c**
1	did you feel	you would feel	would you feel
2	dropped off	picked up	taken off
3	landed	had landed	was landing
4	caused	had caused	had been causing
5	so	so much	such
6	couldn't	hadn't	wasn't
7	Ideally	Luckily	Obviously
8	staff	attendants	crew
9	Injured	People injured	The injured
10	come around	get over	pass out

✓ **Go online** to check your progress

Only when the last tree has died, and the last river has been polluted, and the last fish has been caught will we realize that we can't eat money.
Cree Indian saying

G future perfect and future continuous   **V** the environment, weather   **P** vowel sounds

1 GRAMMAR future perfect and future continuous

a Circle the correct form.

1 Hopefully, we *will be saving / will have saved* enough money to go on vacation by the summer.

2 By this time tomorrow, *we will be traveling / we will have traveled* to Chicago – it's an eight-hour journey, so take something to do on the train.

3 I probably *won't have finished / won't be finishing* the report by Friday – can I give it to you on Monday morning?

4 Don't call between one and two o'clock because we *will have had / will be having* lunch.

5 We *will have had / will be having* five meetings by the end of today.

6 Jack *will be leaving / will have left* for Mexico on Saturday. I'm taking him to the airport.

7 I won't see my children tonight – they *will be going / will have gone* to bed by the time I get home.

8 I've planned a surprise party for Alex – when we get to the restaurant, all her friends *will be waiting / will have waited* for her!

b Complete the sentences with the future perfect or future continuous form of the verb in parentheses.

1 By the end of this month, we *'ll have moved* (move) to our new house, so you can visit us.

2 By this time tomorrow, my parents _____ (fly) over the Pacific on their way to Tokyo.

3 My exams are in May, so I _____ (take) them all by June 1st.

4 Hopefully, you _____ (read) the book I lent you by the next time I see you.

5 If the game starts at 7:00 p.m., we _____ (play) until 8:45 at least.

6 In a year, they _____ (build) the new road, and we'll be able to get to work much quicker.

7 When do you think you _____ (finish) paying your mortgage?

8 Don't call me tomorrow morning because I _____ (attend) an important meeting.

9 It's been raining all morning, but hopefully it _____ (stop) by this afternoon.

10 _____ (you go) to the supermarket later?

c Write future perfect or future continuous questions.

1 when / you / take / your next vacation
When will you be taking your next vacation?

2 what / you / do / this time tomorrow
_____

3 what time / you / get up / tomorrow morning
_____

4 how much TV / you / watch / by the end of the week
_____

5 where / you go / next weekend
_____

6 when / you / finish / your English homework
_____

7 how many times / you / look at your phone / by the end of today?
_____

8 how many hours / you / spend / study English / by the end of the week
_____

d Answer the questions in **c**.

1 _____
  _____
2 _____
  _____
3 _____
  _____
4 _____
  _____
5 _____
  _____
6 _____
  _____
7 _____
  _____
8 _____
  _____

2 VOCABULARY the weather

a Circle the word that is different.

1 below zero   cold   cool   mild
2 damp   drizzling   drought   humid
3 boiling   freezing   hot   scorching
4 breeze   chilly   hurricane   windy
5 changeable   fog   mist   smog
6 pouring   showers   warm   wet

b Complete the sentences.

1 We're having a h*eat wave*_____. It isn't usually so hot at this time of year.
2 Many drivers had to spend the night in their vehicles after they were caught in the bl_____ and their cars got stuck in the snow.
3 People say that there may be a fl_____ if the river continues rising.
4 In some areas there was h_____. The balls of ice were enormous!
5 Last night there was a violent storm and the sound of th_____ woke me up.
6 The government wants us to save water because of the dr_____.
7 In India, the m_____ season usually lasts until October. The rain can be very heavy.
8 The l_____ lit up the sky during the thunderstorm.
9 Hundreds of trees blew down in the h_____, and several buildings were damaged.

c Match 1–9 to a–i.

1 Everyone is hoping for clear ___c___
2 They said the weather will be changeable, ____
3 There were so few sunny ____
4 The forecast is for heavy ____
5 Planes can't take off in this thick ____
6 Driving will be dangerous this morning because of the icy ____
7 Most parts of the tri-state area will enjoy bright ____
8 Many trees were blown down by strong ____
9 We hope the weather will be more settled ____

a roads, so drivers should take care.
b next week – we're going on a cruise.
c skies so that they can see the solar eclipse.
d sunshine today, and it will be warm.
e rain, so the barbecue has been canceled.
f winds during last night's storm.
g so I'm taking my sunglasses and an umbrella.
h fog, so several flights have been canceled.
i periods that we didn't spend much time at the beach.

🔄 **Go online** for more practice

d Complete the paragraphs with the words in each list.

~~freezing~~   heavy   icy   strong

January is one of the coldest months in New York State. The temperature sometimes drops to 32°F, so it's [1] _freezing_ outside, and the roads are [2] _____. There are often [3] _____ winds and [4] _____ rain or snow; during some storms, sleet may fall instead of rain.

breeze   changeable   mild   showers   sunny

In April, it isn't as cold, and some days can be very [5] _____ – around 60°F. There are often rain [6] _____, with [7] _____ periods between them because the weather is very [8] _____. There's often a [9] _____, which can sometimes be very cool.

bright   cool   hail   settled   warm

In June, the weather still isn't [10] _____, and it continues to change a lot: one minute there's [11] _____ sunshine, and the next it rains. Thunderstorms often move through, producing heavy rain and sometimes even balls of [12] _____. In general, it's [13] _____ during the day – around 70°F – but it can get [14] _____ in the evenings, so you need a light jacket.

chilly   clear   drizzle   damp   mist   rain

By October, the temperature starts to fall again, and it can be very [15] _____ outside – only 50°F or 55°F. Some mornings start out with [16] _____ in the mountains and near the water, while on others there are [17] _____ skies and you can see for a long way. Towards the end of the fall, the weather can be rather [18] _____: sometimes just a light [19] _____ and other times pouring [20] _____.

e Write a paragraph about the weather in your country in January, April, July, and October.

3 PRONUNCIATION vowel sounds

a ⃝Circle the word with a different sound.

1	tree	br**ee**ze fr**ee**zing ⃝gr**ea**t h**ea**t wave
2	boot	c**oo**l fl**oo**d mons**oo**n typh**oo**n
3	bike	br**i**ght **i**cy l**i**ghtning m**i**st
4	owl	bl**ow** dr**ou**ght sh**ow**er t**ow**el
5	fish	bl**i**zzard dr**i**zzling ch**i**lly m**i**ld
6	up	h**u**mid s**u**mmer s**u**nny th**u**nder
7	ear	cl**ear** h**ere** w**ear** z**er**o
8	egg	h**ea**t h**ea**vy sw**ea**t w**ea**ther
9	horse	sc**or**ching st**or**m w**ar**m w**or**ld
10	phone	alth**ough** bel**ow** cl**ou**dy sn**ow**

b ◑4.1 Listen and check. Then listen again and repeat the words.

🔍 **Go online** for more practice

| **G** zero and first conditionals, future time clauses | **V** expressions with *take* | **P** linked phrases |

1 GRAMMAR zero and first conditionals, future time clauses

a Complete the sentences with a verb from the list. Decide if they are zero conditional or first conditional sentences. Write **0** (zero) or **1** (first).

---
are   cooks   doesn't answer   doesn't come
~~don't get~~   eat   'll stay   won't move
---

1 Plants die if they *don't get*_____ enough water. *0*

2 If you _____ too many calories, you gain weight. ____

3 I _____ at a friend's house tonight if I miss the last train. ____

4 My sister _____ her phone if she's watching a movie on TV. ____

5 Some dogs bite if they _____ scared. ____

6 If we don't sell our house, we _____. ____

7 If Justin _____ dinner tonight, Karen will be delighted. ____

8 If the bus _____ soon, I'll take a taxi. ____

b Complete the sentences with the correct form of the verb in parentheses.

1 *Bring*_____ your swimsuit if you want to use the pool. (bring)

2 If my wife _____ home before 7:30, she gets caught in rush hour traffic. (not leave)

3 It's raining. You'll get wet if you _____ an umbrella with you. (not take)

4 Don't interrupt Emily if she _____. (study)

5 If you _____ 18 or over, you can vote in a general election. (be)

6 If you can't take me to the airport, I _____ a friend. (ask)

7 If you _____ Jodi Picoult's new book yet, I'll buy you a copy for your birthday. (not read)

8 If I _____ eight hours of sleep, I always feel awful the next day. (not get)

c Complete the second sentence so that it means the same as the first sentence. Use a time expression from the list and no more than two other words.

~~after~~   as soon as   before   if   in case   unless   until   when
---

1 I'll do Pilates, and then I'll take a shower.
I'll take a shower *after I do*_____ Pilates.

2 My boyfriend will arrive at his hotel. He'll call me immediately.
My boyfriend will call me _____ at his hotel.

3 We'll arrive in time for lunch if the traffic isn't bad.
We'll arrive in time for lunch _____ is bad.

4 I'm going to call my husband. He might forget his doctor's appointment.
I'm going to call my husband _____ his doctor's appointment.

5 Sarah is going to pack her suitcase. Then she'll go to bed.
Sarah is going to pack her suitcase _____ to bed.

6 We'll wait for you to get home. Then we'll have dinner.
We won't have dinner _____ home.

7 I might be late tonight, so don't wait up for me.
Don't wait up for me _____ late tonight.

8 I'll go to New York and I'll stay with some friends.
I'll stay with some friends _____ to New York.

d Complete the sentences about you.

1 I'll have dinner after _____
   _____.
2 I'll buy a new car as soon as _____
   _____.
3 I won't go to bed tonight until _____
   _____.
4 I'll go shopping before _____
   _____.
5 I might go out later if _____
   _____.
6 I won't move to a new house unless _____
   _____.
7 I'll finish my English homework now, in case _____
   _____.
8 I'll retire when _____
   _____.

2 PRONUNCIATION linked phrases

a 🔊4.2 Listen and complete the sentences.

1 *First of all* _____, let's see how much money
  we have.
2 I didn't really want to go, but it was _____
  the end.
3 Dress professionally, _____, don't be late.
4 _____ world, everyone would have a
  roof over their head.
5 Don't disturb me _____ important.
6 I'll call you _____ I get home.
7 _____ I'm concerned, there's nothing
  more to say.
8 It was _____ experience that I don't
  really want to think about it.

b 🔊4.2 Listen again and repeat the words. Copy the
rhythm.

3 VOCABULARY expressions with *take*

a Match the sentence halves.

1 Grandparents often **take care of** children ___*i*___
2 Don't **take a risk**, ____
3 Try to **take** all the factors **into account** ____
4 If you get an interesting job opportunity, ____
5 There's a new restaurant opening in my
  neighborhood; ____
6 If you want to be involved in the protest, ____
7 Most people **take pity on** people ____
8 The Olympics **take place** every four years; ____
9 Please don't hurry; ____

a if you think something bad might happen.
b they're always held in a different country.
c they're looking to **take on** a new cook as well as
  several food servers.
d **take advantage of** it.
e who are homeless.
f before you make a decision.
g you can **take your time**.
h you can **take part in** the demonstration.
i ~~when their parents can't look after them.~~

🔵 **Go online** for more practice

b   Complete the sentences with the **bold** phrases in **a**.

1 We didn't _take_ the rush hour traffic _into account_, so we almost missed our flight.

2 Why don't we _____ the sunny weather and go to the beach?

3 My children love drama, so they always _____ the school play.

4 This report doesn't need to be finished today – you can _____.

5 The pilot decided to _____ and try to land the plane on the river.

6 I always _____ my elderly neighbor when he's sick. I visit him every day to check if he needs anything.

7 Most music festivals _____ in the summer months when it's more likely to be sunny.

8 Could you _____ my cat while I'm on vacation?

9 Don't mind Charlie. He doesn't _____ other children very quickly.

c   Match the **bold** phrasal verbs in 1–8 to definitions a–h.

1 When was the last time someone **took** you **out** for dinner? _d_
2 Who was the last person you **took to** immediately? ____
3 Do you **take** your shoes **off** as soon as you go into your house? ____
4 Do you **take your time** doing your English homework? ____
5 In what ways do you **take after** your parents? ____
6 How often do you **take** the trash **out**? ____
7 Have you ever watched the planes **take off** and land at an airport? ____
8 If you could **take up** a new activity, what would it be? ____

a to leave the ground and begin to fly
b to use as much time as you need without hurrying
c to remove a piece of clothing
d ~~to take somebody to a place and pay for them~~
e to start liking somebody
f to learn or start to do something, especially for pleasure
g to remove something from inside, e.g., a house
h to look or behave like

d   Answer the questions in **c** about you.

1 _____
   _____
2 _____
   _____
3 _____
   _____
4 _____
   _____
5 _____
   _____
6 _____
   _____
7 _____
   _____
8 _____
   _____

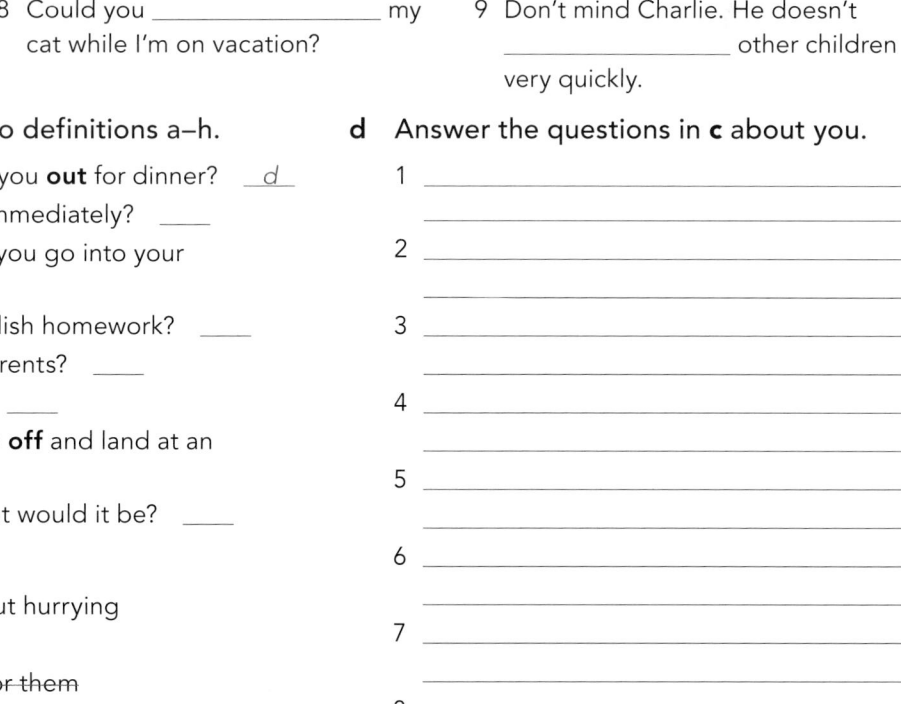

Go online for more practice   Go online to check your progress

5A I'm a survivor

Adventure is just bad planning.
*Explorer Roald Amundsen,
first man to reach the South Pole*

G unreal conditionals   **V** feelings   **P** word stress in three- or four-syllable adjectives

1 VOCABULARY & PRONUNCIATION
feelings; word stress

a How would you feel in these situations? Complete the crossword.

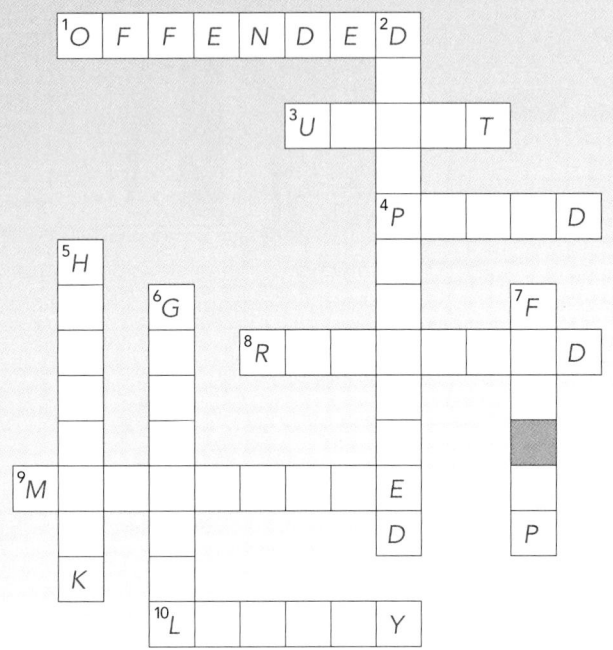

Crossword:
- 1 ACROSS: O F F E N D E D
- 3 ACROSS: U _ _ _ T
- 4 ACROSS: P _ _ _ D
- 8 ACROSS: R _ _ _ _ _ D
- 9 ACROSS: M _ _ _ _ _ E D
- 10 ACROSS: L _ _ _ Y
- 5 DOWN: H
- 6 DOWN: G
- 7 DOWN: F _ _ P
- 2 DOWN: D
- K

ACROSS →
1 Someone told you that your new hairstyle makes you look old.
3 You have an argument with your best friend, and they say they never want to see you again.
4 Your daughter won a painting competition.
8 You think you lost your house keys, and then you find them at the bottom of your bag.
9 You're camping, it's raining, and everything is soaking wet.
10 All your friends are on vacation, and you have nobody to talk to.

DOWN ↓
2 You weren't offered a job after you went to the interview.
5 You're studying abroad and you're missing your family.
6 It's pouring rain and a friend offers to drive you to your home.
7 Your flight has already been delayed three times, and then it's canceled.

b Replace the underlined words with an adjective from the list.

astonished   bewildered   delighted
desperate   devastated   horrified
overwhelmed   stunned   ~~thrilled~~

1 They're <u>very excited</u> to be traveling around South America after saving for so long.
   thrilled
2 When you buy a new phone, it's easy to get <u>very confused</u> by all the different options and contracts.
   _____
3 People were <u>extremely shocked and disgusted</u> when they heard about the terrorist attack.
   _____
4 Andy was <u>amazed</u> when his parents gave him a car for his birthday.
   _____
5 She was <u>so surprised that she couldn't react</u> when she saw the fire damage.
   _____
6 Olivia was <u>incredibly pleased</u> when she got promoted.
   _____
7 My brother was <u>extremely upset</u> when his wife left him.
   _____
8 The soldier's wife was <u>so happy that she didn't know how to react</u> when her husband suddenly arrived home after six months away.
   _____
9 The climbers were <u>losing hope</u>. It was getting dark, snowing heavily, and they couldn't figure out a way down the mountain.
   _____

c Complete the sentences a word from the list.

couldn't believe his eyes   ~~down~~   jumping for joy
scared stiff   sick and tired of   worn out

1 My sister was a little bit
  down after her interview
  exam went badly.

2 I'm _____ always
  having to tell my husband to
  clean up.

3 Javier was _____
  when he saw a big dog
  running towards him.

4 I couldn't sleep on the flight
  from New York. I'm absolutely
  _____ today.

5 Ahmet _____
  when his favorite celebrity
  retweeted him on Twitter.

6 I was _____
  when I got accepted to my
  top choice college.

d Underline the stressed syllable in the adjectives in the list.
Then put them in the correct column.

~~a|sto|nished~~   be|wil|dered   de|ligh|ted   de|spe|rate
de|va|sta|ted   dis|a|ppoin|ted   grate|ful   home|sick
horr|i|fied   lone|ly   mi|se|ra|ble   o|ffen|ded   o|ver|whelmed
re|lieved   up|set

Stress on first syllable	Stress on second syllable	Stress on third syllable
	astonished	

e 🔊 5.1 Listen and check. Then listen again
and repeat the adjectives. Copy the
<u>rhy</u>thm.

f Choose six feelings in **d** that you have
experienced yourself. Write a sentence
about when you experienced each
feeling.

1 _____
  _____
2 _____
  _____
3 _____
  _____
4 _____
  _____
5 _____
  _____
6 _____
  _____

2 **GRAMMAR** unreal conditionals

a Circle the correct form.
  1 Our boss *was* / *would be* more popular if
    he didn't take himself so seriously.
  2 I would have gotten cold if I *didn't take* /
    hadn't taken a jacket.
  3 You *hadn't have* / *wouldn't have* sprained
    your ankle if you'd been looking where you
    were going.
  4 I'd really miss you if you *went* / *would go* to
    live in Seoul.
  5 Vicki *had* / *would have* more friends if she
    didn't complain all the time.
  6 I *had been* / *would have been* really
    disappointed if I hadn't got the job.
  7 He *didn't be able to* / *wouldn't be able to*
    afford a new car if he wasn't living with his
    parents.
  8 We wouldn't have gone to Thailand in
    June if we *knew* / *had known* it was the
    monsoon season.
  9 Jacob wouldn't be so stressed if he *had* /
    would have a more understanding boss.
  10 We wouldn't have gotten lost if we
    had stayed / *would have stayed* on the
    path.

🔵 **Go online** for more practice

b Complete the second and third conditional sentences.

1 We don't go away on weekends because we don't have much free time.
If we had more free time, *we'd go away on weekends.*

2 There wasn't much snow, so we didn't make a snowman.
If there had been more snow, _____.

3 I didn't know the water was so cold, so I jumped in.
I wouldn't have jumped in if _____.

4 He doesn't pass his driver's test because he gets so nervous.
He would pass his driver's test if _____.

5 We missed the last bus because we left the party too late.
If we'd left the party earlier, _____.

6 You get sunburned because you don't use enough sunscreen.
If you used more sunscreen, _____.

7 They hadn't read the book, so they didn't really understand the movie.
They would have understood the movie if _____.

8 I don't earn a lot of money, so I can't buy my own house.
If I earned more money, _____.

c Complete the text with the correct form of the verbs in parentheses.

d Continue the second and third conditional sentences about you.

1 If my parents were billionaires, _____ _____.

2 If I could travel anywhere in the world, _____ _____.

3 If I spoke perfect English, _____ _____.

4 If I had been born in a different country, _____ _____.

5 If I had lived in the 19th century, _____ _____.

6 If I had gotten up earlier this morning, _____ _____.

Would you know what to do if ⁴_____ **(you / get lost) in the mountains?**
The number one survival tip is to stop walking and wait to be rescued. In research done in Canada, however, only two out of 800 lost people actually did this. If ⁵_____ (the others / not keep) walking, a search and rescue team would have found them much more quickly. If they had waited in an open space, ⁶_____ (a helicopter / see) them immediately.
    The most important thing when you go hiking is to tell someone where you are going, so that you can be rescued if anything goes wrong.

What would **you** do if…?

¹*Would you be* **(you / be) prepared if there was an emergency on your plane?**
Think about the last time you flew. Did you pay attention to the safety demonstration? If ²_____ (you / not go) to sleep, you would have heard the flight attendant explain the location of the emergency exits. This information is vital. If there had been a fire, ³_____ (you / have) only about 90 seconds to get off the plane.
    It's unlikely that there will be an emergency on your flight, but if there is, the most important thing is to be ready.

What ⁷_____ **(you / do) if you heard somebody in your house in the middle of the night?**
Imagine you woke up and there was someone in the kitchen. The worst thing you could do is confront the intruder because he might have a weapon.
    Instead you should lock yourself and your family inside a bedroom or the bathroom and call the police. Of course, this would be impossible if ⁸_____ (you / not have) your cell phone with you. So you should always keep your phone fully charged by the side of your bed.

Never look back unless you are planning to go that way.
Henry David Thoreau, author, poet, and philosopher

G *wish* for the present / future, *wish* for past regrets | **V** expressing feelings with verbs or *-ed* / *-ing* adjectives | **P** sentence rhythm and intonation

1 GRAMMAR *wish* for the present / future

a Match 1–8 to a–h.

1 I hardly ever see my boyfriend. _d_
2 My new clothes are always disappearing. ____
3 The weekend has flown by. ____
4 My brother's playing loud music again. ____
5 I'd love to study abroad. ____
6 The kitchen is a mess. ____
7 My neighbors' car is always outside my house. ____
8 Public transportation is terrible around here. ____

a I wish I had a car.
b I wish he would wear headphones.
c I wish you would wash the dishes.
d ~~I wish he didn't work on weekends.~~
e I wish my sister wouldn't borrow them.
f I wish I spoke better English.
g I wish they wouldn't park there.
h I wish it wasn't Monday tomorrow.

b Read the sentences in **a**. Decide if they show that the speaker would like something to be different, or that he / she is annoyed about something? Complete the chart.

speaker wants something to be different	speaker is annoyed about something
1	

c Complete the sentences with *wish* + simple past or *wish* + *would*.

1 My ex-boyfriend is driving me crazy! He calls me every day.
 I wish *my ex-boyfriend wouldn't call me every day.*
2 It's a difficult decision, and I don't know what to do.
 I wish *I knew what to do.*
3 My boss really annoys me. She shouts all the time.
 I wish _____.
4 I didn't get the job because I can't drive.
 I wish _____.
5 I'm fed up with my brother using my computer.
 I wish _____.
6 I can't stand it when my son stays in bed all morning.
 I wish _____.
7 I want to speak to Dan, but I don't have his phone number.
 I wish _____.
8 I hate it when you leave the bathroom a mess.
 I wish _____.
9 I'd love to go away this weekend, but I have to work.
 I wish _____.
10 I have lots of books, but I don't have time to read.
 I wish _____.

d What would you like to be different? What annoys you? Write six sentences with *wish* + simple past or *wish* + *would*.

1 _____
2 _____
3 _____
4 _____
5 _____
6 _____

2 VOCABULARY expressing feelings with verbs or -ed / -ing adjectives

a Complete the sentences with an adjective or a verb made from the word in parentheses.

1 It really _infuriates_ me when people talk loudly on their cell phones on trains. (infuriate)
2 Looking after my sister's three small children is _____ for my parents. (exhaust)
3 Ethan was so _____ when he failed his driver's test. (disappoint)
4 My boyfriend is scared of flying. The idea of getting on a plane _____ him. (terrify)
5 My son is a terrible loser. Not winning something really _____ him. (frustrate)
6 You should try the new Asian restaurant on Main Street. The food is _____. (amaze)
7 I was so _____ when my phone rang during the meeting. (embarrass)
8 His first visit to the theater _____ him to take up acting. (inspire)
9 I find the New York City subway system very _____. I've gotten on the wrong train many times. (confuse)
10 We were _____ that so many people came to our party. (thrill)

b Complete the chart.

verb	-ed adjective	other adjective
1 delight	_delighted_	_delightful_
2 impress		
3 offend		
4 scare		
5 stress		

c Complete the sentences with an adjective from **b**.

1 He was _offended_ when the teacher suggested he might have cheated on the exam.
2 We were _____ when we received a surprise visit from some old friends.
3 She gave such an _____ performance in the movie that I think she might win an Oscar.
4 I'm _____ with your English. You speak really well.
5 The bridge started to move from side to side as we were crossing, which was very _____.
6 She's a little _____ right now because she's taking care of her sister's children as well as her own.
7 I found his sexist comments very _____.
8 Joe's _____ of small spaces – he never uses the elevator.
9 My nieces are _____ – they're very sweet, and they're always making things for me.
10 My boss is good at staying calm in _____ situations.

3 VOCABULARY FROM READING

Complete the sentences with the correct word from a pair in the list.

---
afraid / fear   angry / anger   brave / bravery
encouraging / encouragement
enthusiastic / enthusiasm   ~~excited~~ / excitement
honest / honesty   sorry / sorrow
---

1 My nephew's very _excited_ about his birthday tomorrow.
2 I wish my boyfriend was more _____ – I've caught him telling lies recently.
3 She raised her voice in _____ when she saw the children behaving so badly.
4 I'm not very _____ about the party – I don't really want to go.
5 I wish I had written to my uncle to express my _____ about the death of my aunt.
6 My art teacher is very _____ about my work – she thinks I'm pretty good.
7 The soldier received a medal for his _____ – he had risked his life to protect his unit.
8 The child was shaking with _____ after being chased by a big dog.

Go online for more practice

4 GRAMMAR *wish* for past regrets

a Match 1–8 to a–h. Then complete a–h with the past perfect form of a verb from the list. Use contractions.

bring ~~leave~~ not eat not fall not shout not spend study wear

1 I'm going to be late.   _e_
2 It's colder than I thought today.   ____
3 I feel sick.   ____
4 I failed half of my exams.   ____
5 My leg hurts.   ____
6 I upset my little sister.   ____
7 It's pouring rain.   ____
8 I don't have a lot of money left.   ____

a I wish I _____ an umbrella.
b I wish I _____ so much on that meal last night.
c I wish I _____ harder.
d I wish I _____ at her this morning.
e ~~I wish I'd left~~ _____ ~~home earlier.~~
f I wish I _____ off my bike.
g I wish I _____ a warmer sweater.
h I wish I _____ that seafood.

b Read the situation and write sentences beginning with *I wish* + past perfect.

1 I took the train to work, but it broke down and I was late.
   I wish I hadn't taken the train to work.
2 I left my cell phone on my desk, and now it isn't there.
   _____.
3 I didn't give my boss the report on time, and now he's annoyed with me.
   _____.
4 My girlfriend didn't call me last night, and now I'm worried.
   _____.
5 My friend didn't invite me to her wedding, and now I'm upset.
   _____.
6 We lost our last basketball game, so we won't be playing in the final.
   _____.
7 I was rude to my mother, and now she's offended.
   _____.
8 My son woke me up in the middle of the night, and I couldn't get back to sleep again.
   _____.

5 PRONUNCIATION sentence rhythm and intonation

a ◐ 5.2 Listen and complete the sentences.

1 I wish I'd *applied* for _____.
2 I wish you'd _____ at the _____.
3 I wish I _____ these _____.
4 I wish we'd _____ at _____.
5 I wish you _____ me _____.
6 I wish we _____ on the _____.

b ◐ 5.2 Listen again and repeat the sentences. Copy the <u>rhythm</u> and intonation.

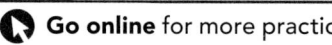 Go online for more practice 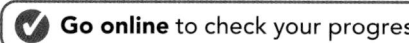 Go online to check your progress

1 LOOKING AT LANGUAGE

Circle the correct comment adverb in the conversations.

1 A How do you recycle your organic waste?
B We don't. *Ideally / Obviously / Unfortunately*, it's impossible to do that where we live.

2 A Who's in charge of emptying the trash cans in your house?
B *Amazingly / Gradually / Sadly*, my teenage son always takes the trash out.

3 A How do you dispose of old electrical devices?
B *Actually / Eventually / Unfortunately*, it's not usually a problem because I rarely buy new ones.

4 A What kind of things do you recycle?
B *Amazingly / Apparently / Basically*, we try to recycle as much as we can.

5 A Can you see any problems with recycling?
B *Actually / Anyway / Obviously*, you need four different recycling bins in the kitchen, but apart from that, it's easy.

6 A What happened to that beautiful old vase you had?
B *Generally / Sadly / Strangely* it broke, so we had to throw it away.

7 A Have they come to empty the recycling bins yet?
B No, they haven't. They always come on Mondays, but *basically / in fact / strangely* they haven't come today.

2 VOCABULARY FROM THE INTERVIEW

Complete the sentences from the interview with a phrase from the list.

| worn out | ~~ended up~~ | falling apart | pretty much |
| off the hook | for the sake | | |

1 We *ended up* _____ filming in 11 countries.
2 He wears his sweaters until they're _____.
3 He keeps his cars until they're _____.
4 He can make _____ anything look beautiful.
5 I don't like to blame one person because that lets us _____.
6 We shouldn't buy new things _____ of it.

3 THE CONVERSATION

Circle the best response.

1 There are plastic bottles that you can eat when you've finished the water.
   a Yes, isn't that awful?
   b Oh wow!
2 There's more plastic in the sea by weight than fish.
   a That sounds pretty cool.
   b I mean, that's so depressing, isn't it?
3 I can't believe how much plastic there is.
   a Yes, it's very scary!
   b Oh wow!
4 They've found plastic in the Marianna Trench.
   a Yes, isn't that awful?
   b I think that's just so amazing.
5 They've found bacteria that have evolved to digest nylon plastic.
   a Its really awful, actually.
   b That's amazing!

4 VOCABULARY FROM THE CONVERSATION

Complete the sentences with a word from the list.

| day | ~~doubt~~ | hilarious | involved | taste |

1 I would without a *doubt* _____ recommend this book.
2 I couldn't stop laughing; it was just _____.
3 I'd really like to get _____ with animals.
4 Reading biographies affects my life and just how I act day-to-_____.
5 But it comes down to _____, doesn't it?

Can you remember...? 1–5

GRAMMAR & VOCABULARY

a Complete the second sentence so that it means the same as the first sentence. Write 2–5 words. Use the word in parentheses.

1 I met John when we were students. (known)
I *'ve known John since* _____ we were students.

2 My son's girlfriend is from Turkey; she's young and interesting. (Turkish)
My son is going out with an _____
_____ woman.

3 There's no doubt you'll save money if you sell your car. (certainly)
You _____
_____ if you sell your car.

4 It started to rain two hours after we started walking. (had)
We _____
_____ two hours when it started to rain.

5 My flight to Las Vegas leaves at 11:00 tomorrow and arrives at 12:15. (flying)
At 12:00 tomorrow, I _____
_____ to Las Vegas.

6 My classes end in May next year. (will)
My classes _____
_____ by June.

7 If the concert isn't sold out, I'll get you a ticket. (unless)
I'll get you a ticket for the concert _____
_____.

8 I got a cold because I went out with wet hair. (have)
If I hadn't gone out with wet hair, _____
_____ a cold.

9 It annoys me when you don't listen to me. (wish)
I _____
listen to me.

10 I regret not visiting The Louvre when I was in Paris. (visited)
I _____
The Louvre when I was in Paris.

b Read the article. Circle a, b, or c.

Thai cave rescue
Boys survive nine days trapped underground

In the summer of 2018, 12 teenage soccer players became trapped deep inside a cave in Thailand with the coach who was taking ⁱ____ them. They had entered the cave to celebrate one of the boy's birthdays, but ²____ rains had flooded the cave, so they couldn't get out. For nine days, the boys and the coach were sitting in complete darkness, which must have been very ³____. They managed to survive by drinking the water dripping from the cave walls and by eating the snacks they had bought for the birthday party. ⁴____, the 25-year-old coach, Ekapol Chantawong, refused to eat any of the food so that the boys would have more for themselves. He helped them stay calm by teaching them meditation. When divers ⁵____ found the boys, they were ⁶____ to see that all the boys were still alive. They were also astonished to find that the boys didn't seem particularly ⁷____ by their experience. The rescue team, on the other hand, was in a race against time to get the boys out of the cave before the ⁸____ rains began. They had also noticed that the level of oxygen in the cave was dropping. The rescue operation took ⁹____ over three days and resulted in all 13 boys being taken safely out of the cave. There was a moment of ¹⁰____, however, when diver Saman Gunan died while he was helping to bring air tanks through the tunnels for the boys.

	a	**b**	**c**
1	after	care of	pity on
2	hard	heavy	strong
3	scare	scared	scary
4	Apparently	Basically	Certainly
5	lately	eventually	gradually
6	bewildered	grateful	relieved
7	stress	stressed	stressful
8	blizzard	hurricane	monsoon
9	part	place	risks
10	anger	sorrow	loss

✓ **Go online** to check your progress

OXFORD
UNIVERSITY PRESS

198 Madison Avenue
New York, NY 10016 USA

Great Clarendon Street, Oxford, OX2 6DP,
United Kingdom

Oxford University Press is a department of the University of Oxford. It furthers the University's objective of excellence in research, scholarship, and education by publishing worldwide. Oxford is a registered trade mark of Oxford University Press in the UK and in certain other countries

© Oxford University Press 2021

The moral rights of the author have been asserted

First published in 2021
2025 2024
10 9 8 7

No unauthorized photocopying

All rights reserved. No part of this publication may be reproduced, stored in a retrieval system, or transmitted, in any form or by any means, without the prior permission in writing of Oxford University Press, or as expressly permitted by law, by licence or under terms agreed with the appropriate reprographics rights organization. Enquiries concerning reproduction outside the scope of the above should be sent to the ELT Rights Department, Oxford University Press, at the address above

You must not circulate this work in any other form and you must impose this same condition on any acquirer

Links to third party websites are provided by Oxford in good faith and for information only. Oxford disclaims any responsibility for the materials contained in any third party website referenced in this work

ISBN: 978 0 19 490694 4 Multi-Pack A with Online Practice Pack
ISBN: 978 0 19 490695 1 Multi-Pack A Component
ISBN: 978 0 19 490684 5 Student Online Practice

Printed in China

This book is printed on paper from certified and well-managed sources

STUDENT BOOK ACKNOWLEDGMENTS

The authors would like to thank all the teachers and students around the world whose feedback has helped us to shape American English File.

The authors would also like to thank: all those at Oxford University Press (both in Oxford and around the world) and the design team who have contributed their skills and ideas to producing this course.

Finally very special thanks from Clive to Maria Angeles, Lucia, and Eric, and from Christina to Cristina, for all their support and encouragement. Christina would also like to thank her children Joaquin, Marco, and Krysia for their constant inspiration.

The publisher and authors would also like to thank the following for their invaluable feedback on the materials: Zahra Bilides, Paz Alonso, Vanessa Ferroni, Dagmara Lata, Sandy Millin, Sarah Giles, Jane Hudson, Yolana Calpe, Rosa María Iglesias Traviesas, Michale Jarvis, Pedro Irazabel Brian Brennan, Robert Anderson, Magdalena Muszyńska, Gyula Kiss, Juliana Stucker, Elif Barbaros, Kenny McDonnell

The publisher and authors are very grateful to the following who have provided information, personal stories, and/or photographs: Alex, Ali, Dominic, Ghislaine, Heidi, Jane, Jeanie, Jo, Krysia, Peter, Tom, Richard Hall p.28, Mike Bench p.39, Sophie Rees p.43, Ali Brookes pp.46–47, Brennan Wenck-Reilly p.57, John Sloboda p.60, Thomas Ormerod p.73, Anya Edwards p.102, Jeff Neil pp.14–15, Marion Pomeranc pp.34–35, Candida Brady pp.54–55, Simon Callow pp.74–75, George Tannenbaum pp.94–95, and The Conversation participants: Debbie Bird, Sarah Baetens, Alice Dillon, Ida Berglöw Kenneway, David Poole, Emma Forward, Simon Warren, Joanne Bowlt, Syinat Tagaeva, Mark Boulle, John Bowlt and Devika Pandit

The authors and publisher are grateful to those who have given permission to reproduce the following extracts and adaptations of copyright material including Noé Colle's teacher who challenged him to write his short story.
p.6 Adapted from "The Q&A interview: Simone Biles" by Rosanna Greenstreet which first appeared in the "Weekend Guardian". Reproduced by permission. p.7 Adapted from "The Q&A interview: Dan Stevens" by Rosanna Greenstreet which first appeared in the "Weekend Guardian". Reproduced by permission. p.8 Adapted from "Would YOU get the job? The 20 toughest interview questions…" by Stephanie Linning, MailOnline. Reproduced by permission of Solo Syndication. p.9 Adapted from "Top 10 weird job interview questions" by Aimee Picchi, CBS News. Reproduced by permission. p.10 Adapted from "Victorian ghost buster is vindicated at last" by Ben Mcintyre, The Times, 1 January 2016, © News UK/News Licensing. Reproduced by permission. p.10 Adapted from "7 Ships That Disappeared Without a Trace" by Claire Cock-Starkey, 5 August 2016, www.metalfloss.com. Reproduced by permission. TBC p.16 Adapted from "Sorting Fact from Fiction: 15 Common First Aid Myths", KG Safety Services. Reproduced by permission. p.19 Adapted from "Confessions of a cyberchondriac" by Anita Chaudhuri, The Sunday Times, 26 April 2009, © News UK/News Licensing. Reproduced by permission. p.20 Adapted from "'She feels like family to me': when age is no barrier to friendship" by Deborah Linton, www.theguardian.com, 9 June 2018. Copyright Guardian News & Media Ltd 2019. Reproduced by permission. p.22 Adapted words from "How to make one piece of clothing work for all ages" by Emily Cronin, Stella, 4th September 2016. © Telegraph Media Group Limited 2016. Reproduced by permission. p.25 Adapted from "Nasa astronaut returns from space younger than his twin", by Oliver Moody, The Times, 3 February 2017, © News UK/News Licensing. Reproduced by permission. p.26 Adapted from "Revealed: The secret to securing the perfect plane" by Gavin Haines, 6 November 2017, © Telegraph Media Group Limited 2017. Reproduced by permission. p.28 Adapted from "Passengers alarmed after bat flies through Spirit Airlines plane: 'I'll never fly Spirit again'" by Mahira Dayal, 6 August 2019, www.yahoo.com/lifestyle/. Reproduced by permission. p.30 50 words from "Departed" by Connell Wayne Regner, © Connell Wayne Regner. Reproduced by permission. p.30 Adapted from "Alone" by Verity Park from https://fiftywordstories.com. Reproduced by permission of the author. p.30 Adapted from "Paper Tiger" by Katya Duft, https://fiftywordstories.com. Reproduced by permission. p.31 Adapted from "Fond of Hard Rock" by Noe Colle from https://fiftywordstories.com. Reproduced by permission. p.36 Adapted from "Are you as environmentally friendly as you think? Personality quiz" by Ben Ambridge, www.guardian.com, 14 May 2017. Copyright Guardian News & Media Ltd 2019. Reproduced by permission. p.38 Adapted from "Climate Stories Project" http://www.climatestoriesproject.org, copyright Climate Stories Project 2019. Reproduced by permission. p.42 Adapted from "Why are deadly extreme sports more popular than ever?" by Leo Benedictus, www.guardian.com, 20 August 2016. Copyright Guardian News & Media Ltd 2019. Reproduced by permission. p.45 Adapted from "Travels' biggest bang: 10 incredible volcanoes that are great to climb" by Amy Horsfield, www.wanderlust.co.uk, 17 February 2017. Reproduced by permission. p.52 Adapted from "What is your biggest regret? Here are people's devastatingly honest answers" by Emma Freud, www.theguardian.com, 31 October 2017. Copyright Guardian News & Media Ltd 2019. Reproduced by permission. p.57 Adapted text and photo from "Segmented Sleep" by Brennan Wenck-Reilly, www.brennanwenck.com. Reproduced by permission of the author. p.59 Adapted from "The expert's rules for a great night's sleep" by Anna Maxted, The Times 21 July 2018, © News UK/News Licensing. Reproduced by permission. p.62 Adapted from "Why you should listen to music while you work" by Mike Wright, 7th September 2017. © Telegraph Media Group Limited 2017. Reproduced by permission. p.62 Adapted from "The surgeon's cut: what do doctors listen to in the operating theatre?" by Homa Khaleeli, www.guardian.com, 5 August 2015. Copyright Guardian News & Media Ltd 2019. Reproduced by permission. p.65 Adapted from "The Power of Music for Sleep and Performance" by Dr. Michael Breus, www.thesleepdoctor.com. Reproduced by permission. p.69 Adapted from "How to win any argument using science" by Victoria Woollaston, MailOnline. Reproduced by permission of Solo Syndication. p.73 Adapted from "The best way to spot a liar… or is it?" by Professor Thomas Ormerod, © Thomas Ormerod. Reproduced by permission of the author. p.76 Extract from "Stay Safe" from www.met.police.uk. Reproduced by Courtesy of the Mayor's Office of Policing and Crime. p.78 Adapted from "The 15 Unluckiest Dumb Criminals Ever" by Andy Simmons and Priscilla Torres, originally published in Readers Digest, www.rd.com. Copyright © 2018 by Trusted Media Brands, Inc. Used by permission. All rights reserved. p.79 Adapted from "Man shocked to learn his identity has been stolen to con women" by Rosie Hopegood, www.themirror.co.uk, 1 April 2018. Reproduced by permission of Mirrorpix. p.83 Adapted from "10 tips on how to spot fake news" by Rob Waugh, The Telegraph, 7 May 2019. Reproduced by permission of the author. p.86 Adapted from "18 false advertising scandals that cost some brands millions" by Julien Rath. Copyrighted 2017. Business Insider. 2105571:0719p. Reproduced by permission of Wrights Media acting on behalf of Business Insider Magazine. p.88 Adapted text and cover image from *Fifty Things that Made the Modern Economy* by Tim Harford, Copyright © 2017 Tim Harford, Little, Brown Book Company Limited. Reproduced by permission. p.90 Adapted from "What makes a city attractive?" by Francesca Perry, www.guardian.com, 10 February 2015. Copyright Francesca Perry/Guardian News & Media Ltd 2019. Reproduced by permission. p.92 Adapted text and photo from "Sleepy in Songdo, Korea's smartest city" by Linda Poon, 22 June 2018, © 2018 CityLab, a division of The Atlantic Media Group LLC. All rights reserved. Distributed by Tribune Content Agency. p.96 Adapted from "Quiz: Can you answer the simple science questions parents struggle to answer" by Mark Molloy, 3rd May 2016. © Telegraph Media Group Limited 2016. Reproduced by permission. p.98 Adapted from "Science Fact or Fiction? The Plausibility of 10 Sci-fi Concepts" by Adam Hadhazy, www.livescience.com, 20 September 2013. Reproduced by permission. p.101 Adapted from "From Martin Luther King to Churchill and Obama: the 10 best speeches – ever", Philip Collins, The Times, 25 September 2017, © News UK/News Licensing. Reproduced by permission. p.105 Adapted from "The Voice of Reason" by John Shammas, www.thesun.co.uk, 14 March 2018 © The Sun/News Licensing. Reproduced by permission. p.107 Adapted from "Air France passengers describe mid-air terror as engine disintegrates over Atlantic" by David Chazan, 30 September 2017 © Telegraph Media Group Limited 2017. Reproduced by permission.
Sources: www.businessinsider.com; XX. *The Necklace* by Guy de Maupassant.

Although every effort has been made to trace and contact copyright holders before publication, this has not been possible in some cases. We apologize for any apparent infringement of copyright and if notified, the publisher will be pleased to rectify any errors or omissions at the earliest opportunity.

Illustrations by Peter Bull pp 26, 38, 107, 112; Petros Bouloubasis/Advocate Art p 96; Canary Pete p 8; Stephen Collins p 116; Sam Dedel/Lemonade Illustration p 76; DILBERT © 2000 Scott Adams. Used By permission of Andrews McMeel Syndication. All rights reserved p102; Isla Fletcher p 66 (handwriting); John Haslam pp 132, 133, 135, 136, 137, 141, 142, 144, 155, 157; Matthew Hollings/Illustrationweb pp 118, 153; Peter Hudspith pp 30, 31; Joe McLaren pp 68–69; Willie Ryan/Illustrationweb pp 16, 152; Garry Walton/Meiklejohn Illustration pp 32–33, 46–47

Commissioned photography by Gareth Boden p 153 (suit, waistcoat, swimsuit); MM Studios pp 19 (mug), 22 (cardigan), 88 (Playstation, Nespresso, HP printer, Gillette razor), 89 (razors); Oxford University Press video stills pp 15, 23 (Huit jeans), 25 (headshots), 35 (the Conversation), 43 (Grace Doyle), 45 (headshots), 54 (Candida Brady), 55 (the Conversation), 63 (Isata Kanneh-Mason), 65 (headshots), 74 (Simon Callow), 75 (the Conversation), 83, 85 (headshots), 94 (George Tannenbaum), 95 (the Conversation), 105 (headshots).

Pronunciation chart artwork by Ellis Nadler

We would also like to thank the following for permission to reproduce the following photographs: Cover: Hobbit/Shutterstock. 123RF pp 19 (woman/ocusfocus), 66 (Cathy Yeulet); Advertising Archives pp 86 (Red Bull), 87 (Olay); Alamy pp 6 (Simone Biles/Aflo Co. Ltd.), (Biles/Erich Schlegel), 7 (Downton Abbey/PictureLux/The Hollywood Archive), 10 (Flannan Island/Ian Cowe), 21 (family portrait/Ashok Tholpady), 25 (astronauts/NASA), 28 (pilot/Hero Images Inc.) (Spirit airlines/Markus Mainka), 34 (Black Beauty/CBW), (Nancy Drew/AztecBlue), (Twilight/CBW), 42 (paragliding/Hemis), (wingsuit flying/Oliver Furrer), 45 (Mount Misti/Pep Roig), (Mount Ngauruhoe/robertharding), 48 (jaguar/Avalon/Bruce Coleman Inc), 49 (footprint/Mode Images), (paddling canoe/Jacques Jangoux), 54 (Trashed/Everett Collection Inc), 70 (Keira Knightley/AF archive), (Meryl Streep/Landmark Media), (Eddie Redmayne/Allstar Picture Library/Warner Bros/AF archive), (Frances McDormand/Focus Features/PictureLux / The Hollywood Archive), (Daniel Kaluuya/Warner Bros/Moviestore collection Ltd), 86 (Activia/Keith Homan), 91 (1/Matthias Scholz), (2/Pulsar Imagens), (3/Ceri Breeze), (5/J Marshall - Tribaleye Images), 94 (Boss/jeremy sutton-hibbert), 98 (speed of light/Quality Stock), (invisibility Harry Potter/ITAR-TASS News Agency), (invisibility cloisters/Francisco Martinez), 99 (Neptune/Irina Dmitrienko), 100 (Neil Armstrong/NASA Archive), 101 (Elizabeth I/IanDagnall Computing), (Emmeline Pankhurst/Granger Historical Picture Archive), (Winston Churchill/David Cole), (John F Kennedy/Pictorial Press Ltd), 117 (Eddie Gerald), 121 (NY Diner/Randy Duchaine), 153 (scarf/Valery Voennyy), 159 (calf/Simon Balson), (knee/Fitness People by Vision); British Newspaper Archive p 10 (newspaper Northants Evening Telegraph, 27/12/1900); Courtesy of Steve Bustin p 79; Captainbijou.com p 94 (MOM Brands/Farina cereal), 159 (thigh/Paul Doyle); Sarah Bench p.39 (Mike Bench); Stewart Cohen/stewartcohen.com p 73 (security officer); Courtesy of Anya Edwards p 102; Corbis p 159 (bottom/Kidstock/Blend Images); Getty Images pp 7 (portrait/Matthias Clamer), 29 (birth on plane/Anadolu Agency), (baggage claim/Peter Cade), 40–41 (AFP), 42 (bungee jumping/Image taken by Mayte Torres), 49 (plane Amazon aerial/Photodisc), 50 (woman/Klubovy), 53 (man/Tetra Images), (woman/Klaus Vedfelt), 72 (upsidedowndog), 74 (rehearsal/Digital Vision), 80 (ramen noodles/George), 82 (Chris Graythen), 86 (VW car/Ramin Talaie), 95 (Nike/Prashanth Vishwanathan/Bloomberg via Getty Images), (Apple/Gilles Mingasson/Liaison), 101 (Abraham Lincoln/Archive Photos), (Martin Luther King/Francis Miller/The LIFE Picture Collection), (Nelson Mandela/Pool Bouvet/De Keerle/Gamma-Rapho), (Barack Obama/Alfredo Estrella), 105 (Stephen Hawking/Bruno Vincent), 113 (jasmine/Vincenzo Lombardo), 119 (family at home/Hans Neleman), (cinema/PhotoAlto Agency RF Collections), 120 (baseball player/Yeatts), 121 (NYC gastropub/Lonely Planet), 153 (sandals/Trish Gant), 159 (ankle/FilmMagic), (fist/JazzIRT), (wrist/George Pimentel/WireImage), (waist/MJ Kim); The Guardian/ Eyevine pp 20 (Dilys and Sian/Thomas Butler), 21 (Dave and John/ Thomas Butler), 91 (4/Martin Creed), 107 (Thomas Butler), 111 (Thomas Butler); iStockphoto pp 48 (raft/TheSilverFox), 58 (yawning/icon river), 98 (intelligent machines/Abidal), 121 (NYC pizza/wdstock), 153 (bow tie/Maddrat), 159 (hip/John Sommer); Little, Brown Book Group Limited p 88 *Fifty Things that made the Modern Economy*, by Tim Harford, 2017; Mary Evans Picture Library p 10 (map from *The Sphere*, 19th January 1901); Courtesy Barack Obama Presidential Library p 103; Courtesy of Professor Thomas Ormerod p 73; Reproduced by permission of Oxford University Press p 48 green texture behind Jungle text; p 60 cover image of *Handbook of Music and Emotion*, Edited by Patrik N. Juslin and John Sloboda, 2011; Oxford University Press pp 14, (Jeff Neil), 34 (Marion Pomeranc), (The Hand-Me-Down Horse), 35 (e-book reader), 113 (kitten and vinegar); OUP\Shutterstock p 60 (guitar neck/AlexMaster), (cello bow/Yuriyfx), 61 (guitar/AlexMaster), (saxophone/AGCuesta), (cello/Yuriyfx), (flute/cowardlion); Courtesy of Lynne Parker p 102; Courtesy of Sophie Rees p 43; Mahmud Sahran p 80 ('zebra'); By kind permission of San Antonio Aquarium & Austin Aquarium p 80 (shark theft); Cover image of *Northern Lights* Text Copyright © Philip Pullman 1995, Cover Design by Crush Design, 2011 Reproduced by permission of Scholastic Ltd. All rights reserved; Science Photo Library p 159 (brain/ heart/ kidneys/ liver/ lungs/all Sciepro); Shutterstock Editorial 74 (Old Vic/Alisdair Macdonalds), (Amadeus/Graham Wiltshire), (Four Weddings and a Funeral/Polygram/Channel 4/Working Title/Kobal), 75 (Daniel Day Lewis/Miramax/Dimension Films/Kobal), (Laurence Olivier/Romulus Films/Park Circus); Shutterstock pp 10 (sky/SeaSandSun), 12 (dugdax), 14 (holding pen/leolintag), (oak tree/S Mercer), (cactus/JoMo333), (apple tree/Mazzzur), 18 (Suteren), 22 (slippers/cretolamna), (mini-skirt/Tarzhanova), (shorts/inchic), (T-shirt/Artem Avetisyan), (jeans/Eyes wide), (blazer and chinos/everytime), 23 (shirt/East), 26 (Khairil Azhar Junos), 29 (car lost/Yalcin Sonat), (broken window/Adalet Semsovic), 34 (If I Ran the Circus/Julie Clopper) 36 (namtipStudio), 37 (fossil fuel/Macrovector), (recycling symbol/picoStudio), (tap/Arcady), (temperature/AVIcon), 38 (thunderstorm/Pictureguy), (hurricane/FotoKina), (rainbow/muratart), (blue sky/irin-k), 39 (man/Luis Monlinero), 42 (skydiving/Germanskydiver), 43 (wave background/EpicStockMedia), 45 (Mount Teide/eldeiv), 48 (leaf texture/GoodStudio), 49 (Amazon River/Nowaczyk), 50 (hearts/Markus Gann), (secret tunnels/gracioustiger), (biscuits/The FirstFotoLab), (mountain landscape/Iakiv Pekarskyi), (dog/Csanad Kiss), (Whatsapp background/topform), 53 (Speaker 2/Natali12389), 56 (Rawpixel.com), 57 (candle-stick/S-Belov), 58 (drill/Pavel K), (bed/babsy17), (mites/lantapix), (fly/Potapov Alexander), 60 (violin/AGCuesta), (keyboard/Smileus), 61 (drums/grekoff), (conductor/LifetimeStock), 63 (surgeons/Gorodenkoff), (Dmitriy Samorodinov), 67 (head and speech bubble/olga kryukova), 71 (pathdoc), 78 (handcuffs/DenisProduction.com), 80 (fever/ArtOfPhotos), 90 (night scene/mart), 92 (Songdo/PKphotograph), 97 (Natykach Nataliia), 98 (aliens/Albert Ziganshin), (teleportation/Sergey Nivens), (invisibility cloak outline/Leo Stock Pix), (instant learning/Gorodenkoff), 99 (Pluto/Dotted Yeti), 108 (namtipStudio), 109 (cabbage/matin), (mango/matin), (rose/satitsrihin), (ice lolly/Lucie Lang), (fur coat/lynnette), (fever/ArtOfPhotos), 113 (camembert/picturepartners), (chilli pepper/mexrix), 153 (vest/Quality Master), (fur collar/Karkas), (lace top/Karkas), (cardigan/NYS), (boots/Karkas), 156 (icons/RedKoala), (dock in fog/frankie's), 158 (emoji/flower travelin' man), 159 (heel/ShotPrime Studio), (elbow/ Steven Frame), (nails/Tamara83), (palm/alexandre zveiger), (chest/Daniel_Dash), 160 (handcuffs/grmarc), 162 (walking in city/Rawpixel.com); Courtesy of Dr Neil Stanley p 59; Reproduced by kind permission of Summersdale Publishers, photo from *Lost in the Jungle* by Yossi Ghinsberg p 48 (*from left to right* Kevin Gale, Tico Tudela and Yossi Ghinsberg © Kevin Gale); Brennan Wenck-Reilly/www.brennanwenck.com p 57 (night view of San Francisco, *From Angel Island*); From John A. Love, *A Natural History of Lighthouses*, Whittles Publishing, 2015, ISBN 978-184995-154-8 Photo © Steven Gibbons p 10 (three lighthouse Keepers *from left to right* Thomas Marshall, Donald Macarthur and James Ducat).

WORKBOOK ACKNOWLEDGMENTS

The authors would like to thank all the teachers and students around the world whose feedback has helped us to shape American English File.

The authors would also like to thank: all those at Oxford University Press (both in Oxford and around the world) and the design team who have contributed their skills and ideas to producing this course.

Finally very special thanks from Clive to Maria Angeles, Lucia, and Eric, and from Christina to Cristina, for all their support and encouragement. Christina would also like to thank her children Joaquin, Marco, and Krysia for their constant inspiration.

The authors and publisher are grateful to those who have given permission to reproduce the following extracts and adaptations of copyright material: p22 Adapted from *Mini Sagas* by Brian Aldiss (ed.), *The Daily Telegraph*, © Telegraph Media Group Limited 2013. Reproduced by permission.

The publisher would like to thank the following for their permission to reproduce photographs: Cover: Hobbit/Shutterstock. Alamy Stock Photo pp6 (interview/ Mariusz Szczawinski), 15 (Tet Festival/ Danita Delimont), 27 (children watching solar eclipse/Cavan), 35 (bookcase/David Askham), 39 (rescue team/Royal Thai Navy/UPI), 50 (knee/Fitness People by Vision), 50 (calf/Simon Balson), 53 (rehearsal/ Keith Morris), 57 (Grand Central Station/Steve Tulley), 59 (reporter/Hongqi Zhang), 62 (bank/Clarence Holmes Photography), 63 (traffic/D A Barnes), 64 (Lagos/Ton Koene), 64 (Mahatma Gandhi/Dinodia Photos), 70 (Marie Curie/Lebrecht Music & Arts), 72 (Oprah Winfrey/PictureLux/The Hollywood Archive); Getty Images pp7 (driving/Hero Images), 11 (Bermuda Triangle/Lightguard), 17 (friends walking/ Hinterhaus Productions), 22 (empty plate/Blend Images - JGI/Jamie Grill), 26 (sleeping/Peopleimages), 26 (birthday/Caiaimage/Paul Bradbury), 30 (shopping/ urbazon), 40 (tired/Motortion), 43 (playing guitar/Inti St Clair), 44 (cello/Greg Dale), 44 (keyboard/Dave King), 50 (ankle/Jason LaVeris/FilmMagic), 50 (wrist/George Pimentel/WireImage), 50 (waist/MJ Kim), 50 (fist/JazzIRT), 53 (Juilliard Orchestra/ Hiroyuki Ito) 68 (researcher/Westend61) 73 (walkway/SandyTambone); iStock.com p50 (hip/John Sommer); OUP pp36 (burrows/Toby Burrows), 44 (soprano/posztos), 44 (bass/Tetra Images), 44 (choir/posztos), 44 (flute/Triff), 44 (violin/Dario Sabljak), 44 (saxophone/horiyan), 44 (drums/misha), 44 (orchestra/Ferenc Szelepcsenyi), 49 (cat/Voraorn Ratanakorn), 63 (Detian Waterfall/4045), 67 (Kolkata/Radiokafka), 71 (Aconcagua/Johnathan Esper), 71 (baby/alice-photo), 71 (teacher/Monkey Business Images), 72 (storm/Wesley Aston), Science Photo Library pp50 (brain/Sciepro), 50 (kidneys/Sciepro), 50 (liver/Sciepro), 50 (bottom/Ian Hooton), 50 (heart/Sciepro), 50 (lungs/Sciepro); Shutterstock pp4 (tourists/Atstock Productions), 5 (Rio De Janeiro/ SNEHIT), 8 (angry boy/Alexxndr), 9 (Mars/Jurik Peter), 15 (learning sign language/ Andrey_Popov), 16 (house/Christopher Meder), 19 (plane cabin/Vetal), 21 (London/ Javen), 22 (woman/Antonio Guillem), 22 (argument/VGstockstudio), 23 (father & daughter/Iakov Filimonov), 23 (clothes shopping/Syda Productions), 25 (reading/ Halfpoint), 26 (beach/aveseen), 26 (train journey/Alexey Sizov), 26 (office worker/ Muk Photo), 26 (couple eating/Monkey Business Images), 26 (meeting/Monkey Business Images), 26 (traveller/AJR_photo), 28 (snowy street/FashionStock.com), 29 (Brooklyn/Brian Goodman), 30 (grandfather & grandson/Rawpixel.com), 32 (Machu Picchu/lovelypeace), 34 (flight attendant/Sergey Smolentsev), 34 (hiker/David Varga), 34 (sleep/Monkey Business Images), 35 (sad girl/fizkes), 37 (businessman/ William Perugini), 37 (insomnia/Sergey Mironov), 41 (library/SpeedKingz), 41 (cycling/Brian A Jackson), 41 (sandcastles/oliveromg), 41 (construction worker/ Dmitry Bunin), 42 (business meeting/VGstockstudio), 43 (boy in tree/KaliAntye), 44 (orchestra/Martin Good), 45 (Swan Lake/Jack.Q), 45 (croissant/Yakobchuk Viacheslav), 46 (missed train/encierro), 47 (bike accident/B-D-S Piotr Marcinski), 47 (plane window/Travel man), 48 (rainy picnic/Robert Wydro Studio), 49 (cake/ Irina Kuzmina), 49 (garlic/Volodymyr Plysiuk), 49 (roquefort/grafvision), 50 (nails/ Tamara83), 50 (elbow/Steven Frame), 50 (thigh/sozon), 50 (chest/cristovao), 50 (heel/ShotPrime Studio), 50 (palm/Alexandre Zveiger), 51 (two boys/sima), 55 (hacker/Gorodenkoff), 56 (motorbike/Rose Makin), 57 (signing/Kritsana Karakate), 58 (cooking/Rawpixel.com), 58 (referee/Vlad1988), 59 (photographers/Denis Makarenko), 60 (kitchen staff/wavebreakmedia), 60 (office/Monkey Business Images), 61 (woman/Stock image), 61 (field/Elenamiv), 62 (vinyl/Rawpixel.com), 65 (dinner/Monkey Business Images), 65 (Mongolian yurt/peachananr), 69 (people with masks/2p2play), 69 (using tablet/Yakobchuk Viacheslav); Shutterstock Editorial pp25 (recovery of plane/Depo Photos Via Zuma Wire), 72 (Sidney Poitier/ Anonymous/AP).

Illustrations by: John Haslam pp31, 33; Matthew Hollings p16; Roger Penwill pp11, 36; Willie Ryan p12.

Commissioned photography by: Oxford University Press video stills pp 10 (the Conversation), 24 (the Conversation), 38 (the Conversation), 52 (Looking at Language), (the Conversation), 66 (Looking at Language), (the Conversation),

Pronunciation chart artwork by Ellis Nadler

Although every effort has been made to trace and contact copyright holders before publication, this has not been possible in some cases. We apologise for any apparent infringement of copyright and, if notified, the publisher will be pleased to rectify any errors or omissions at the earliest possible opportunity.

American English File

Third Edition

4

MULTI-PACK A

Student Book | Workbook

Christina Latham-Koenig
Clive Oxenden
Kate Chomacki

Paul Seligson and Clive Oxenden
are the original co-authors of
English File 1 and *English File 2*

OXFORD

UNIVERSITY PRESS